"Soft Porn" Plays Hardball

Its Tragic Effects on Women, Children & the Family

Judith A. Reisman, Ph.D.

Huntington House Publishers

Huntington House Publishers
P.O. Box 53788
Lafayette, Louisiana 70505

Library of Congress Card Catalog Number 90-84932
ISBN 0-910311-92-7 Trade paper
ISBN 0-910311-65-X Hard back

Printed in Colombia

Table of Contents

Dedication

In the larger sense, this book should serve as a flashlight for many endangered American families, cleansing the dark and secret places of husbands, wives, and children. In a more personal vein, it is dedicated to my mother and father, Ada and Matt, who taught me (by example) that our unparalleled inheritance of freedom and opportunity was paid for by the lives of millions of Americans. These gifts dictate a lifetime commitment to truth.

Acknowledgments

There are so many people who have distinguished themselves by their personal and professional assistance in sharing their own knowledge and in helping to bring this book to the public. I would be remiss, however, should I lose this opportunity to mention a few of these folks by name: Dr. Tom Landess, Dr. Linnea Smith, Dr. W.R. Coulson, Dr. John Court, Dr. George Comstock, Dr. Gordon Muir, Dr. Emanuel Landau, Dr. Franklin Osanka, Pat Buchanan, Laura Lederer, Dr. Richard Zakia, Edward Eichel, Gladys Dickelman, Susan Orr, Richard Dryer, Jim Wootton, George Mercer, Larry Crain, John Whitehead, Randy Shaheen, Kristin Kazyak, Douglas Alexander, John Rabun, Robert Heck, Virginia Armat, and Don Turner.

My thanks to my brave publisher for his generous spirit and commitment to the truth, to Barbara Banks for her willingness to be pleasant day after day, and to Laura Carroll, my editor, who without murmur, made sense and sensibility out of a manuscript with more added scribbles on it than original typed text.

Deepest gratitude to you chosen few who must remain nameless who labored in the cold and damp, who kept the bill collectors at bay, who made the flowers grow, and who held my hand and opened my days to the sun.

Thank you all. That which is useful in this book reflects the collective wisdom and labor of many good people. I alone am responsible for the body of ideas put forward here as well as any errata which may have inevitably crept in during the rush of publication. Should you, kind reader, somehow come upon some such slippage, do be generous and drop a line to me for correction in a future edition. Warmly, Judith Reisman, Ph.D.

Epigraph

Hefner's airbrushed centerfold "was their mental mistress . . . they often saw her picture while making love to their wives. She . . . was always available at bedside, was totally controllable, knew the perfect touch in personal places, and never said or did anything to disturb the mood before the moment of ecstasy.

Each month she was a new person . . . catering to various whims and obsessions, asking nothing in return. She behaved in ways that real women did not. . . . It was a convenient way to carry on a relationship. For the price of the magazine . . . [Hugh Hefner] provided old men with young women, ugly men with desirable women, black men with white women, shy men with nymphomaniacs. He [triggered] imagined extramarital affairs of monogamous men, supplied the stimulus for dormant [or impotent] men, and was thus connected with the central nervous system of *Playboy* readers nationwide."

Gay Talese, *Thy Neighbor's Wife*

Part I:
Soft Porn's Agenda

Chapter 1

"... A CLEAR AND PRESENT DANGER"

Former U.S. Surgeon General, Dr. C. Everett Koop, declared pornography a "crushing public health problem . . . a clear and present danger . . . blatantly anti-human. . . . We must oppose it as we oppose all violence and prejudice."[1] Serial rapist-murderer Ted Bundy illustrated this danger in January 1989 when he talked to psychologist Dr. James Dobson on the eve of his execution. Bundy maintained that "drug store pornography" helped change a vulnerable boy into the brutal mass murderer of over thirty women and girls:

> This is the message I want to get across, that as a young boy, and I mean a boy of twelve and thirteen certainly, that I encountered . . . in the local grocery store, in a local drug store, the soft-core pornography that people call "soft-core". . . . [W]hat I am talking about happened twenty, thirty years ago in my formative stages.[2]

Moments before he was electrocuted, Bundy warned America about the sadosexual material children consume today:

> What scares and appalls me, Dr. Dobson, is when I see what's on cable TV, some of the movies and some of the violence in the movies that comes into homes today, with stuff that they wouldn't show in X-rated adult theaters thirty years ago . . . as it gets into the home to children who may be unattended or unaware that they may be a Ted Bundy.[3]

What did Bundy have to gain by this confession? He was about to die. On the threshold of death, he predicted a future that most academicians, sociologists, psychologists, and sexologists still ignore:

> There are lots of other kids playing in streets around this country today who are going to be dead tomorrow, and the next day and the next day and next month, because other young people are reading the kinds of things and seeing the kinds of things that are available in the media today.[4]

Scholarly studies confirm Bundy's observations. Toxic sadosexual media floods America today. Adults are not its only audience. In fact, a recent Canadian study found adolescents using pornography more than adults.[5] Younger and younger children are exposed to sadosexual stimuli on television, in comics, music videos, film, and books. Children by the millions are being trained by documentably more violent media than anything Ted Bundy saw as a boy.

What happens to masses of children raised on blood-chillingly violent sexual images—toxic images? Sex was not graphically displayed until the early 1970s. In 1959 Bundy was thirteen years old and *Playboy* (1953) was the only "soft-core" sex magazine a boy would have been likely to find in a local drug or grocery store. *Penthouse* did not appear on newsstands or in stores until September 1969. By then Bundy was in his early twenties. He had already raped, and apparently murdered, numerous young girls and women.

WHAT WILL TOMORROW'S SEX CRIMINALS LOOK LIKE?

Dr. Koop had warned that pornography "can prompt violence in people already leaning toward deviancy."[6] Bundy and his generation used *Playboy* to stimulate their undeveloped sexual emotions. Typical of its impact on most serial rapist-murderers, *Playboy* took Bundy beyond his own immature, inexperienced imagination. It comes as a surprise to most people that in the 1950s and 1960s, *Playboy* typically mixed shiny layouts of smiling, naked women, colorful sadosexual cartoons, and photo stories of sex, rape, and pain. Articles, letters, and graphics glamorized sexual deceit, rape, and even sex with children. National rape and child abuse statistics reveal that Bundy was not unique in his response to these stimuli. There were and are other "Bundys."

If Bundy represents the worst effect "drug store" pornography had on the vulnerable youth of the 1950s, what is the worst we ought to expect from children influenced by later, more explicitly violent sexual images? Our current harvest of serial rapist-murderer-mutilators are over twenty years of age—roughly the age of *Penthouse* (1969). *Hustler* (1974) has been a regular image in some children's lives for more than sixteen years.

The availability of increasingly more graphic magazines to new generations of innocent consumers should concern anyone. It is generally accepted that premature exposure to sexually stimulating images affects children negatively. Should we not expect a crop of offenders who reflect what they learned in the newer, more graphically explicit and violent sex publications? These offenders would be identified by a special brand of brutality copied from their early sadosexual indoctrination. If so, *Penthouse/Hustler*-type magazines and their video spin-offs have had the impact we would expect. The current flood of sexual atrocities scarcely resemble those which *Playboy*-reared men in their forties and fifties had seen as boys.

If pornography has the effect this theory claims, the future will bring an avalanche of sexual violence unsurpassed in our nation's history. And this is happening. Recall the rape, murder, and decapitation of little nine-year-old Adam Walsh in 1984 and the vicious rape and genital mutilation of an eight-year-old Tacoma, Wisconsin boy in 1989.[7] And, on 26 October 1990 the Associated Press reported a nine-year-old in Norman, Oklahoma whose genitals were mutilated and an eye was gouged out. Police called for *Hustler* to be taken off local store shelves following the discovery that a recent issue featured a scene where a child endured a similar torture.

The "fantasies" displayed in soft porn magazines are too often blueprints for brutal crime. The Pollyannas who argue that sadosexual pictures do not encourage and stimulate anger, aggression, and crime in some children and adults should, as they say, wake up and smell the coffee. Or, start reading the reports—like the FBI study which found that nearly all serial rapist-murderers admit pornography as their major interest.[8]

The media falsely allege that Bundy was unusual among

the new cadre of serial rapist-murderers. Yet most of these men have admitted an often blind, consuming passion for pornographic stimuli. Perhaps the most tragic aspect of Bundy's story is that it is not news. His testimony about the critical role that pornography played in his life and in his crimes actually typifies the confessions of most incarcerated serial rapist-murderers.

INCREASING BRUTALITY

A significant portion of society's concern about soft porn should be leveled toward the chilling increase in sexual violence so brutal it compares only to the marauding male hordes of primitive folklore. Although centuries of civilization should separate our enlightened society from the days when savages freely tortured, raped, murdered, pillaged, cannibalized, and destroyed the lives of men, women, and children, today the term "wilding" has become commonplace to describe the growing phenomena of our own brand of subhuman sadosexual violence.

In 1989 a young woman jogger was the victim of a notorious gang-rape-battery-mutilation by a horde of teenage boys in New York City's Central Park—dubbed "wilding." Six weeks later a group of high school star athletes from an affluent New Jersey suburb raped and violently sodomized a mildly retarded juvenile. The young sports stars used a broomstick and a miniature baseball bat in carrying out their sexual attack on the innocent girl.

The New York and New Jersey attackers' common view of rape and sex transcended racial, economic, and geographic differences. These boys are part of the *Playboy/ Penthouse/Hustler* generation conditioned to view sexual violence as a part of a fun night out. These brutal attacks occurred during the same year that *Playboy* celebrated thirty-five years of changing American boys into its revolutionary brand of American sexuality:

> *Playboy* freed a generation from guilt about sex, changed some laws and helped launch a revolution or two.... So you may not think it immodest of us to say *Playboy* is the magazine that changed America.[9]

Immodest? Perhaps. But correct. *Playboy* (first issue, December 1953) radically changed America by altering its view of sex. Gang rape, "wilding," and Bundy-like assaults reflect a view of sex learned at the knee of the *Playboy* culture.

SEXUAL VIOLENCE BECOMES ACCEPTABLE AND FUN

Most people identify "fun sex" with *Playboy*'s approach to women as "bunnies"—or sex toys to play with. What most people, including most *Playboy* consumers, do not recognize is the darker side to *Playboy*'s humor. Its highly orchestrated and heavily promoted sexual assault on "the girl next door" has been thoroughly documented. Standard fare are jokes about women drugged (or gotten drunk), then raped; jokes about gang rape; and, jokes about the rape of coeds, girlfriends, unconscious patients, students, secretaries, maids, neighbors, and children. *Playboy* publisher Hugh Hefner bragged about eradicating the diligently erected Judeo-Christian barrier that once helped to protect "good girls" (the Madonna) from being viewed as "bad girls" (the whore):

> In the prudish moral climate of the Fifties, *Playboy* unabashedly championed sexual liberation. Before *Playboy* women were typecast either as Madonna or as whore. But the wholesome, unselfconscious sexuality of *Playboy*'s "girl-next-door" Playmates conveyed—to men and women alike—the unsettling and exciting message that nice girls like sex, too.[10]

The "nice girls like sex" message has also helped change "nice boys'" attitudes toward sexual violence against "nice girls" (even the view of rape as "rough sex"). In May 1988 the Rhode Island Rape Crisis Center asked seventeen hundred sixth- to ninth-grade students about rape. More than half of the boys and girls considered sex to be acceptable after six months of dating—even if rape was necessary to achieve this. Roughly half of the children agreed that if a boy spends ten to fifteen dollars on a girl, he has the right to force a kiss. Sixty-five percent of the boys and 47 percent of the girls said forced sex was acceptable if a couple dated for six months. Without realizing that "forced" sex is rape, nearly a quarter of the boys and a sixth of the girls accepted rape if a boy had spent money on a girl.

What does it mean when boys and girls grow up believing "rough sex" is just erotic play? According to the *Washington Post* (6 May 1988), of 1,035 rapes reported to the Rhode Island Rape Crisis Center in 1987, 79 percent of the victims were raped by someone the woman knew. Moreover, experts estimate one in four girls and one in seven boys will be sexually assaulted before they are eighteen years old—generally by a relative or another trusted acquaintance.[11]

In 1988 Michigan reported on 681 juveniles convicted of sexually assaulting younger children. The average age of the offender was fourteen! The average age of his victim was seven! Almost 60 percent of the sexual assaults involved penetration, and further, "93% of the [juvenile] offenders were acquaintances, friends, baby-sitters, or relatives of the victims."[12]

The horror of this new wave of juvenile sexual assaults is just the tip of the iceberg. On 11 October 1984 the *Washington Post* reported that a high school girl was raped in a boys' school bathroom while at least ten other boys looked on cheering. The *Boston Herald*, on 28 June 1984, ran a story that a twelve-year-old Pawtucket, Massachusetts boy raped a ten-year-old girl on a pool table in a reenactment of the infamous "Big Dan" pool table gang rape of a woman. The "Big Dan" pool hall case had recently received wide media coverage.

SEXUALLY IMPAIRED CHILDREN

Mimicking pictures in their mother's pornography magazines, a nine-year-old boy and his seven-year-old brother penetrated and killed an eight-month-old baby with a pencil and coat hanger in St. Petersburg, Florida, according to a report in the *Buffalo News* (24 April 1984). Similarly, on 21 July 1990 the *Washington Post* reported on a ten-year-old boy who watched an X-rated film then raped an eight-year-old girl and her four-year-old sister. Does anyone seriously deny that American children are increasingly victimized by toxic media—sadosexual stimuli? How can society, particularly the media, continue to deny that children have been receiving clear instruction and stimulation from pornography, in rape and murder? When Shakespeare sought to stir Hamlet's murderous uncle to action, he had Hamlet whisper, "Ah, the play's the thing!" Today, the film and video industries are the "play," which stirs viewers to action.

The key question is, what "play," is stirring sadosexual violence against women and children? When did the script become so mutant? Consider this: If youngsters suddenly began to attack elderly people coast-to-coast, we would question how their view of the elderly had changed, and we would research when and where the change began. Since children have begun to sexually attack women and children coast-to-coast, we should ask how their view of women and children was changed, so that we may research when and where that change began. This is just what we have purposed to do in this book.

By 1970 the *President's Report on Obscenity and Pornography* already identified extensive use of pornography in the informal sexual education of younger children. In *Teenage Sexuality* (1979), Dr. Aaron Hass found most children had been exposed to some form of pornography. Out of more than six hundred children, 91 percent of the girls and 99 percent of the boys had examined "pornographic" books or magazines. Forty-two percent of the girls and 58 percent of the boys had seen a "blue" movie. Both boys and girls frankly reported being aroused by reading explicit material or viewing explicit photographs. Further, not only were they aroused, but more critically, many admitted they attempted to copy what they saw and read. *Playboy* was the pornography most youngsters mentioned using. In 1979 Hass found that youngsters viewed the magazine's information as believable:

> Many adolescents turn to movies, pictures, and articles to find out exactly how to have sexual relations.... The children said "you really learn a lot ... in the *Playboy* advisor ... I wanted to learn the real facts.... These magazines give me something to go by."[13]

Youthful sexual experimentation has long been encouraged by Kinseyan sex experts such as Dr. John Gagnon. Writing in *Sexual Scene*, Gagnon gives a glowing recommendation of *Playboy* for children. As a past colleague of Dr. Alfred Kinsey, founder of the Kinsey Institute in Bloomington, Indiana and author of the famed Kinsey Reports, Gagnon is a major player in the contemporary promotion of Kinseyan sex education in the classroom. He and co-author William Simon describe *Playboy* as a "Boy Scout Manual" of sexual etiquette. Both sexologists are pleased with *Playboy*'s "creating (highly conventional to be sure) scripts for the playing out of sexual dramas."[14] It is our responsibility to know what "sexual dramas" the children are "playing out."

A NEW MIND SET TOWARD RAPE

As *Playboy* laughed about drugging and raping girls and women, the *Playboy* manual provided rape etiquette for their little "Boy Scout" readers. While in college, the leaders of each generation show a propensity and a willingness to change their view of rape. In 1984 Neil Malamuth and James Check reported on a study in which they showed UCLA college males a series of films depicting three common rape myths: 1) the victim enjoyed the rape, 2) the victim deserved the rape, and 3) the victim was not harmed by the rape. Prior to viewing the films, the students had expressed normal, non-violent sexual attitudes. After the films, more than half of the college men claimed they would rape a woman—if they were sure they would not get caught.[15]

It is common knowledge that rape is now practiced sexual "etiquette" for many college males. In campus rape, "Joe College" acts out suggestions which are historically found in *Playboy*'s "Boy Scout Manual" and its "highly conventional . . . scripts," including the more recent categories of campus rape, boyfriend rape, date rape, acquaintance rape, gang rape, and, now, "wilding."

The nature of these attacks indicate that Joe College knows many of the women he rapes—the very "nice girls" whom, in the past, he protected. Now the conventional rapist frequently knows not only the co-eds he rapes, he is also well-acquainted with the families of his victims, suggesting a whole new middle-class script that reflects a conventional twist to rape and retribution. Victims are often left with the sense that not even father, brothers, and the police themselves will serve as her protector.[16] Note that in cases of rape, the convicted felon is not required to be tested for AIDS, which introduces a new element to the victim's violation. The new *Playboy* sexual script always defends offender's rights over victim's rights.

The Hass findings of the spectrum of *Playboy*'s consumers support the marketing statistics that identify millions of children living in the homes of *Playboy/Penthouse/Hustler* consumers. Given this fact, it is significant that in 1985 *USA Today* claimed the "'*Playboy* Advisor' is USA's most widely read . . . sex education resource." The "*Playboy* Advisor" is a regular *Playboy* feature that advises juvenile and adult consumer on everything from oral sex and cocaine protocol to selecting fashionable cars, clothes, travel spots, and wines.

Playboy's "etiquette" requirements for juvenile sex and violence are reflected in the escalation of reported juvenile sexual violence between 1960 and 1969. Popular periodicals like the *Reader's Digest* showed concern when the FBI Uniform Crime Reports revealed:

> Between 1960 and 1969 the number of forcible rapes committed by males under 18 had increased by 86 percent. It could be concluded that some force impelling toward sex crime has been operating on younger males in the United States.[17]

The *Reader's Digest* was justified in its concern. Juvenile sex crimes have statistically skyrocketed since 1969. And remember, children rape available children. Parents seldom report the rape of a young child by their elder child. I have worked with scores of victims, who as children, were assaulted by an older sibling. Understand that the pornography seen today by nearly 100 percent of our youth creates walking targets out of women and children—a holocaust of outrage and carnage never seen before in any free, or even enemy-occupied, western nation.

Chapter 2

A NEURO-CHEMICAL ADDICTION

In one episode of his television series "Bill Moyers' World of Ideas," Moyers spoke of the Nazi use of "literature, plays, and movies" to literally program a fascist people. "The transition from things imagined to things real is a very easy one," he said, "and men, no less than children, will suit action to fantasy." (12 September 1988) The pornography fantasy in literature, plays, and movies has helped create what some outspoken feminists call "sexual fascism" in the United States.

The Japanese-American poet David Mura writes in his award-winning essay *A Male Grief: Notes on Pornography and Addiction* (1987) that "flesh" can provide the same stimulating and addicting effects as a chemical drug. Scientists are just beginning to understand Mura's poetic reference to the relationship between seeing pornography ("flesh") and the brain's release of its own intoxicating chemicals ("drugs").

"Start with the premise that a person—generally a male—may be addicted to pornography," Mura writes. "This addiction may be part of a larger addiction to any number of other sexual 'highs.'" Some of these include adultery, promiscuity, visits to prostitutes, homosexual or bisexual activities, anonymous sex, exhibitionism, voyeurism, and so on.

Says Mura, "At the essence of pornography is the image of flesh used as a drug, a way of numbing psychic pain. But this drug lasts only as long as the man stares at the image."[1] Both the highs and the lows of the pornography fantasy affect the minds and imaginations of adult and adolescent consumers. According to Mura, winner of the Milkweed Creative Non-Fiction Award, the pornographic fantasy first attracts, then like tranquilizers and stimulants, the fantasy becomes an addiction:

> Those who stand back from the world of pornography can not experience this falling, this rush. . . .
> But for the addict the rush is more than an attraction. He is helpless before it. Completely out of control[2]

However, as is the case with all drugs, the promised happiness and relief lasts only momentarily:

> [H]e has sex with his wife while fantasizing of another . . . and a rush of excitement does occur.
> But afterwards the unhappiness returns, the drug has worn off. And the addict becomes angry. . . .
> [T]hat person has not done what he thinks that person should do—take away his unhappiness[3]

The "eye" of fantasy, writes Mura, leads to darkness, despair, and desperation. To get the pornographic high, one must also feel other emotions such as shame, fear, and anxiety. Fun sex it is not.

Underneath all the assertions of liberty and "healthy fun," the casual user senses anxiety and shame. In the addict, fear, loneliness, and sadness fuel the endless consumption of magazines, prostitutes, strip shows, and X-rated films.

In pornography one often experiences a type of vertigo, a fearful exhilaration, a moment when ties to the outside world do indeed seem to be cut or numbed. That sense of endless falling, that rush, is what the addict seeks again and again.[4]

Mura has used poetic language to describe an intoxicated, disoriented central nervous system. Pornography is media-induced stress.

THE BRAIN'S RESPONSE TO STRESS

The human brain experiences conflicting and confusing images and information when viewing pornography. Airbrushed pictures of cosmetically and surgically "perfect" nude women gaze with professional coyness at the consumer from pages that include jokes of male impotence and castration, rape, adultery, child sexual abuse, religious ridicule, and even pictures and jokes of women and children being tortured or sacrificially murdered. Each month's sadosexual stimuli is meshed with advertisements for autos, liquor, and fashion.

Serious articles and interviews with famous, authoritative male figures imply (by their appearance in the magazine) that pornography is acceptable and an important element in a powerful world. By definition the collection of such a multitude of conflicting sexual and scary, value laden stimuli in one sitting would tend to disorient the human brain.

In such a state, how is it possible that a soft porn consumer could isolate and determine which image or idea is arousing him moment by moment, second by second? To have some idea of how boys and men respond to soft porn images, it is necessary to ask how boys and men respond to live women and girls provoking them in the same manner. Sex research, criminal record, classical and contemporary literature, and even the Bible all concur on how normal males respond to a teasing nude female.

Further, how does the brain of a man or a boy respond to murderous, or other anxiety-provoking images? Tragically, we would presume in light of the research by world renowned medical doctor Isadore Rosenfeld, who warned that "the stress and guilt" of illicit sexual conduct can be fatal: "80 percent of all deaths occurring during intercourse do so when the activity is extramarital."[5]

The last few decades of research have produced massive discoveries in the field of neurology and brain studies have clearly established the fact that every human really has two brains: the "left" and the "right" hemisphere. The right hemisphere is often called our "emotional" brain and the left our "thinking" or rational brain. Studies in split-brain behavior established the rush of pornography as a neuro-chemical response experienced primarily by the right brain.

"Every second, 100 million messages bombard the brain carrying information from the body's senses." Only a few of these are heeded by "the conscious mind." Only the most important—or exciting—sense information gets through.[6] This suggests why pornography has such an impact on people—young and old. When one reaches a state of emotional arousal faster than the body can rally its adaptive reactions, a form of stress follows. Briefly, the male body is designed to respond—or adapt—to blatant female coital signals by engaging in sexual intercourse. Anything which increases sexual stress (e.g., sexual signal, sexual shame, sexual fear) triggers known physiological mechanisms. In an instant, anxiety mobilizes the body into a "chain reaction of defenses with a single aim: to put the body in top physical condition to cope with the emergency." Chemicals seep into the pituitary gland, releasing a stress hormone known as adrenocorticotropic hormone (ACTH). Scores of other neuro-chemicals are sped into action as well, notably adrenaline and noradrenaline. The bronchial tubes relax and open for deeper breathing. Blood sugar is increased for maximum energy. The heart beats faster and contracts strongly; stress will "arouse [all] vital organs."[7]

A vital organ is any single structure of the body that performs some specific function, like kidneys, lungs, heart, and sexual organs. So anything that stresses the body, good or bad, will alert the gate keeping organs of sight, sound, and sex.

Muscles contract and blood pressure rises. The eye pupils dilate "widely" to improve vision as the body organizes to meet an emergency. At red-alert, in a flight-or-fight mode, we can "now perform feats of strength and endurance far beyond... normal capacity."[8] This high arousal-anxiety state would be a normal, although not always automatic, biochemical response of a male to a live or pictorial female coital sex cue.

So, let us consider what is happening to a man or boy turning the pages of *Playboy*, *Penthouse*, etc., or viewing a sadosexual video. His brain is processing images and words of diverse sex signals and emotions, a composite of stimuli, which affects a neuro-chemical response throughout his entire body.

In a manner of speaking, if his left brain (rational hemisphere) had any control over the situation, it would be telling his right brain, "You dummy, that girl is only pretending to lust after you—in fact, she's not even real. Why is your heart beating so fast, and why are your eye pupils dilating so wildly? She is only another man's creative fantasy. Get out of this sleazy strip joint or put those pictures away before your wife (mother, girlfriend) comes in!"

CAN A PICTURE VIOLATE THE HUMAN SPIRIT?

"Violence and pornography, which is a felony against the human spirit, are the atrocities of despair," said former U.S. Surgeon General C. Everett Koop?[9]

Given some known physiological responses to anger, fear, sex, and shame, the question we should ask is at what point does a picture violate the human spirit? Our emergency defense system is triggered during any high arousal state. One could measure a person's vital signs for the difference between "reading" *Time* magazine and "viewing" *Playboy*. In this test, if one responds similarly to both *Time* and *Playboy*, a level of desensitization (or habituation) has generally been reached. When the brain adapts to a novel sensation, arousal is dramatically reduced. It is then necessary to seek out more novel, exciting experiences (i.e., more hostile, violent, shameful pornography) in order to satisfy the desire for that "high."

Koop, speaking of violence and pornography-related atrocities, said, "The people who commit them have an appetite for outrage. They devour what we cling to as civilized life."[10] He referred to pornography and violence as one, deliberately choosing words of stress and anxiety. Writing in the *Color Atlas of Physiology* (1981), Drs. Despopoulos and Silbernagl gave us another description of the body's physiological stress responses similar to what could also be a response to pornography:

> Stress occurs when the physiologic activity of the organism increases faster than the adaptive responses. For the immediate reaction to a [pornography-related] stress, many biologic substances are generated and made available (e.g., epinephrine, glucose). . . . In response to physiologic "stress" (fight-or-flight) . . . [there is] mobilization of defenses. . . . [11]

Moreover, the central nervous system (CNS) treats sexual and violent stimuli nondiscriminatively. In response to violent or sexual stimuli, males and females create "brain chemicals" including adrenaline, a kind of naturally produced morphine. In addition, males produce testosterone, a steroid that fuels both creative energy (sex) and destructive energy (violence). (Females produce estrogen and a minute amount of testosterone. Estrogen does not generate aggressiveness.) The authors of *Sex and the Brain* (1984) note that "rapists and exhibitionists have higher testosterone levels than is normal"—and that testosterone levels go up before sex.[12]

This is expected since sex signals generally produce tension. Tension releases a flood of testosterone in normally functioning males—young and old. When one is neuro-chemically charged, it is left to the thinking brain—largely the left hemisphere—to figure out why the brain/body responds with or without an "arousal high" to the nude photo of Miss November. There are times, as noted earlier by Dr. Rosenfeld, when the stress induced by trying to determine the "whys" behind the response is deadly.

THE INTOXICATION OF STRESS

As noted earlier, neurologists now know that the right, or visual, hemisphere is primarily our "feeling" agent (e.g., passionate, emotional, irrational), while the left, or speech, hemisphere is our "thinking" agent (e.g., analytical, organizational, self-governing). Recent data strongly suggest that females are normally more "bilateral" than are males. It has long been known that males are particularly dependent on their right hemisphere, responding, for example, to visual stimuli with more vigor and speed than females. This is perhaps a required ability due to the male-as-protector role to provide superior, visual-spatial skills.

World renowned neurologist Jerre Levy sheds some light on male susceptibility to pornography, saying that "because of the difficulty [males] may have in communicating between their two hemispheres, they may have restricted verbal access to the emotional world."[13]

Although the impact of consuming promiscuous, sexually-oriented entertainment has been made light of in the last four decades, brain researchers nonetheless note that "the sex hormones are among the most subtle and powerful chemicals in nature. And it is only in the past ten years that scientists have begun to get a handle on how profoundly throughout life they affect the human brain/body system."[14]

Say Smith and deSimone, "Crime, one should bear in mind, is committed by the brain . . . [which is connected to] sex, aggression, testosterone, and so on. . . . Males . . . are gamblers. And their patterns of inheritance and the play of sex hormones within them are under much less firm control [than females]."[15] When in stress, humans secrete hormones that attempt to provoke the brain/body to excitement. To do so we generate an adaptive—a natural, neuro-chemical high. But pornography, as a stress cue, tricks the brain into a flight-or-fight arousal state. Exposure to pornography generally increases one's heart rate, respiration, blood pressure, and the like. It is very dangerous to refer to this arousal state as "sexual drive," however, since it will tend to include a mixture of emotions such as fear, anger, shame, and more.

So, intensity of arousal (in most, if not all, cases) increases in proportion to one's level of stress. This is why after a night of conjugal love, Jane and John may think, "I was more aroused to that 'blue' movie than I am to Jane (or John). I must not love Jane (John) anymore!" Quite the contrary. When in love—after the first flush of newness and insecurity has passed—one should feel a sense of trust and faith. Responding to a "sex" cue experienced in a state of fear, anger, or shame should trigger—temporarily—a "higher" arousal state than would "normal," no longer new, conjugal love and trust.

Many potentially fine marriages have broken apart on the rocks due to such confused thinking about pornographic or similarly exciting adulterous adventures. What one often believes to be *sexual* chemistry stirring in the loins upon meeting the "right one" may really be our *neuro-chemical* warning that risk is imminent—run!

While research is needed to focus on the issue of the neuro-chemistry of pornography, such "common sense" data exist in professional literature. Moreover, these observations have been found very useful in the practical realm. Many who have heard me lecture about these points have responded to this information as though the proverbial light bulb just clicked on in their brains—also referred to as the "Ah-ha!" response. Quite a few men (and some women) followed this remark with a resolution to head back home to a sadly neglected spouse!

This theory of fear/anger/sex rests on the additional evidence that the chemistry also works in reverse. Just as love is often found to alleviate ailments such as headaches, skin rashes, and ulcers, emotional sexual stress has been found to trigger similar dysfunctions. While some angry and fearful people misinterpret themselves as being sexually aroused, other sexually aroused people misinterpret themselves as being angry or fearful. For example, some number of child abuse cases have been known to involve a parent whose incestuous urges were displaced into non-sexual battery or verbal assault of a daughter or son. Or, some overwhelmingly sexually frustrated folks are known to devote themselves to intense physical or intellectual labor, believing, for example, they are driven only by the desire to succeed professionally.

Repeatedly, consumers of pornography define its impact upon their nervous systems—upon their lives—as an intoxicant. Back in 1948, misled by supposedly scientific facts disseminated by Dr. Alfred Kinsey and others, Joe College was additionally misled by his own brain's response to pornography and the promise of "sexual freedom." He did not realize that confusion, fear, shame, or even hate were emotions interwoven into his real and imagined sexual experiences. And he did not understand that just as emotion is connected to one's eyes, heart, fingers, and lungs, it is also connected to one's groin. The college male pornography consumers of the past generation were blind-sided by a product that appeared to be affirming rather than robbing them of their true sexuality. They gained a sexual revolution, and never knew what they lost along the way.

Chapter 3

A MAGAZINE LAYS SIEGE TO A NATION

"This magazine started a revolution." *Playboy*'s strategically placed full-page advertisement appeared on 3 September 1985 in the nationally read *Washington Post*. *Playboy* claims to have shaped the sexuality of American boys and men for forty years, with almost two generations of young males aspiring to an image of fun, sex, and spending in order to gain a pleasurable life-style.

Revolutions, even those given birth to by fantasy magazines, have real-world objectives and consequences. *Playboy* targeted the phallus to win the mind of the American male. The ad claimed that *Playboy* inspired a "social revolution," adding that "for the past three decades, young American men have accepted *Playboy*'s message and spirit as their own."

The magazine's revolution and objective was to get American boys and men to reject their parents' morality and accept *Playboy*'s morality as their own. Successful pursuit of that objective has been the stated purpose of *Playboy* resulting in nearly four decades of our current national epidemic of sexual disorders. The success of *Playboy*'s revolution is evident in the increased number of cases of both old and new versions of sexual diseases. Accordingly, *Playboy* morality deserves much credit for the spiraling rates of impotence, divorce, child abuse, and a host of other national sadosexual tragedies. If today's sexual trauma reflects the message and spirit of *Playboy*, the guru for that spirituality is Dr. Alfred C. Kinsey, along with his disciples Hugh Hefner and the professional spin-offs—sexologists, mass entertainment pornographers, and sex educators.

The foundation for the message and spirit of soft porn

publications was Kinsey's sexual "outlet theory" first touted in *Sexual Behavior in the Human Male* (1948). Dr. Kinsey and his team claimed a man is a man based on his total number of "outlets" or orgasms—referred to as the "total sexual outlet." Coitus with a variety of people and animals of all ages and gender was natural, said the Kinsey gang. They argued voraciously that children need multiple orgasm outlets in order to be sexually healthy.

Kinsey's outlet theory ridiculed man-woman love and healthy, face-to-face, eye-to-eye, lip-to-lip, intimate, and personal heterosexual intercourse. Historian Paul Robinson noted that masturbation and homosexual sex were sexual experiences the Kinsey team touted as better than marital love.[1] But how could Americans, especially the men of post-WWII America, buy such nonsense? The answer lies in the manner of dissemination. While Kinsey's supposedly scientific sex statistics swayed a small academic cadre that included Hefner, it was Hefner who swayed America. Kinsey's radical "recreational sex" claims became a hit with single, college men as thousands of air-brushed photographs of "perfect" nude women winked and wiggled at them in the pages of *Playboy*.

FLAGSHIP FOR A REVOLUTION

The flagship of Kinseyan sexuality was launched in December 1953 and was christened *Playboy* by the captain of the vessel, Hugh M. Hefner. His friend Max Lerner recognized the source of inspiration: "Alfred Kinsey . . . gave Hefner the research base for the . . . '*Playboy* Philosophy.'"[2] What non-consumers do not know (and many *Playboy* consumers overlook) is that *Playboy* has always been much more than a "girlie" or "men's magazine." It has long been a bully pulpit for a world view that judges men according to their tally of sexual conquests. The worldwide prototype for *Playboy*'s male design was publisher Hugh Hefner's own allegedly outrageous sexual life-style.

Trumpeting the Kinseyan ideology since 1953, Hefner and *Playboy* insisted marital love alone was not sufficient for healthy sexuality. Just as Ben Franklin offered an ethical code for coping with life, *Playboy* offered a new set of ethical rules for life. According to Hefner, "*Playboy* freed a generation from guilt about sex, changed some laws and helped launch

Detroit Free Press 20 August 1987

a revolution or two," he declared in the January 1989 "35th Anniversary Issue" of *Playboy*. "*Playboy* is the magazine that changed America."[3]

Hefner, as the ultimate playboy, should typify whatever real benefits his revolution has spawned. After observing the comings and goings of his thousands of sex partners, do American men really believe Hefner is free from the reality of venereal diseases and capable of psychosexual satisfaction? Despite his power over the media and his influence in government, enough information about his personal troubles have leaked out to caution his followers. In the summer of 1988 Hugh Hefner's name appeared often in daily newspapers, the press reporting that he was being sued for palimony and that he admitted long-term drug use. The *London Express* in Great Britain asserted that Hefner was seen performing in a homosexual video. Finally the sixty-three-year-old's "bachelor philosophy" was renounced for marriage to a twenty-six-year-old paramour who recently gave birth to Hefner's child. The libertarian *Detroit Free Press* responded by carving the letters "AIDS" directly over *Playboy*'s famous bunny logo.

The "recreational" sex Hefner advocated was linked indelibly in readers' minds to the spread of AIDS.

AN ARMY OF BUNNY CHEERLEADERS

Prophetically, a libertarian newspaper chose the bunny logo to connect *Playboy* to a sexually transmitted national health tragedy generally seen as a homosexual problem. If *Playboy* served as "the Declaration of the Sexual Revolution," the notorious scissor-eared bunny was its freedom flag. The bunny proclaimed a new liberty for anonymous, guiltless, swinging sex; bisexual and homosexual experimentation; drug use with and without needles; oral and anal sodomy; and, eventually, AIDS. The *Playboy* world became the model fantasy for boys and girls. Russell Miller wrote in *Bunny* (1984) that the strategy of *Playboy* executives went beyond fantasy:

> *Playboy* executives had been talking about taking over the world. "We have our own flag and a Bunny army," Hefner exulted in 1970. *"Playboy* is a . . . world within a world."[4]

Waving his bunny flag, Alfred Kinsey's most influential general marched across society. *Playboy* began conquering Judeo-Christian ethics by capturing callow men in college after college, large and small, secular and religious. With each new triumph, *Playboy* planted the bunny flag of Kinsey's sexual ethics on its new campus territory. It strengthened its military power through monthly reinforcements of fresh, nude pictures, interviews with famous men, cartoons, colorful jokes, and risque talk.[5] Frank Brady wrote in *Hefner:* "Hefner established himself, through *Playboy*, as the pop prophet of a new ethic, guru of the upbeat generation."[6]

The "pop prophet" turned his form of the Kinsey ethic into a mass entertainment enterprise, which today fuels an employment industry affecting millions of lives. *Playboy*'s sex industry and spin-offs have established billionaires in Hollywood, Chicago, and New York mansions while providing jobs for millions of store clerks, advertisers, agents, reporters, photographers, and writers. It has underwritten an entire cinema, art, and photographic industry with paper manufacturers, printers, typesetters, and others necessary to maintain and run these enterprises. And its free-sex-as-entertainment revolution has been instrumental in eventually increasing the demand for and thus the pool of strippers, models, prostitutes, pimps, drug dealers, and cosmetic surgeons.

On the political side, *Playboy* is on record as funding legislators and lobbyists to secure its special interests.[7] And, as with most well-funded special interests, what is on record probably represents only the tip of the iceberg. Hundreds of essays and dozens of books describe the impact of the *Playboy* philosophy upon society since the distraught Marilyn Monroe waved merrily from its December 1953 cover.

Brady noted that *Playboy* centerfolds were being displayed on the walls of locker rooms, gas stations, Army barracks, and bedrooms, "instantly elevating Hefner's status to catalyst of more masturbatory orgasms than probably any other man in history."[8] A close reading of *Playboy*'s official history suggests that Hefner's masturbation revolution was the foundation for his sexual revolution. By dazzling impressionable collegians, *Playboy* marketed promiscuous sex, bachelorhood, and (more subtly, as Brady said) masturbatory behavior via Hefner's air-brushed, nude paper dolls.

A COLLEGE MERCHANDISER'S DREAM

Kinsey's theory of masturbation-for-health gave *Playboy* the tool to overcome two major marketing hurdles.[9] It was a college merchandiser's dream. Prior to *Playboy*, the existing "girlie" magazines had been largely disdained by college males as cheap trash. Moreover, prostitutes were equally scorned and generally seen as diseased, unrewarding, and unacceptable for American college men.

In 1960, while attempting to prove Kinsey's statistics accurate, libertarian sex researchers Drs. Phyllis and Eberhard Kronhausen found in their study of two hundred college males that very few college men frequented prostitutes. "This is contrary to the still-widespread belief that college men depend primarily on paid experiences with prostitutes," the Kronhausens wrote. "As a matter of fact, prostitute contacts start for the college group at a fraction of 1 percent and rise to no higher than 3 percent of the total sex outlet for the older age groups."[10]

In addition, the Kronhausens noted (somewhat critically) that college males in 1960 chose to "save" themselves for the woman they took to wife. Their studies indicated that the average college man of the late fifties and early sixties believed that intercourse was "too precious" to share with anyone other than his future spouse and that marriages worked out better if there was no premarital intercourse. In contrast to Kinsey's report, resistance to premarital intercourse among college men and women was "considerable."[11] The prevailing concept was "no sex without love." Clearly, college females were in full agreement with that notion.

The idea of happiness revolving around orgasms—a Kinseyan concept—therefore needed an aggressive marketing campaign. A sexual fantasy could be advertised as a rite of passage for college males until they found love and marriage.[12] If masturbation could gain an audience, even respectability, *Playboy* could be the masturbatory fantasy source, the regular orgasm outlet advocated by Kinsey. But, the colorful magazine delivered much more to its college readers than youth could anticipate or absorb.

Playboy was not simply a rite of passage but a protocol for living. Robinson had said, "The Kinsey Reports were informed by a set of values and intellectual preferences that, taken together, could be said to constitute an ideology."[13] And, *Playboy* represented the Kinsey values, preferences, and ideology. Moreover, *Playboy* supported Kinsey's claim that "any attempt to legislate sexual behavior was doomed to failure and that the only proper sexual policy was no policy at all."[14]

WARNINGS AGAINST THE "DANGERS" OF CHASTITY

The Kinsey Reports gave structure to Hugh Hefner's "*Playboy* Philosophy," directing *Playboy's* subsequent influence on society. Important men were featured in the magazine, recommending *Playboy's* ethics and values along with its centerfold nudes as stimuli for paper-doll-induced orgasms-at-will. The magazine produced a world of unfamiliar fantasies and frustrations for the college consumer. It prompted immediate sexual arousal and taught Joe College to expect immediate orgasm relief—as in masturbation. Also important, *Playboy* provided a complete consumer protocol. College men learned that with new, sporty cars, travel, liquor, clothes, and women they could buy freedom and avoid disappointment and frustration their entire lives.

The magazine was cheaper than any date and required less time and effort. It was approved of, modern, and "safe." Recall that Drs. Kronhausen reported that the 1950s and early

1960s college boy retained his purity for his bride. With *Playboy* he avoided venereal disease and risked neither a girl's rejection nor exposure due to his temporary bouts of sexual impotence. Now, with Dr. Kinsey's dire warning that men's health required regular orgasm outlets, college-age men had what appeared to be logical, imperative reasons to embrace the radical paper-doll periodical.

Playboy was more fun than any religious tomes, philosophical treatises, and revolutionary manifestos ever published—and it was said to teach sexual well-being. How could a young student calculate the manifold health hazards involved in a fifty-cent orgasm? Could he foresee the change in values and conduct in a nation led by Kinsey and *Playboy*-reared college men? In 1978 Thomas Weyr quoted Hefner's analysis of the effect of *Playboy* on a new generation of leaders:

> "I think it can be said with reasonable certainty that no other single thing in popular communications has had more influence on the changing social-sexual values in the last twenty-odd years than *Playboy*. Without question. And its influence is far more dramatic than most people realize, especially on young people growing up, both male and female. . . . *Playboy* is almost twenty-five years old. The generation now running society is the first *Playboy* generation—the first to grow up with this significant influence on their lives—and their influence has been felt across society."[15]

It is hardly surprising that the socio-sexual ethic of *Playboy* "fits" Kinseyan sexuality, for as a college student, Hefner says he was "indelibly impressed by the famous Kinsey report on American sexual behavior."

College youth were helpless to counter Kinsey's supposedly scientific warning of the maladies of chastity taught by thousands of university professors in every field. In 1954 the sexually tolerant Margaret Mead wrote the following about Kinsey's claims:

> A generation of young men who restricted their sex activities, not from conviction but because they believed others did, have been left defenseless by the Kinsey report. . . . Other critics of our present-day customs are worried by the increase in crime, especially juvenile crime, often

> failing to see that the new climate of [Kinseyan]
> opinion has hardly arrived, that as yet it only
> affects a very small number of teachers, judges,
> social workers, physicians, and a small number of
> adolescents who have been reared in the special
> kind of frankness and ease toward which we seem
> to be moving.[16]

Little did Mead, who had been a sexual freedom advocate in her own right, anticipate the popularization of Kinsey's sexual ethic in *Playboy*. Here was a body of visual, visceral literature for the "generation of young men ... left defenseless by the Kinsey report." The "frankness and ease toward which we seem to be moving" received a massive push in *Playboy*, as "teachers, judges, social workers, physicians," and adolescents memorized pages of the new "climate of [Kinseyan] opinion" month after month.[17]

Kinsey preached early sexual experimentation as necessary for a full and happy adult sex life. Hefner, citing his mentor, sermonized on the socio-sexual values of early sex, attacking chastity and marriage. Weyr, a *Playboy* admirer, worried that *Playboy* created an anti-chastity dogma asking, doesn't this "generation have a totalitarian strain running through it [making] chastity obsolete and its practice difficult?"[18]

In 1954 Mead said that Kinsey's early sexuality creed was just beginning to impact our society. This helps us understand the change in the views of juvenile sexuality now taught in the popular media, the entertainment industry, and our grammar schools. It also clarifies a key reason why the percentage of sexually active teenagers rose from 10 percent in 1950 to 50 percent and more in some groups by 1980. The upward trend in out-of-wedlock births among our teens is off the charts, and the United States is on record with the highest incidence of single, teen motherhood in any Western country.[19] The work of Alfred Kinsey advanced abnormal and subsequently harmful beliefs about human sexuality. Hugh Hefner, utilizing the vehicle of *Playboy*, invaded the American psyche with those beliefs.

Chapter 4

FINDING THE FANTASY PLAYBOY

A fantasy "playboy" heart beats within every editorial decision and advertising strategy put forth by *Playboy*. The question is: Who is the fantasy playboy and is he really copied by men and boys in real life? The supposed archetype of and creator for the myth is Hugh Hefner. But where do we find this playboy? Public relations hype and marketing strategy aside, is the fantasy playboy a sexually enhanced man? Is he, on the other hand, contemptuous of women, one who can play it cool? Is he passionate and committed, or does he detach himself from emotional experience? Are men who try to be playboys more manly? Or, are those who judge themselves by its standard themselves victims of the playboy fantasy? Do *Playboy*-type fantasies frequently facilitate degrees of impotency in some consumers?

Judging by magazine ads (e.g., "What kind of man reads *Playboy*?"), photos, and editorial comments, the model playboy is always sexually and professionally successful, happy, detached, and unattached. While the majority of *Playboy* readers are married, the fantasy playboy is free of binding marital and familial commitments. The playboy has the money necessary to create and maintain the facade of desirability to untold numbers of very eager, very young, beautiful, white (occasionally spiced with light black, Hispanic, and Asian) sex partners. His *Playboy* guidebook provides "authoritative" sex and drug counsel, while marketing expensive cars, clothes, furnishings, and exotic travel necessary to complete his playboy image.

In a 1961 interview, Hugh Hefner said:

> Our reader buys a "total package" when he picks up
> *Playboy*—advertising as well as editorial . . . every

thing within *Playboy*'s pages should create a consistent impression of the good life to which *Playboy* is dedicated.[1]

This new world view of the "good life" has been exposed by Judeo-Christian moralists, political .conservatives, libertarians, feminists, and others as fascism with a modern face. It was humanist psychiatrist Rollo May who labeled *Playboy*'s trafficking in naked women as "the new sexual fascism":

> Open an issue of *Playboy*, that redoubtable journal reputedly sold mainly to college students and clergymen. You discover the naked girls with silicated breasts side by side with the articles by reputable authors. . . . An image of a type of American male is being presented—a suave, detached, self-assured bachelor, who regards the girl as a "*Playboy* accessory" like items in his fashionable dress. . . . *Playboy* is basically antisexual . . . the new sexual fascism. . . . Noninvolvement (like playing it cool) is elevated into the ideal model for the Playboy.[2]

Playboy's "total package" offers its consumers fantasy men, women, and children cavorting about in a mythological world in which everyone gets to play. The fantasy playboy lives in a third world of sexuality—where women, young girls, and children live for his pleasure and to do his will. Virginity never exists by choice and is an illness to be cured. Hefner said he broke the barrier between Madonna and whore. The underside to this view is that now all women, including wives, daughters, and mothers are also whores, therefore rape is humorous, for it is a way of giving women the sex they want but are too embarrassed to admit or request. Even children and animals may be represented as existing to sexually service the needs of the playboy fantasy superstar.

THE WORLD THROUGH THE EYES OF *PLAYBOY*

A complete picture of the playboy's world is based on what *Playboy* visually depicts and omits in its pages. Examining the monthly visual data, especially the roughly thirteen thousand cartoons drafted over forty years, playboys give little to their world and take much. Juxtaposed to the serious monthly interviews with recognized government, sports, and entertainment leaders, the playboy is photographed

photographed and cartooned as accessing his power primarily to buy and control people. His lovers, secretaries, wives, housekeepers, patients, nurses, students, and children all exist for his sexual entertainment.

The only elderly women allowed to exist in the *Playboy* culture are ugly, old wives, a sex-obsessed and ridiculed "granny," and a sweet, plump, whorehouse madame who markets young girls and women. Elderly men are generally cartooned as child molesters, impotent sexual adventurers, or old fools chasing young nurses and nubile girls hoping to achieve a sexual experience. Childbirth and children are unwanted accidents. *Playboy* is consistent in its ridicule of the single mother left to care for the child. Those children who appear in the pages, having survived the abortions promoted and humorized by the pornographers, are cartooned in sexual relationships with adults—kin or non-kin. Boys are depicted as sexually curious, eventually becoming porn consumers and playboys themselves to keep the industry alive.

Clergy are cartooned as child rapists, religion is faith-fully cartooned and spoofed, and satanic photo stories glamorize tales of sexual demons. The proper role of government, says *Playboy*, is to liberate us all from any sexual taboos and from laws restricting or banning illicit drugs. All government authority is shown as corrupt, without exception, and democratic only on the surface. Sex is currency in all decision making.

Equality of personage in the *Playboy* visual world translates into cruel, dominant women. Power is in the hands of only white, college men and a few black athletes or entertainers. Being top dog—like Hefner—is everything. The top man ultimately controls the lives of other people. *Playboy* and its spin-off pornographies work to erode empathy and remorse in consumers—the qualities that humanize man and prevent him from becoming a heartless bully.

One could add much more to this picture of *Playboy*'s visual world particularly in light of its recent forays into more sadosexual violence, excretory and similarly deviant attempts at "humor" and sophistication. A fair question is, could the total package of one "girlie" picture magazine have helped generate the malignant, drugged, and sexually violent "good life"—which the *Detroit Free Press* linked with AIDS?

WHEN PLAYBOYS GAIN POWER

Hugh Hefner's self-professed claim to fame should be kept in mind: "The generation now running society is the first *Playboy* generation." Based upon the data (e.g., letters to the *Playboy* editor from senators, congressmen, theologians, lawyers, entertainers, organization leaders, and the VIP list of Hefner's friends and supporters), this *is* largely a *Playboy*-reared society. And it is a Kinsey-reared society as well. Hefner and Kinsey share the responsibility for a generation of powerful, influential playboys. Such men tend toward heterophobia—fear and distrust of the opposite sex—widespread drug use and addiction, impotence and homosexuality, suicide, astronomical divorce rates, epidemics of venereal disease, and AIDS. Boys become juvenile runaways and possibly develop patterns of behavior that identify rapist-murderers.

Both Kinsey and Hefner battled for the elimination and liberalization of sex laws. The concept of "victimless crime," criminals' rights, and blaming the victim were products of the Kinsey/Hefner effort. Eventually tens of thousands of criminals, primarily sex offenders, were paroled back into society. The post-1953 Kinsey/Hefner view of sexuality promised to reduce sexual frustration, thereby eradicating every kind of delinquency and unhappiness.

The measure of success for Kinsey and Hefner can be seen everywhere. Post-Kinsey/Hefner, the profession of "sexology" was created to cope with a massive increase in cases of sexual disorders. Building on its fraudulent research base, sexology crept into higher education, medicine, counselling, therapy, law and public policy, sex and AIDS education curricula, and political lobbying. While the sexuality profession owes its origin and credibility to Kinsey and the Kinsey Institute, it may be said that sexology owes its economic success and massive popularity to Hugh Hefner. Hefner preaches, glamorizes, and visualizes Kinseyism every month in the pages of *Playboy*.

THE *PLAYBOY* MODEL

As noted, the fantasy model for Hefner's playboy is the publisher himself. Hefner's editorial control and his world view defined every detail of his paper fantasy, and to understand this playboy—and the rest of soft porn—Hefner, missionary for Dr. Alfred Kinsey, must be analyzed and understood. Russell Miller wrote in *Bunny* that Hefner was captivated by Kinsey:

> In 1948, the first Kinsey Report was published. Hefner read every word and wrote an enthusiastic review for the *Shaft*, [University of Illinois campus newspaper] attacking the hypocrisy of public attitudes toward sex. Kinsey's findings, indicating that 86 percent of American men experienced sexual intercourse before marriage, 70 percent had intercourse with prostitutes, and 40 percent indulged in extramarital intercourse, revealed an extraordinary discrepancy between private behavior and public attitudes that Hefner thought was truly shocking.[3]

Kinsey's figures, based on a sample disproportionately weighted by homosexuals, prisoners and other social deviants, were believed by Hefner, a callow young student. Kinsey's false statistics on masturbation, bisexuality, homosexuality, virginity, adultery ("swinging"), and child-adult sex became Hefner's own world view. Kinsey blamed Christianity and Judaism for all the world's ills. His paradise would be attained when the archaic sexual restraints imposed by Judeo-Christian morality were destroyed. Only then would everyone be happy. Hefner was inspired.

In *Reaching for Paradise*, biographer Thomas Weyr cites the young Hefner as chaffing under his own religious restrictions. A God-fearing Methodist who accepted "traditional values," Hefner painfully endured his own virginity and the sexual restraint imposed by his fiance, says Weyr. To abandon his moral foundation, Hefner required, as did most 1950s American Christian and Jewish males, a new god, a new moral view, a "religious" justification for adopting new standards.

Kinsey, says Weyr, became Hefner's new god, his guru, and the Kinseyan cult began:

> If the beginning of social upheavals can be pinpointed in time . . . then the publication in 1948 of Alfred Kinsey's report on male sexual behavior marked the official start of the second American sexual revolution. For Hugh Hefner, as for most American collegians, [the revolution was] the appearance of Kinsey's book. . . . For Hefner, Kinsey

was the confirmation of his own vague feelings, first discovered in the two years he spent in the army.[4]

The first Kinsey book, Hefner feels, "produced a tremendous sexual awakening largely because of media attention. . . . I really view Kinsey as the beginning. Certainly the book was very important to me. . . ." Conscious or not, Hefner approached *Playboy* with a prophet's fervor. Sex was good, abstention almost a moral wrong.[5]

The Kinsey Report marked the beginning of scientific probing into the sexual process, a probing based on statistical method more than on Freudian intuitive insight. Hefner recognized Kinsey as the incontrovertible word of the new God based on the new holy writ—demonstrable evidence. Kinsey would add a dash of scientific truth to the *Playboy* mix.[6]

Throughout his life, Hefner cited the "scientific" Kinsey reports about male and female sexuality extensively. In college, he accepted Kinsey's data and arguments for elimination of nearly all sex laws. Weyr quotes Hefner's college essay, which paraphrases Kinsey's report, in which the student "wrote a term paper for a criminology course on Kinsey and U.S. sex laws.'If successfully executed they [the laws] would have virtually everybody in prison' he wrote and suggested major revisions in the penal code." Later these were adopted. [7]

It is doubtful Hefner realized that while he had paraphrased Kinsey, Kinsey had paraphrased (or plagiarized) his friend and colleague, pedophile and child-adult sex advocate Rene Guyon (*The Ethics of Sex Acts*, 1948) on the topic of sex laws. The motto of the Rene Guyon Society (an international pedophile organization) was "sex before eight or else it's too late."[8]

THE MONTH BY MONTH ASSAULT ON VIRGINITY

Kinsey swayed both Hefner's intellectual and philosophical allegiance and his personal sexual behavior. His biographers all agree that until the Kinsey Reports, even after his army service, Hugh Hefner was an average, American guy—which meant sexually inexperienced. Corny as it sounds now that we've become accustomed to wide-spread adolescent sexuality and pregnancy, at eighteen years of age this leader of sexual liberation, said Miller, "never touched a drink in his life, never smoked, never swore and was a virgin." In fact, said Miller, the first time he made love was to his fiance at the age of twenty-two.[9] "The first time was in college. It was with the girl that I married," said Hefner in a 11 January 1976 interview with the *Sunday Plain Dealer*. Miller, asserting the power of one man's vision to change another man's life, claims the Kinsey Reports transformed Hefner's Puritan values, giving him the confidence to delve into pornography and to insist on having sex with his reluctant fiance prior to their wedding night:

> It was the Kinsey Report that aroused his interest in sex as a subject of legitimate study, rather than the source of considerable frustration in his courtship of Millie. He began avidly reading medical journals, nudist magazines, marriage guidance handbooks, books on sex law, and any work with a vaguely erotic or pornographic content. That summer . . . Millie acquiesced to his urgent pleading to "go the whole way."[10]

Miller writes that Hefner said he later felt betrayed when he discovered that Millie had been sexually unfaithful prior to their wedding, and it has often been said that the *Playboy* world he created was an act of revenge for this betrayal.

ATTACK ON RELIGION AND AMERICAN SEX LAWS

To pinpoint Hefner's guiding philosophy, most of his biographers cite the first *Playboy* issue. In that December 1953 issue, the publisher outlined his ideology. As recently as December 1987, Hefner reiterated what he felt were the most important statements in his "*Playboy* Philosophy." Clearly Kinsey is still alive and well and shaping American men and laws.

> Church-state legislation has made common criminals of us all. Dr. Alfred Kinsey has estimated that if the sex laws of the United States were conscientiously enforced, over 90 percent of the adult population would be in prison. . . . A sexually hypocritical society is an unhealthy society that produces more than its share of perversion, neurosis,

psychosis, unsuccessful marriage, divorce and suicide ... shame and suppression in the early years of
life and you will reap frustration, frigidity, impotence
... repression ... producing frigidity, impotence,
masochism, sadism.[11]

Things were certainly not perfect under the guidance of
religion, pre-Kinsey—after all attempting to civilize man has
never been a simple task. However, if we honor Hefner's
1953 challenge, we should compare the two hundred years of
problems allegedly caused by the Judeo-Christian sexual
ethic to the current problems caused by forty years of Kinseyism
and the *Playboy* philosophy. Since Hefner claims his magazine shaped American men for at least one generation, if not
two, we should now see very few cases of "perversion,
neurosis, psychosis, unsuccessful marriage, divorce . . .
suicide ... frigidity, impotence ... masochism, [and] sadism."

Unfortunately, in a post-Kinsey/Hefner era, every one
of these measures are documented as escalating dramatically,
while whole new mutant forms of sexual violence (serial
rape-murder), masturbatory (autoerotic) fatalities, sexual diseases (AIDS,) and the like have emerged from the Kinsey/
Hefner world view. This is to be expected. As the men Kinsey
called typical American males were largely sexual deviants,
homosexual activists, imprisoned sex criminals, and such, it
is no wonder Kinsey (as quoted by Hefner) could find that
"over 90 percent of the adult population would be in prison"
if sex laws were enforced.[12]

Hefner correctly believed his magazine would
popularize Kinseyism. In his words, cited by Weyr, they were
"filling a publishing need only slightly less important than
one just taken care of by the Kinsey Report."[13]

HEFNER INTRODUCES THE FANTASY WOMAN

What kind of world would fantasy playboys have
without fantasy women? The absurd idea that women were
sexually "inhibited" ignored the fact that Americans had just
swept away two generations of the "white slave trade" (a
massive industry prostituting poor women and children). The
Third World today generally keeps women in virtual slave
status and much of Europe winks at the women's movement,
holding fast to long-preferred views of women's inferiority.

Sex was not explicit in mainstream media until 1948 when *Playboy* entered the American entertainment marketplace. Said Hefner, "women's magazines wouldn't run bikini pictures. . . . Nudity was unknown in the women's field . . . what we were doing was really counter-culture at that time" (*Sunday Plain Dealer*, 11 January 1976). Miller recalled "that time" when World War II films, novels, plays, and song lyrics focused on love of family, romantic love, and marriage:

> Sex was not yet making an appearance in popular lyrics, but it was certainly on everyone's mind. To a generation brought up to believe that sex was furtive and dirty, the Kinsey reports were a revelation. If *Sexual Behavior in the Human Male*, published in 1948, was a shocker, the report on female sexual behavior that followed five years later was a sensation, revealing to America a remarkable truth; nice girls did. And, on the vinyl-upholstered back seats of two-tone automobiles . . . more and more young men were discovering to their surprise and delight, that Kinsey was right.[14]

Miller neglected to mention that Joe College discovered "Kinsey was right" because youthful behavior had been drastically altered by Kinsey's fraudulent sex data. Would Hefner have broadcast Kinsey's sex theories had he known nearly all the women Kinsey interviewed were already sexually "unconventional"? In fact, a sizeable and apparently significant number of the respondents were working prostitutes—whom Kinsey would have identified as married women! Would Hefner have created *Playboy* if he knew Kinsey lied about men's sexuality, just as he lied about women's sexuality? What if Hefner knew that the male subjects Kinsey used as models of sexuality were primarily convicted sex offenders and homosexuals?

Kinsey's findings were believed by college graduates and hard-hat laborers alike—and his phony sex data on children, women, and men fueled Hefner's prophet-like fervor. *Playboy* touched off a mass sex industry, which has reflected Kinsey's false data throughout its entire existence.

NO EQUALITY IN *PLAYBOY* MONARCHY

Every nation's culture is defined by its body of literature, laws, religion, art, and national symbols and whether its government is a democracy, an oligarchy, a republic, a monarchy, etc.

From the perspective of governance, *Playboy* is a monarchy. Hefner's biographers reveal him holding forth in silken, flowing robes, heavily guarded in his high-walled castle—his principality. Inside the castle a royal court is housed: royal artists, media professionals, and writers who interpret the king's words for the populace. There is a constantly changing stream of royal queens, concubines, and court prostitutes to sexually entertain his guests, and a beautiful princess to inherit the throne. There are multitudes of court jesters, advisors, religious leaders, and royal liaisons to the people.

The kingdom has a "Foundation" that bestows grants and awards to chosen subjects for specific works and research projects beneficial to the image and interest of the king and his kingdom. And it sponsors events, exhibiting charitable concern. Luxuriant food, drink, and drugs flow. As in Mayan times, one young female (a centerfold) is washed, combed, coiffed, and decorated each month in preparation for nude presentation—a regular public inspection in a form of "ritual sacrifice." Few of these young women ever appear in *Playboy* as special beings again. In fact the only *Playboy* centerfold who ever rated a film and book about her life was a young woman who became interesting to the media after her insane husband brutally, sadistically murdered her.

The *Playboy* government is no republic, nor is it a democracy. Though Hefner personally drafted his own constitution via the "*Playboy* Philosophy" and declared love for "equality, fraternity," Brady wrote that the practice at the *Playboy* mansion was quite different, "reflecting the royal" intrigues of the Old World.

> To be seen putting a hand on Hefner's shoulder ... is intimately related to the chair-on-the-left. Upper-level *Playboy* executives who have been attending Hefner's movies for years would not dream of sitting there unless beckoned to do so by Hefner. Somehow, they never are.... The protocol is that of true royalty: no one ... talks to him first.... Hefner maintains the position of control, keeping everyone else in a distastefully subordinate role.... Despite the almost unbearable tension, an invitation ... was a highly prized status symbol, jealously guarded by those who achieved it and fiercely resented by those who were ignored.[15]

Most interesting is the rare description of King Hefner's throne. Despite his many biographers and mansion visitors, and their "hints" of the royal court and throne, only Brady—himself a Hefner devotee—publicly reported this behavior:

> Hefner sometimes keeps his assembled guests waiting for hours before appearing . . . often dressed in paisley pajamas and a yellow silk robe and usually accompanied by his then-current special girl. . . .

> Hefner sits in his chair—which is a huge, deeply upholstered affair with a matching ottoman, making the whole thing something like the size of a bed—like Henry VIII on his throne, his good lady of the moment snuggling up to him. . . . Next to Hefner's chair, on the left-hand side, is another throne, an exact duplicate of Hef's. This is also reserved, and there is a certain mystique about who does and doesn't sit there. . . . Hefner's offhand comments . . . are always answered with the invariable . . . "Love ya, Baby!" . . . There is apparently a curious, unspoken rule which says that only those to whom Hefner somehow silently communicates his approval or beneficence can have the pleasure—or honor—of sitting next to him. No visiting celebrity is ever asked to sit next to Hefner . . . [but is sent to] a high-level chair directly behind him. This is true even when the companion throne chair is empty.[16]

KING OR GOD?

Efforts to examine the royal cloak within which the sex merchant wraps himself are important. Biographers attempt to uncover their subject's psyche in order to understand his conduct. Brady details what other writers have politely noticed, that Hefner's followers laugh at his every "joke," clap at his words, and nod in agreement to his moral pronouncements. They know that the consequences for neglecting such behavior—no welcome at the next mansion soiree—can be suicidal to the health of their business. They drink Pepsi Cola even though they may detest it, show enthusiasm and distaste in imitation of Hefner, and generally supplicate themselves before their king.

Brady and the other biographers mention that the chosen few among Hefner's retinue compete for the hallowed chair beside the sex merchant's throne. Imagine this humiliated entourage, men and women who connive to sit alongside Hugh Hefner. Concluding this modest glimpse into Hefner's imperial etiquette, Brady describes the discourtesy borne by guests who are themselves luminaries:

> Stars and celebrities . . . famous people are then given to know the extent of their relative unimportance. . . . No one speaks to the [celebrity] guest. . . . Walking quickly to his chair, he [Hefner] may occasionally deign to nod to the by-now cowed guest; even more rarely, he may stop to speak a word or two. (This invariably produces a murmur among the throng. . . .) In the minds of the disciples, there is only one god.[17]

What kind of sexuality would such a "god" propose for his people? Would he want other men to experience a healthier life (sexual or non-sexual) than his own? From all appearances, Hefner's life (like Kinsey's) was fraught with desperate insecurity. While both were compulsive voyeurs, Hefner also fits the definition of a sex addict. That is, a man who is unable to control his sexual appetite due to his overwhelming insecurity and inability to experience satisfaction.

Patrick Anderson, another Hefner admirer, notes that Hefner has "slept with hundreds, even thousands, of beautiful young women."[18] However, in a small note elsewhere, Anderson quotes Hefner saying he could never make "love" without drugs. Hefner admitted he felt little or nothing during sex.[19] So, Hefner made "love" with drugs, not women.

Author Gay Talese, in *Thy Neighbor's Wife*, described Hefner as "a sex junkie with an insatiable habit."[20] Dr. Patrick Carnes cites Hugh Hefner as a typical sex addict in *The Sexual Addiction*: "Addicts, at one level, judge themselves by society's standards. Unable to live up to these, they live with constant pain and alienation . . . isolation and constant fear of discovery."[21] Carnes notes the four-step addictive cycle: preoccupation, ritualization, compulsive sexual behavior, and despair.[22]

The Hefner that biographers describe and the life he projects in the pages of *Playboy* both meet psychotherapist Erich Fromm's description of dehumanizing "technocratic fascism":

Pleasure and thrill are conducive to sadness after the so-called peak has been reached; for the thrill has been experienced, but the vessel has not grown.[23]

Dehumanized Man will become so mad that he will not be able to sustain a viable society in the long run.[24]

Fromm points out that a nation of Hefners—vessels engaged in non-intimate sex or sex without growth—leads to catastrophe.[25] The amazing thing about the playboy fantasy is that it could never have taken place in a nation that really believed sex was "dirty." The romantic era had actually elevated sex-in-marriage to a level of sensual honor. The "Roaring Twenties" was hardly a time of repression and sexual inhibition. World War II had unified women and men.

On the contrary, it was this ideal of marital sex as beautiful that motivated college boys and girls to save "it" for marriage and their lifelong partner. Utilizing this groundwork, Kinsey and *Playboy* could argue that sex was good and clean.

The pornographers had to start with a high ideal of marital sex that was beautiful and loving before they could make the argument that sex could not be dirtied merely by the absence of a piece of paper saying one was married.

In fact, until his recent marriage, Hefner consistently defined himself as a "romantic," who was always falling in love. This view of romance could not have been possible unless and until the foundation had been laid establishing sex as beautiful and romantic—in marriage. Despite the disdain of researchers like the Kronhausens for such prosaic, Judeo-Christian values, this sexual attitude can be found in their 1960 research on college men.

Hefner is, in fact, typical of the youth of the 1950s, reared to restrain sexual activity and to delay coitus until marriage. But, *Lady Chatterly's Lover* had been in print since 1928, Ernest Hemingway was hardly anti-sexual, and Freud had persuaded family doctors to lecture on the need for sexual fulfillment.[26] From there, American women's magazines wrote glowingly of "falling in love" with the sunny view of coitus as the wedding night culmination of love.

Despite the enthusiasm over Kinsey's reports, the world really needed no deliverance from a supposedly suppressed ideal of the value of fulfilled marital sexuality. Imagine the surprise and delight of boys in finding that Kinsey was right and that "good girls did it." Sociologist Bernard Barber predicted that Kinsey's claims of normal male sexuality would alter the western male's perception of himself. College-age boys, believing Kinsey's bogus data, would respond with increased "sexual" expectations of themselves and the young women they dated.[27] This, said Barber, was a "self-fulfilling prophecy." Stressing massive sexual activity as normal would increase actual sexual behavior so that everyone would be "normal."[28] Thus, there would be more sexual license among college-age girls after the Kinsey report, than before the report:

> Knowledge about the consequences of our knowledge is doubly important. . . . New knowledge will change the very situation that the scientists are themselves studying. There can be no question that the Kinsey Reports will change the patterns of sexual behavior in American society. . . . [Trapped by] "self-fulfilling prophecies," the scientist gets the results he predicted partly because he predicts them. As it has been wittily . . . said, the Kinsey volume on Men produced the results of the Kinsey volume on Women.[29]

So, following the first Kinsey Report in 1948, a sexual reformation was underway on college campuses across the nation. Unbenownst to the young men who bought the first issues of *Playboy*, love was being shifted not to a modified form of the prevailing Judeo-Christian "family" oriented view but totally away from that view, to one that could be called, anthropologically, a "Third World" view. That is, women's status was to be increasingly devalued and male responsibility, fidelity, and lifelong obligation to one woman undermined.

In the playboy's world, women are a lower species—sexual game (like rabbits) that one goes out to hunt. To alter attitudes of an entire generation of young men toward love and marriage, *Playboy* cast males as sexually primal, predatory, and guiltless animals. In fact, perhaps the most disturbing aspect of this strange, new world *Playboy* helped create is that there really are no men in it. There are only boys playing at being men—playboys. Ages may vary widely, but the emotional maturity and common interest of all males is supposedly the same. In this world, all males are defined in relation to their playful pursuit and fulfillment of sexual release—outlets. All males fall in to one of two camps: either indefatigable sexual superstars or impotent wimps.

Chapter 5

PLAYBOY EMASCULATES THE AMERICAN MALE

Were a woman's magazine to treat men's sexual imagery the way *Playboy* has for forty years, one could logically assume the publishers and staff feared, and perhaps even hated men. One could assume they were bitter women attempting to castrate and dominate men. It is hard to accept that same motivation where the publishers and staff are male. But *Playboy* and its satellites have systematically ridiculed male sexuality, including male impotence, in hundreds of cartoons and articles. While radical feminism hit the scene in the mid-sixties, *Playboy* had been exploiting male sexual fears of female rejection for over a decade.

The marketing strategy of the soft porn business works to undermine long-term, married heterosexual love and commitment—also known as heterophilia, or love and trust for the opposite sex. *Playboy* was the first national magazine to exploit college men's fears of women and family commitment. *Playboy* offered itself as a reliable, comforting substitute to monogamous heterosexual love. Their attack on American men has been devastating. By creating the fantasy image of a playboy sexual superstar, the sex merchants have masked their real goal—total control of the American male.

The resulting male impotence spawned by pornographers has been characterized not only by men's reduced orgasm ability (which for pornography consumers is often true) but by weakening their desire, courage, and ability to tackle the most significant relationships of a man's life. And as Aristotle warned, when the family is weakened, the loss is felt in community, state, and federal leadership. Given enough exposure to high stress sadosexual images and philosophy, regular consumers go from being initially titillated to an unconscious sense of insecurity. Eventually most consumers become vaguely unsure of how (and some totally powerless) to function due to a reduced evaluation of their own self worth.

In contrast to the hundreds of emotionally castrated men who yearned to sit near the Hefner throne, the fully functioning, sexually potent male is a man among men. He is not intimidated by another man's power, money, or control of people—women or men. This is not because the true male has money and power himself. It is because he has the strength of internal convictions and moral fiber. Very often he has won the love of a wife who reaffirms his masculinity. A real man knows who he is and rejects the pornographer's exploitation of women and children. Unlike Hefner, who only feels love when he is on drugs, the sexually self-assured male does not need drugs or extravaganzas to help him feel aroused. He can have a loving, lifetime-committed relationship charged by natural body-chemistry.

Such a man stands in stark contrast with what we know of the father of soft-core pornography. This critical biographical data is necessary to understand the publisher's goals and objectives for his magazine. Consider the way in which Hefner controls all media that turn an eye toward him or his empire. There are rare insights into the real Hugh Hefner. Before his marriage, Hefner's last queen, young Canadian model Carrie Leigh, had threatened to file suit against him. Leigh had released homemade videos that the *London Express* claimed showed Hefner engaged in "disgusting homosexual activities." This was not impossible since Hefner admitted to some earlier homosexual dalliances. Leigh also revealed something that has often been reported and Hefner himself admitted—that she and Hefner regularly took drugs in order to enjoy sex.[1]

Without drug use, Hefner had no sexual feeling. As noted earlier, this means his arousal was never to sex, or making love with a woman, but to artificial chemical stimulation. (He would experience similar excitement from masturbation during drug use.) Only Anderson reprinted Hefner's admission that he was dependent on drugs for sexual excitement. Frank Brady, a "Hefophile," who regularly identified with and glowed with appreciation for the publisher, gingerly avoided the implications of Hefner's drug dependence in his report:

> There has been relatively little written about Hefner's use of drugs, mainly because he prefers not to talk about it. . . . [He] was introduced to amphetamines ("speed") by one of the other *Playboy* executives . . . [finally taking] two or three each hour, even shortly after waking. . . . [He] still consumes a fair amount of bourbon, to this day laced with the inevitable Pepsi. I've seen him drink as many as a half-dozen bourbons in one two-hour sitting.[2]

The latter reveals a poly-drug use pattern. Of the hundreds of reporters who have written about Hefner, none suggest that he might be an impotent poly-drug abuser who uses *Playboy* to try to emasculate other males. Hefner is on record as a user of marijuana and speed (and implicitly cocaine). Like most poly-drug addicts, alcoholism is also a serious problem. He regularly consumed three bourbons an hour. Add alcohol to the reports of Hefner's stated dependence on marijuana or speed to enjoy sex and we have a profile of an emotionally impotent, frightened, chemically addicted man, with massive numbers of sex partners, yielding inevitable venereal and other health problems—including that of impotency.

Brady continues:

> Hefner has a fear of water and doesn't swim . . . declarations of self-satisfaction are mere rationalization; for in reality Hefner was highly pressured, constantly overworked, and often melancholy.[3]

Hefner's publicity—his pipe, sex, and pajamas—suggests a laid-back personality. But information to the contrary leaks out from between the cracks in the castle walls. He is hardly an athlete or fitness-oriented individual. The potent, healthy, normal male is the real threat to the *Playboy* fantasy and to the hidden impotence of its insecure creators. Thus Hefner's initial goal would be to capture the mind of the American male. The *Playboy* achievement would be to have men dependent on their association with *Playboy* et al for their sexuality and potency. Psychiatrist Rollo May said in *Love and Will* (1969) that the sexual revolution changed the nature of men's sexual problems. Suddenly, May said, analysts were finding an increase in sexual impotency even among the young:

> Sex is . . . the source at once of the human being's most intense pleasure and his most pervasive anxiety. . . . [I]mpotence is increasing these days despite (or is it because of) the unrestrained freedom on all sides. . . . External social anxiety and guilt have lessened. . . . [I]nternal anxiety and guilt have increased. And in some ways these are more morbid. . . . [O]verconcern with potency is generally a compensation for feelings of impotence.[4]

May said that the sexual revolution triggered "our schizoid world" and impotence. The psychiatrist was seeing in his clients a new phenomenon—lack of sexual desire (which sexologists now prefer to call "insufficient sexual desire" or ISD). Certainly the preoccupation with male potency, which permeates pornography, contributes to the consumer's fears of his own impotency.

THE ANTI-MALE, IMPOTENCY GOAL OF SEX MERCHANTS

Many people are becoming aware of the anti-woman, anti-child character of pornography and its threat to the health and welfare of women and children. Relatively few people, however, are aware of its deeper structure, the anti-man, impotence goal of all sex merchants.[5]

The cash register could explain this apparent inconsistency. One can go bankrupt if the competition provides a better product at a cheaper price. A good marriage can permanently supply the only product sex merchants have to sell—arousal and masculine fulfillment. Economically it is necessary for the sex industry to do two things: first, it must poison men against the love of one woman, and, secondly, it needs to sexually disable men. Hence, the effort to destroy man's ability to experience natural arousal in an atmosphere of fulfilling, marital committed love.

The initial, youthful exposure to pornography is often accidental. And the subsequent purchase of pornography is generally triggered by youthful curiosity. Often a friend, relative, a parent—even a wife—might buy a boy or man a subscription to a pornographic magazine. Continued pornography use reflects the boy-man's excitement with his fantasy notions of power over women and girls—or as with homosexual pornography—power over men and boys. Many male consumers are easily trained to believe they are being cheated if they have a love life with one woman. Sex merchants intend to displace woman-wife and love. Sex merchants intend to become the consumer's substitute lover!

Playboy has often illustrated this process in its own cartoons. One of the more memorable was a lovely young woman in bed with a man—her spouse it seems. They are having sex, only he has spread a centerfold picture over her body. She looks up, the centerfold separating her face from her beloved and asks, "Are you sure you still love me, Henry?" In another, as a middle age couple is leaving a porn movie, the man says to his aging wife, "I'm leaving you, Ella."

As the consumer's new love life, the sex merchant dominates and insinuates himself into the lives of millions of men and boys. Should men ever understand themselves as victimized by sexually dysfunctional pornographers, the sex exploitation industry would indeed be endangered.

Fear and distrust of the opposite sex are major weapons for achieving the sex industry's anti-male objective. Pornographic fantasies impair the delicate ability of men to love, marry, and to be permanently, exclusively committed to one woman—one family.

Fear and distrust of women renders men increasingly physically and emotionally absent, asexual, sexually promiscuous, impotent, violent, and homosexual. In this condition, robbed of their male power, they become vulnerable to the sex industry, which appears to be on the other side, posing as a cure for their problems. Living in such fear, men are not able to fully mature, love, and commit. Despite the roles they often play as influential power brokers, they are not able to take their places in society as complete, responsible, adult men.

The recent fall of scores of powerful, political, academic, and religious leaders to sexual crimes is an example of this impotence. The sexual dysfunctions of educated males can lead them into emotionally traumatic, even fatal, waters. The need of *Playboy* and other pornographers to co-opt Judeo-Christian morés was, and still is, a critical component for pornography's success. It was necessary to throw out the healthy Judeo-Christian baby (literally) with the murky bath water.

DESTROYING THE WILL TO LOVE

Psychotherapist Erich Fromm points out that man and woman can create life, babies, art, objects, food, and ideas. When one does not create goodness and love, Fromm writes, the desire for transcendence (immortality, or leaving a marker that indicates one's existence) will take on a vicious form. In the following quote, Fromm's use of the term "man" is generic referring to women and men: "The ultimate choice for man . . . is to create or to destroy, to love or to hate. . . . The will for destruction . . . is rooted in the nature of man, just as the drive to create is rooted in it."[6] So impotence has a direct impact on man's need to create love and good.

The choice of love over hate is supported by Judeo-Christian values. Belief in love is the foundation for the biblical call to chastity, fidelity, delayed sexuality, and monogamy. Scripture condemns fornication, adultery, sodomy, and bestiality because of a belief in man-woman, spiritual-physical love. The underpinnings of these morés could be called "unselfish love." Despite the well-known extremes of Puritan and Victorian sexual standards, those societies produced strong nations and vigorous people economically, educationally, genetically, artistically, and governmentally.

Any reasonable analysis of the health and vigor of western society must consider the major influence of Judeo-Christian laws and their unique valuing of women's responsible (rather than men's recreational) sexual morés. Contrary to popular rhetoric, the Judeo-Christian world view legally enforced women's sexual interests. Although hardly perfect, Judeo-Christian sexual law has pioneered women's and children's civil rights. All non-Western societies are still exclusively male oriented, most allowing men many wives and instant divorce while denying women divorce or property rights.

The healthy impact of a Judeo-Christian sexual view on our national well-being is obvious. Pitraim Sorokin, past professor emeritus in sociology at Harvard University, addressed the "vitalizing and enabling power of unselfish love" in contrast to the loneliness and psycho-social isolation that produces suicide:

> The best antidote against suicide is . . . unselfish creative love for other human beings. . . . Love is a factor which seems to increase the duration of life. . . . A minimum of this love is absolutely necessary for survival of newborn babies and for their healthy growth. . . . The bulk of juvenile delinquents are recruited from the children who in their early life did not have the necessary minimum of love. Deficiency of "the vitamin of love" is also responsible for many mental disorders. . . . "Love begets love and hate begets hate." . . . Creative love increases not only the longevity of individuals but also of societies and organizations. Social organizations built by hate, conquest, and coercion, such as the empires of Alexander the Great, Genghis-Khan, Tamerlane, Napoleon/Ceasar, Hitler, have, as a rule, a short life—years, decades, or rarely a few centuries.[7]

"People with the capacity to love have the impulse to love and the need to love in order to feel health," wrote Sorokin's co-author, psychologist Abraham Maslow. "Capacities clamor to be used and cease their clamor only when they are used sufficiently."[8] Erich Fromm, quoted in the same volume, declares that man's sanity depends on the necessary fulfillment of uniting with and being related to other living beings:

> The experience of love does away with the necessity of illusions. . . . Love is in the experience of human solidarity with our fellow creatures, it is in the erotic love of man and woman, in the love of the mother for her child.[9]

Sexual behavior must be understood within the framework of love (or the absence thereof). Historically we know that men are too easily trained to be hostile, violent, and ugly. Modern male sexual behavior educated by the *Playboy* philosophy to be exploitative often becomes explosive. Men who are filled with illusions become disappointed and destructive of the integrity of the loved one. Following up on Fromm's comment about illusion, Sorokin warned that hostility, sadism, and distrust reflect a hunger in the soul—leading to physical and mental ill health. Love requires integrity and trust. This nation believes in love in marriage, and as millions of divorces confirm, love is crushed by the insensitive or the coarse.

CREATING RAGE TOWARD WOMEN

The strategy of the pornographer is to create coarse men, men who are insensitive, fearful, and distrustful of women. The emptiness of a heterophobic soul triggers impotence and rage in men toward men, women, children, and western views of sexuality. The pornographers' success is seen in the proliferation of the hate literature called pornography or erotica[10] and by the tragic state of man-woman relations. The current pitiful condition was not always so. There was a time when even though women did not have equal access to the boardroom, their values were largely yielded to—even respected in the bedroom.

The effects of the Kinsey/Hefner philosophy were predicted in 1969 when psychotherapist Rollo May forecast that separating intimacy from sex would lead to male hostility and impotence:

> In an amazingly short period following World War I, we shifted from acting as though sex did not exist at all to being obsessed with it. . . . From bishops to biologists, everyone is in on the act. . . . [Note the] whole turgid flood of post-Kinsey utilitarianism. . . . Couples place great emphasis on bookkeeping and timetables in their love-making—a practice confirmed and standardized by Kinsey . . . [m]aking one's self feel less in order to perform better! My impression is that impotence is increasing . . . it is becoming harder for the young man as well as the old to take "yes" for an answer.[11]

May's earlier notice that excessive concern with potency could perhaps be a "compensation for feelings of impotence" has since been supported by other specialists. Do personal problems, concerns, and compensations regarding impotency occupy the minds of the staffs and publishers of the magazines? Since roughly half of American males have experienced some form of impotence[12], the sex industry is exploiting perhaps man's greatest fear.

Normally in marital love, a trusted, loved woman easily allays her man's sporadic impotence. The two will be together

forever, therefore, they have time. They have other interests
and responsibilities equally or more important than orgasms.
A loving wife will soothe and reassure her spouse. His love for
her will manifest naturally, and usually, the two will defeat
the problem, sharing another experience foreign to the promiscuous heterosexual or homosexual male—the power and
sexual potency of lifelong committed love.

On the other hand, the impotent, unattached, or promiscuous male will often seek reassurance by turning to the
widely available excitements and pseudo-intimacies of the
pornographer's paper dolls. This way he can fail or succeed
in secrecy. He is often sure the "right" woman will free him
soon from compulsive masturbation. The reality is that no
woman with whom he mates can permanently match his
pornographic illusions. He has worked himself into a state of
anxiety, which eventually contaminates all sexual contacts.
Even the transient experience of impotence, Silber explains,

> creates such anxiety, worry, and insecurity over
> future performance that suddenly the man finds
> that what was simply a transient event is now
> persisting. [He] usually feels aroused sexually, but
> his penis simply doesn't cooperate.[13]

As symptoms such as premature climax or inability to
maintain his arousal state begin to manifest, pornography
becomes the crutch man frequently uses to justify himself as
a sexual being.

CASTRATION HUMOR FEEDS FEARS

Dr. Bernie Zilbergeld, who later was commissioned by
Penthouse to write about the benefits of pornography, had
earlier warned that pornography would destroy heterosexual
relations. He especially pointed to *Playboy* cartoons as
encouraging impotence:

> Humor is the basic source of education. . . . And
> sexual humor bolsters all the old crap and the old
> fears. It counts. Sex is loaded with anxiety, even
> for ten-year-olds. . . . Cartoons that poke fun at
> impotence or other male inadequacies "would
> outweigh any supportive things said in the
> advice column. Cartoons are simply more
> compelling. . . ." [Even Paul Gebhard, a co-author

of the Kinsey report, admitted,] "Any cartoon with
an impotence theme would distress an impotent
male to some extent and perhaps plant the seed of
worry in another male's mind."[14]

Those familiar with the study of impotence are aware of
its shocking escalation during these free sex and pornography
decades. A man's fear of impotence is consistently cited as the
very cause for his temporary and permanent impotence. And
performance anxiety is a key sexual fear identified by men.
Associated with performance anxiety is the male fear that his
phallus is inadequate, misshapen, or even ugly.

Strangely enough, sex researchers fail to confront the
reality that forty years of Kinseyan sexual freedom has
resulted in higher—not lower—rates of impotence. In order
to illustrate the defects of Judeo-Christian sexual morés,
Kinsey tended to overstate nearly every male-female sexual
problem. Yet on the issue of impotence, he reported in 1948
a baffling incidence of impotence of only "0.4 percent of the
males under 25, and less than 1 percent of the males under 35
years of age"[15] even among his bizarre, criminal, and
homosexual volunteers. In 1965 the Kinsey team reported
impotence rates of more than 60 percent among similar sex
offender groups. By 1969 Rollo May was impressed that
impotence was increasing. And by 1970 Dr. David Reuben
said 100 percent of the male population experienced
impotence at some time, and chronic or repeated impotence
"probably affects about 30 to 40 percent of men at any given
time."[16]

IMPOTENCE MEANS "WITHOUT POWER"

Impotence literally means "without power." If it is even
vaguely true that from 1948 to 1970 men went from less than
1 percent impotence to an average of 30 to 40 percent
impotence, masses of men had been robbed of their "power"
by something or someone. By 1970 Kinseyan philosophy had
influenced American males for twenty-two years and
Playboy magazine for seventeen years. Despite women's
liberation and the availability of heterosexual sex, free, and
without guilt, male sexual disorder had definitely undergone
a change for the worse from 1948 to 1970. Whatever the
precise increase in this disorder, and despite women's rights
to multiple orgasms, the sexual revolution has continued to

torment men with impotence. By 1979 historian Christopher Lash would write in the *Culture of Narcissism*:

> Whether or not the actual incidence of impotence has increased in American males—and there is no reason to doubt reports that it has—the specter of impotence haunts the contemporary imagination. ... Today impotence typically ... [is a] generalized fear of women that has little resemblance to the sentimental adoration men once granted to women who made them sexually uncomfortable. The fear of woman ... reveals itself not only as impotence but as a boundless rage against the female sex. This blind and impotent rage, which seems so prevalent at the present time ... when men still control most of the power and wealth in society yet feel themselves threatened on every hand—intimidated, emasculated—appears deeply irrational ... even Mom is a menace.[17]

It cannot be over stressed that while *Playboy* has denigrated women and children for four decades, its real target has been to deliberately and methodically control men by controlling their male sexuality.

Chapter 6

A CAMPAIGN TO ELIMINATE THE NICE GIRL

For thousands of years, Western religious thought has reflected the Bible's demands that men and women refrain from adultery in order to create and ensure the stability of families and nurture healthy children. This arrangement would fulfill God's plan under the belief that regular coitus with a fit marital partner would control what was seen as the baser nature of man. This self-discipline and self-control would bring them into service to God, family, and nation. Aristotle himself argued that society could only reflect the family—for better or worse.

Playboy dealt with these notions about marriage and family in its first issue, Christmas 1953. The new college man's bible warned them to beware of the marriage "trap," showing the m instead how to get "clean" sex from Jane Co-Ed.

The magazine is designed to sexually arouse. Without a sex partner and without the availability of a wife, however, millions of boys and men were commonly given to bouts of masturbation with the smiling paper dolls as "partners." But in 1953 masturbation was still considered juvenile and humiliating. To admit the obvious masturbatory function of *Playboy*, would be the death knell for both it and the evolving sex industry.

So, the magazine's strategy was fourfold: (1) to sexually stimulate readers, (2) to discourage marriage, (3) to encourage orgasms via masturbation, and (4) to glorify promiscuity—"recreational sex."

It worked. Today males often remain single and have sex exclusively with paper dolls and with numerous "nice girls" who "like sex, too." He knows, and they know, that women still want him to "pop the question"—even if only so they can say "no." Today's girlfriends frequently cook, clean, and sew for their guy, have sex in any number of positions he wishes to try (with video enhancement if he so desires), and seldom dare mention the "M" word (marriage). If she becomes pregnant, unlike the 1950s when the girlfriend would run out and buy a full white wedding gown, she will generally be expected to visit the local abortion clinic to rid herself of the little "inconvenience" and be back at work by Monday. Some men might share the expenses. After an abortion, the demoralized couple will soon split up and return to the brutal, disease-laden, singles scene. Welcome to Hefner's sexual fantasy world.

In the 1950s, when "nice" girls had sex, few people knew about it. Despite Kinsey's phony data, most women tried to maintain their virginity until marriage—or until they had sex with their fiance. Remember, pre-Hefner, both boys and girls looked upon virginity as a valued condition.

HOW TO SEDUCE VIRGINS

Realizing this, the first *Playboy* issue gave men step-by-step directions on how to trick girls out of their virginity. Here, primarily virginal Judeo-Christian college boys were reassured that real men are never virgins and that the more girls they "deflower," the more good deeds they have done. In its maiden issue, *Playboy* directed men to seduce virgins and move on, as a "bee" pollinating many flowers (virgins) but not remaining long with any one. At the first inkling of feelings, cautioned the magazine, flee! The same pioneering issue included an essay entitled "Miss Goldigger," a terrorist attack on marriage.

In our day of genital herpes, AIDS, new forms of syphilis, a strain of gonorrhea that eats penicillin alive ("Saigon clap"), and a host of other venereal diseases and heterosexual dysfunctions, the public may now see that the *Playboy* philosophy was fatal even to some of its casual adherents. Typical *Playboy* advice ominously rings hollow with almost forty years of deadly, disease-ridden sex counsel. The anti-virginity doctrine, authored by "Frankenstein Smith," has been preached since 1953 from the *Playboy* pulpit in text, cartoons, photos, articles, jokes, film and record reviews, and wine and cheese recommendations. Readers might encounter anti-marriage sex advice anywhere in the magazine or in its numerous video and magazine spin-offs:

> All sophisticated playboys are interested in virginity.
> . . . Most men realize that virginity is an unpleasant little matter to be disposed of early in life . . . you are actually doing the girl a service. Some may suggest that you are trying to deprive them of something— trying to take from them a cherished possession. This is nonsense. Actually, you are giving them a new freedom—a means of enjoying life more fully. . . . Some difficulties have arisen because of the confusion (in female minds) between virginity and purity. The two have nothing to do with one another, and it is important that you point this out at the proper moment. Thus, armed with our convictions, we are ready to begin. First, of course, we must select a suitable subject. . . . Once we've found our subject, we are ready for the approach. . . . [don't bother with non-virgins because] it robs you of the special pleasure of spreading the good news—and that, after all, is what this article is about.[1]

PLAYBOY 1987: ONLY VIRGINS FOR "SAFE SEX"

The general sexual depression afflicting our nation can be seen in today's sexual despair. Cases of AIDS, genital herpes (affecting, some studies claim, nearly 50% of college women[2]), and venereal diseases (striking 2.5 million teenagers yearly) exceed the amount of major childhood disease cases reported each year. This would suggest the blatant tragedy of Playboy's "recreational sex" advice, believed and practiced for decades by millions of boys and men. In 1987 the Playboy advisor James Petersen (a USA Today poll called him "USA's most widely read men's sex education resource" [27 September 1985]) offered a revealing reply to a letter on how to avoid AIDS.

By all means, have sex, Petersen said, but use "safe sex" practices. For "safe sex" strategies he recommends to consumers: "Date virgins, or very young lovers, or people who were monogamous for the past decade, and you cut down your chances of being exposed to the virus" (May 1987).

From 1953 to 1987, the nation's most widely read men's sex education resource had educated boys and men to detest monogamy and fidelity, teaching them instead how to seduce virgins and then discard them. Yet now, while the nation pays a heavy price for these decades of *Playboy* propaganda, the most widely read men's sex education resource suggests the use of "virgins or very young lovers." Just how young is "very young?"

Typically, Petersen writes with the reader's good time in mind. Subsequently, advising sex with "virgins" (plural) and "very young lovers" (also plural) is the way to achieve a good time while avoiding self-exposure to a deadly disease (clearly regardless of whether or not the virgins or very young lovers may be exposed). Petersen does not advise readers to abstain from sex. Or to marry the virgin or the youngster. Petersen should be well aware that the data on juvenile sexuality suggests seventeen-year-old girls are frequently sexually active, and that few "*Playboy*-type" women over twenty-one are still virgins.

Implicitly, Petersen's advice is to locate *very* young females for sex—since these are the safest sex partners. The same advice—to deflower virgin after virgin—was offered to readers in 1953. Petersen shows no concern that the playboy himself might be AIDS or otherwise venereally infected. Male readers are again advised to seduce, have sex, and move on—to other "virgins" and "very young" girls—plural.

Playboy encouraged readers in 1953's essay, "Virginity," to seduce as many virgins as possible, but to avoid forced "r-a-p-e." The article instructs readers on how to maneuver and trick the "subject" into sex, voluntarily forfeiting her virginity. Again and again, if you are falling in love, the advisor says, abandon the girl immediately and locate another "subject" to have sex. Such advice was good for *Playboy* marketing. A consumer closes the magazine in an aroused state and turns to either masturbation, sex with the wife, or the next woman (virgin) to "help." Said Weyr:

> Unless you are wholly undersexed, you cannot come away from *Playboy* without feeling, "Shouldn't I be having sex now?" The pressures of sexual conformity are huge. Options exist only in the variety of sexual experience, not in its narrowing, or, God forbid, in chastity or partial abstinence. . . . There is never any "counterthinking" in matters of sex; no argument for the joy of fidelity, or the closeness

between man and woman without penetration and orgasm. Tenderness is noticeable chiefly in its absence, despite Hefner's vigorous espousal of "romanticism."[3]

THE END OF BREACH OF PROMISE

Some people have been known to protest that *violate* is too strenuous a word to describe the process of orchestrating a young girl into bed with the single intention of ending her virginity. This suggests how coarsened our society has become. Webster's definition of the verb *violate* is: "To infringe on; to break or disregard, as a promise. . . . To desecrate, as a sacred place." Webster does not mention extreme violence such as rape, assault or torture—the image we might rather conjure when we consider the act of violation.

Until the 1940s, violated young girls could legally press "breach of promise" suits, identifying and disgracing the "cads and bounders" (and their families) who trampled on a young girl's trust and vulnerability. (Today, our enlightened society debates the "discriminatory nature" of the long held tradition of withholding public release of an alleged rape victim's name and identifying her alleged assailant—further evidence of the casual attitude toward violation.) The modern American playboy, however, need not worry. He may lie about his intentions without concern about recourse or retribution. There is no longer any legal resource for young women through which psychosexual battery damages can be repaired. This powerful—though seldom used—protection for females is gone, purged from the legal codes. Instead, playboys have been trained, directed, and schooled in artful abuse of trust. En masse, the playboy has been conditioned to detach himself from emotional concern for his victims or hesitation about his actions.

LETTER-FRAUD MISREPRESENTS FEMALE MORALITY

British psychiatrist, Peter Dally, while generally supportive of pornography, noted in *The Fantasy Factor* that the sex magazines relied heavily on phony letters to entertain and instruct their readers:

> *Penthouse*, a "soft porn" magazine that claims a
> monthly circulation of five hundred thousand in

Britain alone, categorizes its letters under various
subheadings, such as "Rubber Delights," "Pain and
Punishment," and so on. . . . Most of these letters give
the impression of being written in the editorial offices, their style is so similar . . . some of the letters
may be genuine.[4]

It may be negligent to think Petersen and others do not
doctor and write their letters, particularly in light of a rare
public admission regarding fraudulent *Playboy* letters. Miller
reveals in *Bunny* that the magazine did falsify its text, casually
lying about the source of material that filled the letters
section:

The first letters were all written and answered by
Playboy staffers . . . only a few readers had sex on
their minds: for every letter asking advice about sex,
there were seven or eight asking about wine, or
cufflinks or sports cars. Sex questions were largely
concerned with dating etiquette and deflowering
virgins [finally leading to queries on] fist-f--ing, and
the caloric content of sperm . . . there would always
be dozens of anxious inquiries about the average size
of the penis. It was the subject that dominated the
correspondence and no amount of reassurance that
size was not related to performance stopped readers
fretting that theirs was not big enough.[5]

Moreover, there was a period of time when the "*Playboy*
Forum" was penned by Anson Mount, once Hefner's religion
liaison, eventually becoming *Playboy*'s sports writer. No one
could complain that the "*Playboy* Forum" was boring when it
made its debut in June 1963. Indeed, the ideas being
exchanged were astonishing for the times: there were outrageous letters from young girls describing the pleasures of
group sex, advice from priests on the benefits of premarital
sex, and wild sex stories from Southern sheriffs. Many of
these letters were written by the Forum's ingenious editor and
signed with names chosen from the telephone directory.
Miller justifies the magazine fraud by observing that Mount
was eventually replaced, becoming the college athlete re-
cruiter for *Playboy*'s All-American Team.

For a magazine that. claims iconoclastic honesty,
Playboy's lies and fraudulent advice went unrecalled. If these
were phony checks or bad tires, the law would intervene,
enforcing a manufacturer's recall, and the public would have

reason to be wary of future products marketed by that manufacturer. How does a magazine recall lies about young girls,
women, and priests? By printing a retraction?

There were no admissions and no corrections by the
magazine. Taxpayers spend millions of dollars to finance
Playboy's translation into Braille and its placement in our
nation's libraries because of its claim to be a serious journal
concerned with truth and social responsibility. Yet, the
magazine is not expected to adhere to journalistic standards of
reporting. *Playboy*'s structure allows it to be less candid than
the *Communist Daily Worker*, or the *People's World*. Despite
the media's efforts to sanitize the image .of Hefner, some
rather incriminating information on the magazine's censorship strategies has seeped through. In his book, Brady
reprinted a telling memo the *Playboy* editorial staff received
from Hefner:

> In the future, pick the Letters To The Editor on the
> basis of their interest value. Do not feel obliged a la
> *Time Magazine*, to give both sides and to include a
> lot of stuff that is negative about the magazine. We
> assume that most of our readers dig us, so we don't
> have to include lots of letters calling us homosexuals
> or sex nuts. . . . Pick the letters, as I said, for . . . what
> they continually do to build the image of the maga-
> zine.[6]

VIOLATING THE PUBLIC TRUST

A magazine that alters photos, slants articles, censors
letters, purges writers, and presents a uniform visual and
textual bias on critical social issues would be called
"propaganda." But *Playboy* is also regarded as a "fantasy"
magazine. So, there was no suggestion that Mount's
outrageous fraudulent letters—attributed to the pens of "young
girls"—were the product either of their editor's sexual
disorder, his pedophilia, or other amoral appetites. It was seen
that the Mount letters already had established a belief system
and a pattern of sexual behavior for their readership. A
process of sexual "creativity" had begun in "*Playboy* Forum,"
and "*Playboy* Letters," and it would be continued—if not by
Mount, by other editors or readers whose "creative" juices he
had stimulated. Miller noted later that even after Mount left
"Forum" for another department

> the genuine letters that were pouring into the *Playboy* Forum were quite as extraordinary as those dreamed up by Anson Mount . . . masturbation, buggery, penis envy, lesbianism, impotence, abortion . . . [a girl's alleged sexual use of the crucifix, later seen in *The Exorcist* and orgasm with a fly. . . .] [7]

Based on Hefner's command to censor and discard the "wrong" sort of letters to the editor, the magazine would likely not print letters that revealed abuse or impotence as a result of the *Playboy* philosophy. Mount's fraudulent letters could, as Dally suggested, be an accepted practice. There is no more reason to believe these "genuine" letters of seductive cheerleaders, mothers, and co-eds than there would be to believe Mount's letters.

Hugh Hefner himself called into question the honesty of sex magazine letter writers in his "Philosophy IV" writings. Noting the "psychosexual pathological implications" of readers who wrote that they enjoyed spanking their wives, he said "girlie" magazine claimed such mail came "from females, too." Displaying his distrust of other pornography magazines, Hefner added, "at least the letter writers claimed to be female."[8]

Hefner doubted the gender of the letter-writers. He said those who enjoy "spanking" reveal sexual pathology. Today's "*Playboy* Letters" section is filled with accounts of brutal acts of spanking and other sadism. Hefner has already programmed "psychosexual pathology" into the trough at which *Playboy* readers feed. In the November 1976 "*Playboy* Advisor," Petersen published a letter allegedly written by a young "high school cheerleader" in which she described how much she enjoyed her boyfriend beating ("spanking") her with a wooden paddle while she was naked and Mom watched. (Mom "looked at her watch and told him to start spanking. Thirty minutes later he stopped. My bottom was . . . .")

Years of reviewing such letters leads me to judge this letter (and many others) as a plant—written with the publication's own editorial hand. The advisor, Petersen, tells the "girl" that sadism is fun and he recommends better ways to increase the pain. Examining Petersen's advice one finds an on-going attempt to normalize what Hefner called the "psychosexual pathology" of sadism. And there are on-going attempts to normalize child sexual abuse and a broad spectrum of other behaviors, including illicit drug use and incest.

Letters have a documented impact on readers—most firmly believe the stories are real. Black poet Susan Lurie addressed the importance of these dishonest letters in *Take Back the Night*:

> The pornographers have her report a need to be "filled with male desire," and sign female pen names to their misogynistic fantasies in an effort to convince their public that pornography is simply "explicit sexuality" and reflects what is sexually fulfilling to men and women alike.[9]

BROKEN IMAGES OF HEALTHY HETEROSEXUAL LOVE

For over thirty-five years Hugh Hefner parlayed Kinsey's sham pan-sexual statistics into male entertainment. The Kinsey/Hefner sexual view has become modern "sex education" in public, private, and parochial schools. It has influenced child rearing, legislation, psychology, and the behavior of college boys and girls, spouses, divorcees, parents, doctors, teachers, and national leaders. If it is true that whoever controls men's sexuality controls men, then the sex industry controls much of today's society.

The wedding ring ends the continuation of a playboy life-style and much of the control the magazine wields over a man. Women with a good self image are vocal about their contempt for men who stash paper dollies nearby for a sexual charge. The real world test of forty years of fraudulent Kinsey/Hefner sexual education is reflected in the rates of heterosexual dysfunction manifested in divorce, impotence, homosexuality, sex addiction, rape, serial rape-murder, incest, drugs, alcohol, and AIDS.

In 1987 a twelve-year-old child was raped, beaten, and left dead in a dumpster. Her only recognizable feature was a gold cap on her front tooth, engraved with a *Playboy* bunny. While most children don't have teeth replaced with embossed images of the *Playboy* bunny, most children are marked by both the science of Kinsey and the entertainment of Hefner.

Playboy was the first mainstream magazine to popularize illicit drug use and rape—even rape of children and virgins—by college men. As noted earlier, in 1953 the magazine began teaching rape trickery. This continued up to 1987 when the most widely read advice column in the United States recommended having sex with virgins or very young lovers to avoid AIDS. Today, sexual harassment, trickery, and sexual sadism are endemic.

Since *Playboy*'s letters had been written by editors in the past, one can assume sadistic tales of young high school cheerleaders were also planted by the advisor or his staff. Author Susan Lurie agrees with publisher Hugh Hefner, that he and his magazine reveal a psychosexual pathology. Men like Hefner, implies Lurie, will sign female pen names in order to convince the public that perversion is joyful to men and women alike.

Chapter 7

THE FAMILY: *PLAYBOY'S* GREATEST FEAR

In the wake of the AIDS and herpes scare, families and marriage are considered even more important to the vast majority of Americans. But to the *Playboy* empire, and the *Playboy* mentality, those values are anathema. Said Hefner:

> We want to make clear from the very start, we aren't a "family magazine." If you are somebody's sister, wife or mother-in-law and picked us up by mistake, please pass us along to the man in your life and get back to your *Ladies Home Companion*. . . . I don't want my editors marrying anyone and getting a lot of foolish notions in their heads about "togetherness," home, family, and all that jazz.[1]

Hefner, the alleged outspoken opponent of censorship, declared his editors and writers would not dare support notions of "'togetherness,' home, family, and all that jazz"— nor marry. Brady reported:

> The male *Playboy* staffers, for the most part, were divorced or unmarried, and they used the magazine as an entry to meet the women they photographed and wrote about. . . . Nearly all staff members . . . conducted wild parties and had a wonderful time. . . . Many of the parties had the ambience of a fraternity smoker, and the group seemed more typical of high school or college students than men in or entering their thirties.[2]

Stephen Byer, a past corporate vice-president in charge of all *Playboy's* marketing activities, wrote in *Hefner's Gonna Kill Me When He Reads This* that while few *Playboy* employees were married, some had been divorced. By 1972, when Hefner's attack on marriage began to bear fruit, marriage was still "in"—but not at *Playboy*. After writing that nearly all secretaries regularly provided sexual services to their bosses at *Playboy* (the cartoons, he said, were a realistic description of their work place), Byer testified that at *Playboy* headquarters:

> Other activities involved instances of hanky-panky, homosexuality, divorce and drugs, not to mention the clothes-freaks. . . . Take, for example, the area of divorce. Between 60 and 80 percent of the people I came in contact with had been divorced at least once.[3]

The after-glow of World War II was characterized by the most advanced-to-date male-female egalitarianism of the 1950s. People were celebrating the church on the hill, the white picket fence, the suburban home, and the nursery. During the era of the child-centered society, woman was "superwife" and mom and, most essentially, the lifeblood of the nation.

Playboy was carrying out a different agenda—its aggressive program of "heterophobic" sexuality, crafting a fear of marriage, family, and children. Apparently it was a fear reflected in the *Playboy* staff "typical of high school or college students" although these men are now well past thirty, forty, fifty, and even sixty years. Safety and power for men existed only in a playboy, party-time bachelorhood. Said Weyr:

> Critics argue that *Playboy*'s anti-sexuality fomented male fears of women and prevented men from finding fulfilling relationships by building a protective wall against the dangers and terrors of sex. Perhaps so. But millions of men [and boys] bought *Playboy*'s message that sex was safe and fun anyway. And even those who didn't, who feared sex or commitment, must have found much of the *Playboy* message soothing. . . . Much of *Playboy*'s sexual tone was subliminal. It emerged from the total package more than from any individual piece.[4]

THE FORTY YEAR WAR AGAINST MARRIAGE

When that *Playboy* message was first introduced, women's magazines were carrying monthly articles about how to make hubby happy, how to keep him and her family healthy, and how to be a better—and more attractive—mother, wife, and citizen. Vance Packard is one of the critics who noted Hefner's role in turning men against women's sexual sensibilities. In his best-selling book *The Sexual Wil-*

derness, Packard wrote of the difference between the *Playboy* genre and women's magazines in the mid-1960s:

> Some of the more sophisticated male magazines provided their readers with material that exhibited glowering hostility. . . . A good deal of their content seemed designed to denigrate females. The mood was often competitive or defensive. . . . In contrast, the leading U.S. women's magazines during the 1960s devoted very little space to trying to put the male in his place. Instead, when discussing male-female relationships they seemed to be trying thoughtfully to understand what was going on.[5]

What "was going on" was largely *Playboy*, the sophisticated "major magazine" for future male leaders. *Penthouse* was not yet in existence. Celebrating a self-centered Eros, *Playboy* institutionalized the war between women and men, waging a forty year assault against marriage, the family, and heterosexual love.

Until the early 1950s, mature men were not expected to subscribe to sex magazines. College males laughed at men who used sex pictures for arousal. However, with the roster of famous leaders writing for the magazine by the 1960s American men had largely bought the package. By the early 1970s, when a young man married, if he was a *Playboy* consumer, he was generally expected to ritualistically pass on his collection of magazines to another bachelor, give it to a college dormitory, or to toss it into the trash before the wedding night. It seems useful to recall what Paul Robinson said about Kinsey's view of marriage:

> Marital intercourse, was even more rudely confined to a single chapter toward the back of the book, where it received about one-third the attention devoted to homosexual relations. . . . Thus, there can be no doubting Kinsey's intention in the Male volume of dramatically promoting the significance of homosexuality in the total experience of American men.[6]

Women (and even most men) were aware of the offensiveness and intuitively recognized the peril of a fantasy paper doll collection for a couple and their future. After a short marital mourning period, most men of the '60s viewed their paper dolls nostalgically as an adolescent era. Magazine subscription data on marriage and the age of readers reveals that fewer married men bought these publications, and fewer "bachelor" products were sold, lowering advertising revenues and overall profits.

Yet, by the late 1970s and 1980s married men had begun keeping their *Playboy*, *Penthouse*, and *Hustler* collections, even bringing them out of closets, basements, attics, and garages, and into their woman's domain. By the 1980s, women shared the marital home—the bathroom, the bedroom, the living room—with their husband's naked paper dolls. Men were no longer embarrassed to have their pornography; and their wives were often bullied, embarrassed, and tricked into living with it. The consumer had been taught in the magazine the language of coercion: "Don't you have a sense of humor?" "Are you jealous of a pretty girl?" "I got it for the articles!" "You are just repressed!" etc. What happened? Recall the power of *Playboy* on the imagination and on the nation. The last pages of *Reaching for Paradise* bear repeating:

> No intelligent reader can do without it and pretend to any serious understanding about the United States . . . one of the few bully pulpits left in a nation increasingly fractious and fragile, growing unsure and uncertain of what it is and where it is headed. . . . Hefner has become a genuine folk hero . . . his messianic streak, make[s] him endearing. For many young Americans, "Hef" and his life-style are the stuff dreams are made of.[7]

UNDERMINING WOMEN'S SEXUAL ETHICS

Playboy's "messianic" marketing strategy worked. Substituting Kinseyan "facts" for feminine feelings, *Playboy* undermined woman's sexual ethics and her influence on marriage and society. With articles, "letters," photos, and polemical cartoons, Hefner swayed millions of young consumers who were unsure of where they were headed.

The sexual revolution was supported by the post-World War II economic and industrial revolution, which stressed the "buy now, pay later" ethic. Young couples left their home towns and traveled to new jobs, new opportunities, and higher incomes. Corporations routinely provided substantial salaries to executives who uprooted their families—"upward mobility" increasingly became the cliche of the times. For the first time in history, a society had produced so much merchandise that its citizenry could never purchase all the inventory on merchants' shelves. Everyone needed consumers badly.

In the midst of such massive geographic mobility, the eradication of a woman's personal sovereignty in her own home and bedroom was taking place. Women had no notion that marital and family survival was often intimately tied to their network of close family members, long-time school chums, and co-religionists. Without family, friends, or religious ties, without people who knew and loved them, millions of young women—and their children—became totally dependent upon the good will of husbands for both economic and psychological survival.

It makes sense that the research on wife battery finds the battered wife frequently isolated from such a support system, from those who could come to her defense and who would bring swift penalty and another perspective to a battering husband or father. Women of the fifties had been generally prepared to give up notions of professional careers to care for their husbands and children. They often attended college to meet a man who shared their desires for a knowledgeable albeit material life, and to prepare themselves for a career as an educated wife and mother. But the new sexuality was being taught throughout colleges and universities in psychology, sociology, family life courses, hygiene—everywhere.

How could women have known that the very colleges that educated them would also help destroy their command over their sexual lives, that the new sex experts would undermine women as the experts on how they feel about sex? What kind of attitudes and conduct could one expect from men taught the new sexual theories in college and reared on anti-woman, anti-marriage magazines? Kinsey and Hefner both pirated woman's rights, yanking her sexuality out from underneath her with the December 1953 issue of *Playboy*. In 1989 Hefner wrote about that first issue:

> Back in 1953, when I had this brash idea for a new men's magazine who would have bet that we'd be holding an anniversary celebration 35 years later? Certainly not I. The first issue of *Playboy* was undated, because I wasn't sure there'd be a second. But we've managed 420 issues since then ... and *Playboy* has become a fixture of the cultural landscape, an

institution as universal as Disneyland and Coca-Cola.[8]

For nearly thirty-five years college book stores housed racks of *Playboy* and male and female college students showed their sophistication by subscribing. In 1968 *Playboy* was claiming more college males as readers than any other magazine. By 1972 *Playboy* was quoting (in ads which read, "What Kind of Man Reads *Playboy*?") Simmons Market Research data stating that "*Playboy* reaches 3 of every 4 males in college and 1 of every 2 men under 53 in professional and managerial occupations—more than any other magazine." College professors lectured on the new sexual freedom to what the *Playboy* ad called "men on the move up." By the 1960s, Hefner and Kinsey's data had carved out the new sexual "truth" for university educated men and women. Vance Packard documented this shift in attitude:

> In the mid-1960s one of the fastest-growing major magazines, *Playboy*, dedicated itself to extolling the hedonistic, sensual way of life. A professor of philosophy at a college in North Carolina told me, "I teach philosophy from Socrates to Hefner." . . . The professor said that *Playboy* was then the most widely read publication on campus and added, "I read it because the students do."[9]

Packard pointed out the "wavering role of religious doctrine in controlling specifically the process of sexual awakening" and noted that while religious youngsters had restricted premarital intimacy through the mid-1950s, by the 1960s "the traditional armor seems to be crumbling."

> Clergymen have been arguing the pros and cons of *Playboy*'s highly permissive and hedonistic philosophy in, of all places the pages of [*Christian Century*]. An Episcopal minister in Raleigh, N.C., wrote that *Playboy*'s philosophy "has opened many doors for me and has caused some deep and exciting thoughts as well as discussion."[10]

LOSS OF THE MOTHER'S IDENTITY

Taught at college that they were to be sensual, at a loss to find support for sexual ethics within much of the organized religious world, and wanting desperately to attract and please husbands and to protect marriages, women began increasingly to slip into states of depression. Work-saving home aids and overproduction of consumer goods all created less honor for the "non-material" woman (wife and mother) and more honor for the "woman who works" (outside the home).

The growing view repeated often in *Playboy* text and imagery was that women at home did not work and they were a form of old-fashioned parasite and prostitute. Men were told that vacuum cleaners, washers, dryers, and miracle cleaners—or maids—would handle household problems. Dry cleaners sewed on suit buttons and put the right amount of starch in shirts, fast foods could be popped into the oven, and decorators could be hired to furnish homes. Wives were becoming a useless expense unless one had children—an idea that the Kinsey/Hefner life-style strongly opposed.

However, even here, nursery schools could care for children, so a man could expect his wife to work outside the home and remain a chef in the kitchen, a mother in the nursery, and a sexy, (young) hussy in the bedroom. Women swapped tales about husbands who arrived home from air-conditioned offices where secretaries catered to every whim. Hubby would glance over the spotless (un-air-conditioned) home his wife had cleaned, note his four happy children and his sumptuous meal on the table, only to complain about the weeds in the yard and ask her: "What did you do all day?" Soon, responding to the stories they read and heard from sexologists, pornographers, and foreign films about the fun and harmlessness of shared sex, some husbands wanted to play at "wife-swapping." The era of "open marriage" and "swinging" began.

With woman struggling for her identity under the crumbling foundation of a wife and mother's role, men began to assert their new-found sexual dominance. Now they would have their paper dolls waiting at home along with their wives. To that end, *Playboy* provided monthly sex experts, important athletes, and other such men for overall magazine credibility. Anti-woman/child propaganda was masked as humorous commentary in articles and cartoons and as "art" photography.

Photographs of infants were displayed as centerfolds. Was it a joke? The data says no, that all females were sex targets and that adult sadistic sexual abuse of children was glamorized. (See Part II for documentation.) Wives were constant sources of scorn, and belittled as sexually inhibited, fat, ugly, bestial—or as glamorous whores. Working women were similarly portrayed as abused and raped if they were in low paying jobs and cheated on if they were in high paying professional jobs. Illicit drugs and illicit sex were promoted as a viable sophisticated pleasure for all readers.

But what of men? While VIP's gave interviews, the real propaganda and training came from the monthly editorial cartoons. Here, in almost every image of male sexuality, men were covertly threatened, mocked, jeered, or ridiculed—impotence, impotence, impotence. Men are laughed at as "too late with too little." Today, millions of judges, legislators, clergymen, fathers, brothers, sons, and husbands have been nurtured, trained, and educated in the sex industry ethic. *Playboy* is correct in saying that it produced the current male society and sexual life in the United States.

FREEING MEN FROM THE DIVORCE BURDEN

Nothing could have set the stage more effectively for the forty-year war against marriage than the very first pages of *Playboy*'s December 1953 issue. Here, as noted, "Miss Goldigger" trashed marriage. Allegedly a factual essay about the horrors of marriage and the virulence of wives, readers were warned that women only marry to get alimony:

> In the frivolous days of black market booze and short-skirted women, a man knew where he stood. . . . Career girls were uninhibited, wives were faithful, and alimony was reserved for the little floozies who periodically married and divorced millionaire playboys as careless with their lucre as their love. Today, with taxes astronomical, both sexes Kinseyfied and all well-heeled millionaires holed up in Texas, alimony has gone democratic. In other words, it can happen to you too, brother.

Playboy advocated a form of no-fault divorce for the first time in any major publication. "The marriage doesn't work. Maybe it's the guy's fault; maybe it's the girl's. Could be neither one is to blame. . . ." It is common for revolutionaries to create a bogey-man to shoot at. Looking back one can see in the creation of "Miss Goldigger" the beginning of Hefner's legal and financial campaign for "no-fault" divorce and the elimination of alimony. He won, and this change in law helped create today's largest growing poverty group—single mothers and their children.

The hostility to marriage in the magazine images formed its power base. If men had to please wives in order to have sex, the publication would be crippled. Women did not like *Playboy*. It and they were natural enemies. Since the married playboy cancelled his subscription, marriage was a marketing nightmare for *Playboy*. Hoping to end that mutual dependence between women and men, Hefner appealed to the emerging leaders, the young men who would lead others. Hefner's magazine was touted in advertisements as having a unique appeal. *Playboy* had the

> "Man in the Hathaway Shirt with Eyepatch" snob appeal . . . that made the country great in the first place, instead of settling for job security, conformity, togetherness, anonymity and slow death.[11]

Togetherness, job security, and marriage were considered slow death, a threat to the reader's masculinity. The discretionary goods advertised by the magazine—liquor, travel, stereos, cars, cigarettes, fashionable clothing, men's cosmetics, marijuana growing units and wrapping papers, and sex-aids, including the magazine itself, and subsequently its clubs and casinos—all depended on unattached or irresponsible men. Single, divorced, separated, frustrated, and insecure men meant maximum profit. Thus, fanning the flames of male discontent was a critical marketing effort. The married men of the 1940s who were loved, fed, clothed, looked after, and who saved money to invest in their children's education and the couple's retirement were a low-profit venture. In contrast, with divorce came lawyer's fees, profits in sale and resale of properties, completely refurnished and new apartments, therapists for all parties, guilt purchases for the children, sex-aids, and finally the cosmetics, clothes, and entertainment necessary to locate another spouse. This was the beginning of a whole new way of living, called "serial marriage."

CREATING LONG-TERM, SINGLE MALE CONSUMERS

College males could move society out of its togetherness—"save" mode into the "me" generation—a loneliness-"spend" mode. Pornography would not succeed

without the credibility and the leadership of the college male.
Dr. Philip Kotler, a marketing specialist and professor at
Northwestern University, served as an advisor to *Playboy* for
some time. In his watershed book, *Marketing Management*,
Kotler talked about the small group "change agent," a sales
phenomenon commonly understood in marketing:

> The powerful influence of small groups on indi-
> vidual attitudes has been demonstrated in a number
> of social-psychological experiments . . . [David
> Reisman found] a tendency for individuals to be
> influenced increasingly by their contemporaries in
> the definition of their values rather than by their
> parents and elders. . . . [Marketers] stimulate new,
> specific wants.ι . . . Ignorance of the product calls for
> extensive information dissemination; inertia calls for
> repetitive advertising; and psychological resistance
> calls for subtle thematic advertising designed to
> overcome resistance.[12]

What did Kotler mean when he said, that "psychological resistance calls for subtle thematic advertising designed to
overcome resistance?" "Miss Goldigger" preached the sex
industry's sermon to the bread-winning, marriage-minded
male from the very beginning. The message was that only
wimps wed: "All woman wants is security. And she's perfectly willing to crush man's adventurous, freedom-loving
spirit to get it." Perhaps not quite as subtle a theme as it ought
to have been, but obviously it worked.

Millions of married men bought the magazine's
message, unaware they were the ones targeted for
emasculation. Once he could create a male fantasy, a men's
paradise, as Weyr had noted, Hefner became a hero. For
"many young Americans, 'Hef' and his life-style are the stuff
dreams are made of."[13]

Capturing and controlling America's men has been
relatively easy for the sex industry. As opposed to other
revolutionary manifestos, *Playboy* (using thematic
advertising to overcome resistance) was easy to read, month
after month, year after year. In *The Hearts of Men*, Barbara
Ehrenreich examined the magazine's propaganda:

> The playboy did not want his "traditional role" back;
> he just wanted out. Hefner's friend Burt Zollo wrote
> in one of the early issues: "Take a good look at the
> sorry, regimented husbands trudging down every

> woman-dominated street in this woman-dominated
> land. Check what they're doing when you're out on
> the town with a different dish every night. . . . Don't
> bother asking their advice. Almost to a man they'll
> tell you marriage is the greatest. Naturally. Do you
> expect them to admit they made the biggest mistake
> of their lives?"[14]

"This was strong stuff for the mid-fifties," said Ehrenreich. "*Look* had just coined the new noun 'together-ness' to bless the isolated exurban family."[15] Sociologist Jessie Bernard also commented on the changes occurring in modern marriages in her watershed book *The Future of Marriage*:

> Studies made in the 1930s and 1940s . . . reported
> results more favorable for the egalitarian marriage
> than do those made in the 1950s and 1960s. Whereas
> more of the egalitarian than of the non-egalitarian
> marriages were found to be happy in one of the early
> studies, in the 1960s, egalitarian marriages were said
> to be "confused, irresponsible, and characterized by
> an inability to resolve problems." . . . Something
> seemed to have happened either to the researchers or
> to marriages between the early and the later studies.[16]

Something *had* happened to both the college-educated researchers and to marriages. The greatest common denomi-nator affecting researchers and marriages alike was the impact of the Kinsey Reports and *Playboy* on college males and females. In fact, Bernard called collegiate men, the "bell-weather of the future."[17] The college men who had worked to become model husbands in model marriages, responsible for family and nation in past generations, suddenly had to have their freedom.

PLAYBOY BACKS LEGAL ASSAULT ON DIVORCE LAW

With *Playboy* as its financial patron, an army of young, college-educated lawyers worked to eliminate the legal protections their great-grandfathers had previously embed-ded in American divorce law for women and children. From December 1953 on, *Playboy* maintained a practice of frequent reports to readers on the progress of its efforts at a divorce revolution. The excitement of experimental illicit sex made friendly marriages appear boring. Young people throughout the nation (especially husbands) said good-bye to their spouses: "We don't have the chemistry anymore. Look at the excitement I'm missing. Love must be over." Leonore Weitzman summed up the new situation in *The Divorce Revolution*:

> In a single decade, divorce in America has been transformed by a legal revolution that has brought unexpected hardships for divorced women and their children. Between 1970 and 1980, 48 states adopted some form of no-fault divorce law. . . . [Now] divorced women and their children suffer an immediate 73 percent drop in their standard of living, while their ex-husbands enjoy a 42 percent rise in theirs. For women, especially young mothers and older homemakers, no-fault divorce is a financial disaster. . . . The new rules for divorce are changing the rules of marriage itself, redefining the behavior, expectations and commitment of husbands and wives.[18]

Within roughly two decades, Hefner's campaign to end alimony was won. In this new atmosphere, men seeking social approval from other enlightened men discarded their "old" wives for young ones with financial ease. Belief in men's responsibility to love, honor, and cherish until death diminished. Fathers increasingly neglected and abandoned their children. Child support went unpaid. Single mothers, well below the poverty line, quickly took in lovers, searching for a husband and a father to their children, often exposing the children to further despair and increased sexual and violent abuse. Their numbers began to increase the welfare rolls, swelling the ranks of families on public assistance—and creating a totally new element of the homeless. No longer was it only the old, drunken bum who slept on street corners. By the mid-1980s, abandoned women and their small children comprised the new wave of "homeless families."[19] Things have not worked out quite as "happily ever after" for children and society as promised by the sexual revolutionaries.

In 1989, with the last Playboy Club closed and the aging Hefner married, some journalists have hailed the end of the era of permissive sex. That just isn't happening. Our nation's laws, public policy, education, drug, and sexual morés have been dramatically altered. Until the country identifies the key sources of our socio-sexual malignancy, the Kinsey/Hefner legacy will continue to flourish in unanticipated forms, setting down new shoots, planting new, stronger roots, and destroying wholesome family life.

Ellen Goodman, feminist columnist appearing in major newspapers across the nation, claimed Hefner displayed a saying over his threshold: "If you don't swing, don't ring." She observed that the man who canonized "marriage is a trap . . . death" was marrying his latest centerfold and closing the last Playboy Club. The general attitude of press reports about Hefner's marriage seemed to be that a happy, sexually satisfied Hefner was now taking on marriage in his quiet old age. In a July 30, 1988 *Washington Post* article, "Say It Ain't So, Hef!" the correspondent quoted Hefner as telling him to: "Talk about the end of the sexual revolution." Goodman, looking at Hefner's trip to the altar and fear of AIDS, argued the nation was closing the door on *Playboy* and on our licentious past.

Certainly the sexual revolution has taken a major blow with AIDS and other incurable, sexually-transmitted diseases. However, the continuing spiral in child sexual abuse and the increasingly bizarre and brutal forms of sexual violence seen in heterosexual and homosexual rape, pornography, and mainstream entertainment do not signify a return to Judeo-Christian morals and an end to sexual dysfunction.

The end of alimony and the emergence of no-fault divorce are only two fascinating scores of the Kinsey/Hefner union after decades of *Playboy*'s "hate marriage" propaganda. In "Miss Goldigger," the author warned that with "both sexes . . . Kinseyfied," all women, from "Plain Jane" to "chorus cutie" were sexually available. This made marriage old-fashioned, expensive, and unnecessary. The 1953 article alleged, "All American womanhood has depended on alimony as a natural heritage" and *Playboy* would finally correct that.

Sex merchants hate happy marriages for pragmatic reasons. The pornographies had few sales among happily married men, too many could bankrupt the sex industry. Economic preservation dictated necessary exploitation of traditional, provable male fears—fear of failure, fear of impotence, fear of rejection, fear of women. If pornography

could adequately stimulate men's frustration, fear, and disappointment with women, males could prefer the less
threatening "relationship" with the sexy magazine images.
Then, the magazine and its products would sell, profits would
be secure and increase—and each month's paper-dolls would
roll over to make room for other paper-dolls. It was critical for
the sex industry to create an atmosphere where women and
men distrusted and feared one another, a situation known as
"heterophobia": fear and distrust of the opposite sex.

Historically, the most successful hate propaganda
campaigns have been waged with humor as a primary weapon–
specifically through cartoons. However, until *Playboy* began
its anti-female and anti-family campaign in 1953, no nation
had ever experienced the wide scale heterophobic, "sexist,"
and pedophile propaganda found among its pages.

Chapter 8

DRUGS SUBSTITUTED FOR LOST AROUSAL

In 1989, when we finally understood that our children were its major victims, our nation declared a war on drugs. That war for our children's lives will not be won without understanding the current and past involvement of *Playboy* and subsequent sex merchants in liberalizing laws on illicit drugs and promoting drug use. Glamorizing massive drug use by pornographers is consistent with their anti-Judeo-Christian philosophy.

We have discussed recent scientific data on the brain's ability to trigger the body to produce mind-altering, psychotropic chemicals. These neuro-chemicals are responsible for our self-defense mechanisms. They also produce healthy states of arousal, natural "highs," in the course of committed, trusting heterosexual relationships. The sex industry, having seen the economic necessity of separating male consumers from the possibility of fulfilled marital sexuality, promoted marital dissatisfaction and "heterophobia" (fear of the opposite sex). Having undermined their consumers' natural internal responses to normal sexual stimuli, pornographers offer external arousal and escape substitutes. These external substitutes include not only the confusing sex-violence-fear images—provocative centerfolds soliciting copulation—but also promotion of licit and illicit drugs.

If pornography disorients one's natural sexual responses and triggers abnormal levels of neuro-chemical stimulation, it would have been expected that the nation's number one playboy was involved in unusual varieties of sexual experience—with drugs to supply his fatigued natural arousal functions. As noted earlier, former Hefner girlfriend, Carrie Leigh, revealed that she and Hefner regularly took drugs in order to engage in sex. Sympathetic biographer Brady confirmed Hefner's admitted need for drugs during sex. Under the circumstances, it is reasonable to find that *Playboy* has been a primary promoter and crusader for the liberalization of illicit drug use. Hefner has been involved in at least two fatal drug investigations involving illegal drug use, apparent suicide, and drug overdose by his former private secretary and by a *Playboy* bunny.[1] Both Hefner and his daughter, Christie, are on record as using illegal drugs. Hefner declared in a 1976 newspaper interview that, not only did *Playboy* play a leading role in the sexual revolution, but that the magazine "is the major influence" in moves toward a "more reasonable attitude toward drugs."[2]

An examination of *Playboy*'s role in the democratization of the drug culture is long overdue. Unless we understand who bears responsibility for the current drug epidemic, we can hardly expect to take control over the chaos. Moreover, simple justice requires that those largely responsible for today's "recreational" view of drugs be named for the violence they have caused to the entire nation.

PLAYBOY: GIVING DRUG USE A NEW LANGUAGE

In the late 1960s and early 1970s an unprecedented litany of drug language and argument suddenly materialized across the country, provided by new drug "experts." Reporters, college professors, and their students celebrated the alleged love, sex, and friendship resulting from drug use. Writing in *Marketing Management,* Philip Kotler, a *Playboy* consultant and professor at Northwestern University, explained that in order to persuade people to be "venturesome," to try "risky situations," marketers must provide some personal influence to affect public change. People need to hear new language about the taboo idea over and over again. Media advertising cannot do the whole job, said Kotler:

> It underscores the desirability of creating advertising messages designed to supply early adopters with ways of verbalizing their opinions to others [to prove] the innovations relative advantage, or the degree to which it appears superior to previous ideas.[3]

Acceptance of illicit drugs required learning a new

"language." Unlike most of the Third World in which psycho-tropic drugs of different types have largely been endemic for centuries, the Judeo-Christian ethic generally had viewed drug use as morally "sinful." Some limited use of certain alcoholic beverages (such as wine) had been considered permissible within a certain religious and familial frame-work. However, until the easy availability and promotion of hard liquor in this century, the pathetic "town drunk" remained a symbol of the relative success of alcohol abstinence morés.

The word *recreational* became key to changing drug use conduct. *Recreation* was distorted to justify illicit drug use. Webster defines *recreation* as involving a "refreshment" of body or mind, engagement in a physically or emotionally healthy and "building" activity. Use of drugs does not qualify. However, the "recreational" terminology moved illicit drugs out of the sinful category by giving users a moral argument for its use. Users claimed private rights to pursue a recreation that was alleged to be scientifically proven harmless and would not interfere with others.

Together with the idea of drugs as "recreational" went the argument for "responsible" consumption—a contradic-tion in terms. For how can one be responsible while engaging in illegal entertainment? Along this line, responsible "use" of drugs was distinguished from problems with irresponsible "abuse." This meant that there could be a proper use of marijuana just as there was proper use of wine. Another word co-opted by the legalization movement was *do*. One did or was "doing" drugs.

Again, *do* is defined by Webster as "to bring about; to produce, as an effect or result . . . to work at; as, to do odd jobs." The sense of action and productivity as in "trip" is incorrectly given to acts of consumption. (One does not "do" food or water, one eats and drinks.) Hence, some of the many words used to unlock resistance to drugs were *recreational, do, use,* and *abuse.*

Citing drug "expertise," which was barely a few years old, experimenter-users taught readers a pro-drug use doctrine. They quoted obscure (and unverified) research studies that were allegedly conducted in Yemen, Jamaica, and Peru. Ivy League professors, college men and women, and

New York lawyers naively confused the excitement of their personal drug experiences with the value of public policies that legalized illicit drugs. These self-styled experts cited "populations of well-balanced American LSD, cocaine, and/ or marijuana users" whom they vaguely identified as alive and well. Massive, nationwide drug use was going to end violence, war, jealousy, and sexual possessiveness. Tripping about in a light and cloudy stupor, the nation would continue to produce the highest quality of life in the world, and we would all be happy.

PLAYBOY WELCOMES THE PROPHET OF LSD

In 1962, Harvard instructor, Dr. Timothy Leary, waxed intellectually ecstatic about drug use and by 1967 was popularizing LSD to the nation's children. Provided with a grand entry into college dormitories on the backs of American's football heroes in the *"Playboy* All-American Pigskin Preview," *Playboy* provided its pulpit to Leary in September 1966. Here, alongside Leary's sermons on the joys of LSD, were famous football players calling passes and looking fit, celebrating their success as macho males.

The reader, stirred by his identification with and desire to be one of these great athletes, was simultaneously examining drug jokes, child-adult sex jokes, and provocative, arousing nude females. In such an emotional and cognitively vulnerable state, many consumers would be temporarily susceptible to Dr. Leary's majestic claims for the drug "experience."

Unfortunately, having been reared in a western nation with no real exposure to wide scale drug use, Leary was as ignorant as his followers of the long—or even short range—effects of LSD, or any other illicit drug on individuals and society. Yet that did not dampen his enthusiastic cry for its general use. In December 1969, Leary appeared in another *Playboy* "pop-up" article surrounded by and covered with exquisitely illustrated flowers and mushrooms. His words, encased in this frame of exquisite, colorful, three-dimensional posies, were presented like poetry, honored and honorable. The article itself, "Episode & Postscript," was a call to idealistic action, a demand for justice and humanity. Leary's tale was historical. He had written a passionate LSD guide for *Playboy* readers in 1966. During that time, however, "what I said and wrote was censored." Leary had encouraged family drug sessions, that is, use of LSD by children and adults. He complained:

> In December 1965, I was arrested in Laredo, Texas, along with my wife, Rosemary, my daughter, Susan, and my son, Jack, for the possession of less than half an ounce of marijuana. . . . When I speak of this deliberate desire to encourage young persons to sever the conditioned reflexes that tie them to the values of their parents, I am not speaking metaphorically.[4]

Here was Leary, "popping up" on both sides of this colorful magazine page, a handsome, gentle guru, smoking a water pipe, bedecked in flowers and myrrh. Never denying that parents and children were drug users, Leary alleged that he, his wife, and children had been the subjects of cruel, abusive arrest. Leary created "trip guidebooks" for especially youthful non-users, and *Playboy* helped him disciple new converts.

> The first step was to persuade people to take the drug. Leary aimed his message at those whose hearts and minds were still up for grabs: the younger generation. He saw himself as the orchestrator of a mass cultural phenomenon. His goal was to encourage large numbers of American youth to decondition themselves . . . with large helpings of LSD. . . . To those in the inner circle it quickly became apparent that the psychedelic movement would be sold . . . [like] Madison Avenue.

> Leary not only hyped LSD as a shortcut to mystical enlightenment but also fused it with something that had proven mass appeal: sex. In his 1966 *Playboy* interview he discussed psychedelics [as] "erotic politics" and "hedonic engineering." Acid was portrayed as a "cure" for homosexuality and a means of inhabiting a supremely sensual reality.

> "In a carefully prepared, loving LSD session," Leary stated, "a woman will inevitably have several hundred orgasms. The three inevitable goals of the LSD session are to discover and make love with God, to discover and make love with yourself, and to discover and make love with a woman. . . . That is

> what the LSD experience is all about. . . . The sexual
> impact is, of course, the open but private secret about
> LSD."[5]

So said Leary in *Playboy*'s 1966 "Pigskin Preview" issue. *Playboy* marketers knew it would be their biggest selling issue of the year, an issue that would be snatched up by young boys, athletic hopefuls, "those whose hearts and minds were still up for grabs: the younger generation." A young lad reaching up for his football heroes in September 1966 would catch *Playboy*, sex, and drugs. What were boys being programmed to receive? "When I grow up, I, too, can be stoned while I execute an extravagant forward pass, to the exquisite sounds of my centerfold lovers having hundreds of orgasms?" Strong—and indelible—fantasies programming vulnerable youngsters.

> Leary had a knack for telling his audiences exactly
> what they wanted to hear. . . . . "It's all God's flesh
> . . . LSD is always a sacrament: whether you are a silly
> thirteen-year-old popping a sugar cube on your boy-
> friend's motorcycle, or a theatrical agent giving pot
> to a girl to get her horny . . : or even a psychiatrist
> giving LSD to an unsuspecting patient to do a
> scientific study." Leary's pronouncements were
> calculated to seduce and frighten.[6]

Leary and *Playboy* realized that while many thirteen-year-old girls might not be reading *Playboy*, it was likely that many of their boyfriends were. These boys internalized Leary's exciting drug message while embracing All-American athletes and adoring centerfold paper dolls. Soon a "small change agent" group of sex/drug believers emerged. By stacking pro-drug letters to the editor and editorials, censoring meaningful anti-drug information, and by providing seed monies and continuing funds to the National Organization for the Reform of Marijuana Laws (NORML), *Playboy* promised friends, family, and the nation peace, love, better sex, "relevant" education, sex education, and a splendid quality of life.

> Marijuana smokers across the country suddenly materialized with a litany of apparently logical grounds for legalization of marijuana. It would not lead to mass use; it would only be used by consenting adults; it would not lead to use of stronger drugs; it was less toxic than liquor; adults used liquor, and grass was youth's "drug of choice"; primitive

cultures used it and thrived; it was good for sex; it was needed
for medical purposes; it was non-addictive, and on and on.
Few people understood that we were careening around the
bend to an avalanche of drug wars and national devastation.
Even fewer people understood the role of *Playboy* and its
pornography satellites in creating a drug-using, youth population.

In 1984 Dr. Robert Dupont, White House Drug Chief
from 1973 to 1975, was completely unaware that "crack"
cocaine would become a major peril when he quoted these
statistics in his book, *Getting Tough on Gateway Drugs*:

> Drug use in America today is a major threat to our
> health, productivity and quality of life. Drugs, in-
> cluding alcohol and tobacco, now cause 30 percent of
> all Americans to die prematurely. Drug use costs the
> national economy over $100 billion a year, with
> much of that cost attributed to lost productivity.
> Among America's young adults ranging in age from
> 18 to 25, which is the segment of our population that
> uses drugs most heavily, 41 percent used marijuana,
> 20 percent used cocaine, and 84 percent used alcohol
> during 1982. Nationally, we have 57 million people
> who have used marijuana at least once, 20 million of
> them are now regular, current users of a drug which
> was a rarity in the United States 20 years ago . . .
> America's teenagers, polled by George Gallup in
> 1983, . . . ranked "Drug Abuse" number one [as a
> threat to their generation].[7]

How did the United States fall so quickly into the abyss
of drug use? What transpired to emasculate the behavioral
models of what were, historically, the only three socializing
agencies: 1) church, 2) family, and 3) schools? Curbs on
hedonistic indulgence and support of American values were
conventionally taught in these three social and cultural
institutions. Until recently parents, churches, and schools
supported each other, and it was commonly understood that
parents who were good role models would produce law
abiding, God-fearing, socially productive children. However,
parents who seldom drank a glass of wine and who took their
religion seriously, if warmly, as well as those who were
atheists or alcoholics, have often found themselves confronted with an adolescent or young adult who used drugs.

There is not sufficient space here to discuss the drug

mis-education forced upon youngsters in our nation's schools. Since drugs were being taught about in class, parents wrongly assumed their children were learning about the harm of all illicit drugs and the need to avoid all such toxins. Little did the nation understand that these three socializing agents—responsible for child development for centuries—no longer had the final say on their children's moral development.

Nor did the nation realize that this move toward massive drug use was aided and abetted by the same man who displayed the tragic, naked Marilyn Monroe to sell his first magazine. If the juvenile and adult consumer was buying a "total package," as Hefner said he was, then part of that package was and still is the acceptance of illegal drugs as part of the good life.

In 1976 a sympathetic reporter from the *Cleveland Plain Dealer* interviewed Hugh Hefner about sex. As noted earlier, Hefner funded the National Organization for the Repeal (later, "Reform") of Marijuana Laws, better known as NORML on Capital Hill. As late as 1989, five Washington, DC legislative lobbyists were on record as representing NORML. By association, they would be representing its support agency, *Playboy*, as well. The reporter asked Hefner a provocative question:

> Question: The *Playboy* Foundation has been a major supporter of NORML (National Organization for the Reform of Marijuana Laws) hasn't it?
>
> Answer: We're the major funder of NORML. We had a lot to do with the sexual revolution in the 1960s, but it is less well recognized that as we are moving into a more reasonable attitude toward drugs, and grass in particular, that *Playboy* is the major influence there as well.

The Tenth Anniversary party for NORML was advertised in its monthly journal. On the cover of this important issue was a scraggly Doonesbury cartoon character, laid-back, casually smoking a joint, surrounded by a "LIBERATE MARIJUANA" sign. When a consumer held the booklet so that both the front and back covers were visible an interesting lesson in typical marijuana "humor" and what happens to "stoned," intoxicated art sensibilities is provided.

On the back cover is a "comic strip" (which would be especially appealing to children) called "Typical Tales." This shows a young fellow trying to convince his parents that marijuana is harmless. He becomes so enraged with their refusal to listen to him that, when his mother asks his help in mixing drinks, he shoves her hand and arm into the electric blender, her blood spurting wildly out from the whirling blades. This mutilation tale ends with the mother. casually reading something while her mangled arm rests inside the blender.

Hefner often stated that he used marijuana to improve his sexual life, so it was normal to find his daughter Christie— as the second generation—also documented as a drug user.[8]

However, in May 1987, following the deaths of college basketball star Len Bias (*Playboy* All-American, 1986) and football hero Don Rogers (*Playboy* All-American, 1983) of drug overdoses, *Playboy* magazine initiated mass distribution of what seemed to be a slick anti-drug booklet to coaches in schools and colleges across the nation. In the booklet, *Playboy* appeared, at first blush, to distance itself from its own fifteen years of drug marketing.

This booklet "educating" children about the evils of some-drugs-for-some-people was reprinted from a *Playboy* issue that also advertised *Mello Mail*, a catalog for New York's largest "head shop." *Mello Mail* offered cocaine and marijuana drug paraphernalia along with erotic lingerie and sadistic (S/M) sex "toys." Despite *Playboy*'s knowledge— according to Stephen Byer in *Hefner's Gonna Kill Me When He Reads This*—that even in 1972 the "average" mail order buyer was a seventeen-year-old, and despite its claim to be corporately responsible and concerned about drug use, the magazine was aggressively advertising the drug experience to young people.

Playboy has visibly "stepped-up" its promotion of drugs. One aggressive marketing effort is a monthly advertisement for the Phototron, a light unit designed to grow marijuana indoors. No longer able to legally broker drug paraphernalia, *Playboy* began an on-going monthly ad campaign for the $390 marijuana growing unit. Along with *Penthouse* and the drug magazine *High Times*, *Playboy* has been advertising the Phototron, a structure that produces enough "fresh leaf and bud material everyday" to provide a daily high and shady revenue to numerous child and adult users. Mass promotion of a product—such as the Phototron—that is built to grow marijuana for home or dormitory is in keeping with *Playboy*'s documented role as "America's number one drug promoter."

The role of *Playboy*'s athletic images—its "All American" team—in glamorizing drug use was uncovered by psychiatrist Dr. Linnea Smith, wife of renowned University of North Carolina basketball coach Dean Smith. Dr. Smith has been tireless in her efforts to alert the athletic community to its responsibilities, in order as she says, "to divest from any association with *Playboy* magazine and its pro-drug promotions." Citing the deaths of young athletes from drug use, Dr. Smith has been attempting to raise the consciousness of leaders within the athletic community. (To this end, Dr. Smith and I produced a monograph entitled *Sports, Children, Drugs, and Crime and Violence in Playboy Magazine*.)

When I began my association with Dr. Smith a few years ago, I had no idea I was embarking on a fascinating odyssey into the land of athletics, *Playboy*, and drugs. In January 1986 I received a phone call from Dr. Smith. She had been told by the executive director of the Attorney General's Commission on Pornography of my research on the three main "sex" magazines, *Playboy*, *Penthouse*, and *Hustler*. After confirming the nature of my research, she asked if I would talk to her husband's colleagues, all basketball coaches, about *Playboy*. While *Penthouse* and *Hustler* were surely harmful, she said, famous athletes compete for the honor of annually appearing in *Playboy*'s All-American Team. The pictured athletes were seen to represent what this magazine stood for. The coaches need to know what is in the magazine, she said.

The gathering coaches were the National Association of Basketball Coaches (NABC), whose executive board chairman that year was John Thompson of Georgetown University. (Thompson would later be an Olympic team coach.) The event was the National Collegiate Athletic Association's "Final Four" basketball tournament in Dallas. The top college teams were converging to fight for the 1986 championship title. Just before the play-offs, Dr. Smith and I gave a two-hour briefing to the executive board of the NABC on "Child Pornography and Drugs in *Playboy*." We urged the thirty coaches to boycott participation in *Playboy's* annual All-American Team. It was well-known that these athletic issues were collector's items for juvenile males—serving as behavior and personality manuals as well.

Following our video tape presentation and lecture in Dallas, Chairman Thompson, an early *Playboy's* All-American coach, thanked us, and before all of his colleagues proclaimed humiliation at having voluntarily appeared in *Playboy*. Thompson said he had "never really looked at the magazine" and had not realized that it promoted drugs or that children were sexually exploited in its pages. Thompson now saw for himself that this was indeed the case. He said he would examine whether the association could divest, and since that briefing, Coach Thompson has apparently turned down an offer to be *Playboy* coach of the year.

The *Durham* (N.C) *Morning Herald* reported on 24 May 1987 that other coaches, including Mike Krzyzewski of Duke University, "turned down an opportunity to be *Playboy* coach of the year":

> The magazine editors, who have been receiving rejections more frequently in the last few years, were cautious in their approach. They asked Krzyzewski if he would be interested in being considered. "I told them it just was not appropriate for me to do," Krzyzewski said. Linnea Smith, the wife of UNC coach Dean Smith, has been campaigning to get athletes and coaches to reject *Playboy* because she disapproves of the magazine's literature about drug use. Krzyzewski's wife, Mickie, has supported Mrs. Smith's stance. The magazine's officers insist they have been editorially and financially supportive of anti-drug movements.

While it is difficult to know precisely how many rejections *Playboy* has received in the last few years, several coaches and athletes are known to have individually declined *Playboy*'s all-expense paid honor. Art Chansky, in a mid-1980 *Basketball Times* article entitled, "Hoops, *Playboy* Don't Mix," examined the changing attitudes of athletes toward the *Playboy* All-American team.

> Last summer, North Carolina's Kenny Smith, Navy's David Robinson, Indiana's Steve Alford and Notre Dame's David Rivers declined *Playboy*'s invitations to go and be photographed. . . . The magazine promptly replaced the players with other "All-Americans" on the team and in the picture. . . . "If they don't want to play ball, they're not on the team," a *Playboy* spokesman explained. "Someone else will take their place. "

On 9 August 1986, in the *Charlotte Observer,* sports reviewer Ron Green confirmed *Playboy*'s statement in the undated "Hoops" article, that "If they don't want to play ball, they're not on the team. . . . Someone else will take their place." This happened recently when Mark Price of Georgian Tech said, "No, thanks." Since this 1986 article appeared, *Playboy* has begun to publish a photograph—or illustration—of the chosen athlete as their All-American athlete even if he doesn't "want to play ball."

Dr. Smith also presented her argument for athletic divestment in a July 21, 1986 letter to leaders of the American Football Coaches Association. She repeated much of what she had said to the NABC. Dr. Smith urged the football coaches to reject any media organization that viewed drug use in a positive light.

> Currently the athletic community and general public are stunned and outraged at the sudden, tragic deaths due to cocaine intoxication of two healthy young athletes [Len Bias and Don Rogers]. . . . For almost two decades *Playboy* has been popularizing the idea that drug consumption is expected or normal. The magazine focuses on "recreational" use while ignoring or trivializing potential harmful effects. In addition, the *Playboy* foundation has contributed substantially to organizations lobbying for decriminalization of "recreational" drugs, including cocaine and marijuana. Rejection is essential and urgently needed of all media that gives positive drug information to a society with a drug problem of epidemic proportions.

Dr. Smith assailed *Playboy* for labeling drug use a natural and desirable rite of passage. She identified the role of mainstream media as "perpetuating the myth of risk-free 'recreational' drug consumption." As a medical doctor, and a mental health professional, Smith came down hard on *Playboy*'s most oft quoted drug expert, Ronald K. Siegel, Ph.D., whom she accused of covering up the pathology and dangers of drugs, including cocaine.

Siegel stated in the April 1982 issue of *Playboy* that "As it stands now, the most dangerous aspect of cocaine use is getting caught and suffering the criminal penalties for a narcotic offense." Dr. Siegel wrote his cocaine-is-harmless diagnosis shortly before two of *Playboy*'s own "All American" team—Len Bias and Don Rogers—died of cocaine drug overdoses.

Dr. Smith pointed out that until *Playboy*, no legitimate American publication had brought "positive drug" information to the public—and certainly not to children. She has said that *Playboy*'s sports/sex/drug format must be seen as critical in establishing the current drug epidemic. Smith reiterated Kotler's discussion of the need for a new language when one attempts to change a cultural norm. She said that *Playboy* had created that language for the drug revolution.

Although this chapter on drugs gives short shrift to *Penthouse* and *Hustler*, these magazines also promote drug use. Anything promoted by *Playboy* will be similarly brokered by other sex magazines. However, other "skin" magazines do not have *Playboy*'s influence as publisher of the annual All-American basketball and football championship teams and as founder and patron of NORML. Moreover, only Hefner is seen publicly as an associate and friend of entertainment and political luminaries.

Playboy has threatened Dr. Smith with legal action because of her public statements about its promotion of drug use and depictions of sex with children. A letter was sent to Dr. Smith by Arthur Kretchmer, editorial director of *Playboy*, on 21 November 1986. He refuted Dr. Smith's statements:

> You are . . . on record as having said that *Playboy* encourages the use of drugs. . . . [T]hat is an error. What . . . *Playboy* is against is anti-drug hysteria. . . . Since you are a respected professional, I would think that you'd want to carefully evaluate what you say in public. . . . Your statements have also been malicious, in both the common and legal sense. *Playboy* . . . has a significant role in the lives of young men . . . I'd be less than candid if I didn't advise you that *Playboy* will do whatever is necessary to protect its reputation.

Despite *Playboy*'s intimidation, the unflappable Dr. Smith has continued in her efforts to alert the athletic world to what she sees as its responsibility, since, as Kretchmer said, *Playboy* "has a significant role in the lives of young men."

Playboy's drug advisor, James Petersen, revealed a drug-using magazine agenda. In December 1978 Petersen replied to what he claimed was a letter from a "dope smoker for several years." Having noted Anson Mount's creation of

his own exciting "letters" for his *Playboy* reader's column
and Hefner's censorship directions, one is forewarned regarding *Playboy* text accuracy. This alleged "reader" seeks
help from Petersen in the "*Playboy* Advisor." He reports his
recent addiction to marijuana: "I have been a dope smoker for
several years now, but only recently have I started getting
wrecked on a regular basis." His technical problem is that his
contact lenses hurt his eyes during his chemically "wrecked"
states. What shall I do, he asks?

One reason people read a "letters" column is for advice
about their own concerns. As the official "advisor" and
counsellor representing *Playboy*, Petersen is advising all their
readers. Recall that the publisher and his editors are well
aware that this column is read by young boys and girls
throughout the country. Hass reported on youthful reliance on
the "*Playboy* Advisor."[9] Hefner himself noted his 6 percent
youth readership in the 1960s[10] and past letters from alleged
youth have been printed and answered by Petersen.

In order to understand the *Playboy* agenda, we need to
examine what Petersen does not advise readers as much as
what he does advise. He does not note the writer as marijuana
dependent. He does not recommend that the writer stop using
drugs or get therapy if he cannot stop alone. He does not say
all drug use is dangerous, illegal, and unhealthy. He does not
even admit that the man is having unhealthy side effects from
marijuana use. Petersen certainly does not recommend that
the fellow turn in his dealers, himself, and other users and
throw himself on the mercy of the court.

Instead, the "USA's most widely read men's sex education resource," James Petersen, employs a stereotypical
"clever" response to a drug addict's symptoms of physical,
emotional, and sexual disorder:

> Let's hear it, now: Smoke gets in your eyes. . . . For
> sex, we suggest K-Y jelly or another lubricant. For
> your eyes, we suggest using drops to get the red out,
> or perhaps switching to soft lenses. . . . Whatever you
> do, don't get so stoned that you confuse the eyedrops
> with the K-Y jelly.[11]

In another alleged letter (June 1979), a woman complained to Petersen that she must use marijuana to have an
orgasm during sex. She explained her plight and concluded by
saying that she knew she was a marijuana addict. The writer

knew she was *dependent* on marijuana. "I must overcome it. Any suggestions? [signed] Miss R.I., Big Sur, California."

This is Petersen's advice to the woman who wants to overcome her dependency:

> Cough. Cough. Grass has been America's unofficial aphrodisiac for several years.... Woody Allen's film *Annie Hall* depicts a girl who shares your love of killer weed. There is a danger that an overanxious partner might object to your habit; i.e., are you getting off on your joint or his? ... You don't mention what techniques you and your boyfriend use in lovemaking. ... Just ask your boyfriend to give you a little more [technical] attention. If the thought of a mechanical device doesn't offend you, invest in a vibrator and play with it together.[12]

Petersen arrogantly dismissed the writer's plea for help in her marijuana addiction. True to the *Playboy* position, instead of directing the victim toward drug rehabilitation, Petersen cheerily likens the suffering woman to a fantasy film heroine. Petersen proclaimed the "weed" to be an unofficial sexual aphrodisiac used by creative, bright Americans—like Hugh Hefner himself. As noted earlier, Anderson wrote in *High in America* that Hefner claimed marijuana allowed him to make "love."

"I didn't know what making love was all about for all those years," Hefner said in 1980. "Smoking helped put me in touch with the realm of the senses. I discovered a whole other dimension to sex. I discovered the difference between f--ing and making love."[13] The difference, for him, between sex as a nothing experience and sex as "love" was being stoned. The fantasy and illusion Hefner created so undermined his emotional health and vigor that he thinks drugs and love are the same thing.

Interested in selling itself, *Playboy* must convince its readers that the "tingles" from drug-enhanced pornography are as good or better than loving man-woman passion. Petersen's advice to the suffering woman can be anticipated. It is common form for a group to adopt the values of its leader. If Hefner needs drugs for sex, "Advisor" would naturally tell the world that drugs are needed for healthy orgasms. Lucky is the group with a well-balanced leader.

For the January 1986 *Playboy* photos, Len Bias was

flown down to the *Playboy* mansion where he and the other chosen athletes were wined and dined for several days under its glamorous roof. Testimony from Miki Garcia, Brenda McKillop, and Linda (Lovelace) Marciano, before the Attorney General's Commission, and found in Frank Brady's *Hefner*, confirm the common use of drugs by Hefner, the bunnies, and guests (including college athletes) at the *Playboy* mansion. Booze, drugs, and coerced sex were documented as cultural norms at the mansion.

In September 1984 *Playboy*'s "Pigskin Preview" issue put the spotlight on "Cocaine: A Special Report." One article talked of creating NORCL, the National Organization for the Reform of Cocaine Laws. The magazine provided false, misleading statements about an alleged 10 percent addiction solution. Briefly, the author told the child and adult *Playboy* readers that while 90 percent of society could use cocaine without worry, only an "addictive personality" becomes dependent—or dysfunctional—due to drugs.

Playboy and other similar magazines might not be drug pushers in the legal sense of the term—if they were, they could be arrested by the DEA—but in the actual and moral sense they are certainly drug brokers and promoters. How many fine, strong young men like Len Bias and Don Rogers have paid the penalty for believing the pro-drug nonsense *Playboy* has promoted for decades?

Part II:
Images of Children in
Soft Porn

Chapter 9

CARTOONS AND PHOTOS IN
PLAYBOY, PENTHOUSE, AND
HUSTLER (PPH)

People are usually surprised to learn that *Playboy* and *Penthouse* surveys found adult readers saying the cartoons were their very favorite and most interesting feature (data on favored features were unavailable for *Hustler*). This was one of the key reasons we examined cartoon content in the three magazines for the Department of Justice. Cartoons are especially important to study: all three journals have a significant child readership, and children pay special attention to comics, cartoons, and other forms of illustration.[1]

The National Committee for the Prevention of Child Abuse (NCPCA) chose the cartoon format and "Spiderman" in 1984 to teach children about sexual assault—to warn children about what is appropriate adult-child behavior. The need to look at cartoon behavior in *Playboy* and other porn magazines is especially significant since most children assume that *Playboy* (thus the others also) is "approved." Either they have seen it sold in stores, or Dad and other adult male kin are seen reading or buying the magazines. In the late 1980s, television specials such as "A Current Affair," "Personalities," "Donahue," and "Geraldo" cameoed centerfolds and other nude models, increasing the acceptance of this form of prostitution.

For decades, *Playboy* and its imitators have used comics and cartoons to educate child and adult consumers about sex, teaching them how children should respond to adults who approach them sexually. In fact, NCPCA's *Spiderman* comic visually portrays the common use of "girlie" magazines to sexually entrap young boys. The NCPCA comic described the standard process of child sexual entrapment. A young boy meets an older man in the library. The man is very friendly, helps Spiderman (the boy) with his science project, talks with him, plays games, and finally gets the boy to visit his apartment alone. Once on the couch the man says:

> "Don't you ever stop thinking 'Einstein?' Hey, I've got something to show you that's guaranteed to take your mind off science. Bet you've never seen pictures like those in a stuffy text book. [Shows boy *Girlie* magazine]. Come on, Einstein! let's conduct a little experiment of our own. Let's see if we can touch each other like the people in that magazine . . . ."
> "Please, Skip. DON'T! I've got to go now." [But the young boy was too frightened to leave.][2]

The committee of child abuse experts chose Spiderman as the boy ("Einstein") in order to imprint acceptance in the reader for the comic book's message. *Spiderman* told children the adult was wrong. Children should not have sex with older people. On the flip side of that coin, however, *Playboy* had been using cartoons to "teach" children how to deal with adult-child sex for forty years—since 1954! Indeed, this "girlie magazine" uses cartoons to make children adult sex objects for almost two generations—enough time to make a fundamental difference in what was believed about adult-child sex by boys and girls who grew into the nation's men and women.

PLAYBOY SEXUALIZES SMALL CHILDREN
SINCE 1954

The first cartoon (May 1954) to suggest children are unharmed by sex with adults involved a group of early adolescent boys and two women in a brothel. The *Playboy* artist had a group of young Boy Scouts attempting entry into a bordello. The adult females are shutting the door on the boys, although the eager lads came to have sex. No harm to children from such encounters with prostitutes is suggested (a la Kinsey) and the cartoonist draws lustful looks on their young faces, quite inappropriate to the "Scout" concept and generally inaccurate for normal, naive boys this age. Importantly, while this first cartoon shows young boys soliciting sex, the adult women are refusing.

The next early (August 1954) cartoon should be carefully studied, since it was drawn by the publisher, Hugh Hefner. As the story is a record of one of the few ideas he chose to personally illustrate for his magazine, it betrays Hefner's deep personal interest for it. While this should be analyzed by someone from the psychiatric profession, we shall examine Hefner's cartoon message from a communication perspective.

A cartoon is like a scene in a play, frozen in time. Hefner's cartoon scene has four boy actors. Three of the boys are closely examining semi-nude pictures of women on a burlesque theater display, while the fourth lad is preoccupied watching a dog. Hefner has one of the three boys explain to the others that the reason "Joey" is not looking at pictures of the naked women is: "Joey ain't interested—he's got a sister."

Hefner routinely selected each cartoon that went into *Playboy*, which meant he planted this August incest innuendo. His cartoon tells readers Joey has access to his sister. This suggests either voyeur incest, peeping at his sister in semi-nude, burlesque dress or hands-on incest. The words also imply the older sister is harmlessly servicing her little brother. Hefner's image pushes his emerging myth—that boys are unharmed by sexual exposure to adults, including incest.

At the end of the same year (November 1954), *Playboy* removed all clothing and all pretense in a scene of a prostitute and a toddler. The baby—and this change is important—now solicits from the woman. He holds out his little coin to either pay for or to request sex. The sand in the hour glass could intimate that the child has already been sexually serviced and is now paying.

The woman's hand is poised over the cash register, noting "NO SALE." Is she about to ring up "SALE" or has she determined "NO SALE"? This sleight-of-hand comforts millions of readers who wish to interpret these as innocent, harmless jokes. On the other hand, it also titillates them, for there is a subconscious hunch that the joke is malevolent—and not innocent at all.

Not only is child-adult sex "hinted" at here, but incest is blatantly implied as well. In 1954, long before the advent of "crack houses" where little children would roam about unattended, a small child did not wander far from his mother's side. Hefner knew this of course. Thus, the nude child toddles about, pulling his little toy behind him, in a nude woman's bedroom. The visual incest language is thunderous.

Were this a real child-sex drama, the baby's sex solicitation scene would be the final curtain of three acts. In Act One (May) the older boys wanted sex, but were refused by prostitutes. In Act Two (in August), a young boy is apparently acting out sexually with his older sister. And in Act Three (November), a naked little toddler solicits and pays for sex like the August boys tried to do. Now, however, his female kin is a prostitute, and, we do not know if the tot was refused sex or paid for sex—with sister, mother, or other female relative.

FROM *PLAYBOY* TO SOCIETY'S DECISION MAKERS

So, in one short year of 1954, Hefner brought us from clothed adolescent Boy Scouts, soliciting sex and being refused, to naked toddlers soliciting sex with mom or sis. This Kinsey/Hefner sexual fraud repeated year after year, spread to dozens of magazine imitators. Thousands of vulnerable readers eventually worked in mass media ventures: film, television, women's news, general papers and magazines, radio, video, "fine art," advertising, children's comic books, and the like. Masses of these professionals now creatively "abuse" women and children as entertainment for profit.

The widespread mass media sexual attack on women and children means something is uniformly wrong with the sexuality of thousands of American cartoonists, writers, photographers, broadcasters, songwriters, and other creative media people. And *Playboy* claims the "message and spirit" of these men are its own. Back in 1967, Joe Goldberg quoted Hefner in *The Big Bunny*:

> Being around a certain amount of time gives you a
> certain kind of stability and strength, in the view of
> the community, and you become a part of the scene.

In addition to that, there are the young people who dig us and understand us. The older people who object will be dying off, and the young kids who were *Playboy* fans when they were in college [and grade school] will be the top executives, the presidents of corporations, etc., the decision-makers. So our future seems not only established, but extremely bright. I think that the best is all ahead.[3]

ONE NEEDS "PROBABLE CAUSE" TO INVESTIGATE

On 22 May 1989 the *Washington Times* (the *Washington Post* did not print the story) reported to the public that cartoonist Dwaine Tinsley, creator of *Hustler* magazine's "Chester the Molester" had been arrested for child sexual abuse. Just as one would expect a racist cartoonist to victimize blacks whenever the opportunity presented itself, Tinsley's child abuse cartoons suggested that he molested children when he could.

One's art product is a strong indication of one's attitudes. Tinsley alone produced 145 child abuse cartoons for *Hustler* with violence and rape as the overriding theme. Hefner produced 3,045 child images (1,196 child cartoons and 1,849 child visuals). Roughly three-fourths of Hefner's child materials were sexual or violent. Men who glamorize child sex abuse are revealing pedophile ideas and beliefs. Currently, these men would be completely unable to tell the truth to the press and the public about their motives.

For example, in 1988, Dwaine Tinsley was interviewed for a video called *Rate It X* (available from Women Against Pornography in the Media—California). In the tape, several "Chester the Molester" cartoons are shown. The cartoonist was questioned about the feature:

Q: Who is Chester the Molester?

A: Chester is a character that I do for the magazine [*Hustler*]. You have this dirty old guy who would do anything to trap a young girl ... the younger ones, 10 or 12. [H]e would lay out candy for them like he was trying to trap ... a bird. .... First of all if he's going to trap a little girl the idea for him would be to knock her out or something. .... I mean, he didn't have to ... actually use a club or bat. He could have smacked her, but just the idea of the bat is a little goofier.

What's better than a baseball bat? It was always with him [Note the Glen Ridge High boys used a baseball bat with which to rape the young girl they had kidnapped].

Q: Don't you think that by making him [Chester the Molester] such a lovable, goofy type of guy, that somehow legitimizes what he is doing?

A: No, I don't think I was legitimizing child molesting. Chester was just a goofy kinda guy.

Q: And by laughing at him, it doesn't make it fun on some level?

A: You mean that child molesting is okay?

Q: Not okay. That's too strong a word. But more okay.

A: More acceptable? More palatable? No. I really don't think so. I don't . . . think that people were saying that it's okay to be a child molester. If I thought that, I wouldn't have done the character. . . . Most of the letters I received were "I know he's a nut, really. He's such a goofy guy." . . . Chester . . . has restrictions now . . . he can't go after minors, you know. It's almost acceptable if this goofy guy goes for a woman that's at least 18 years of age . . . it's not such a lovable offense anymore if he goes after a young girl.

As reported in the *Washington Times*, Dwaine Tinsley was convicted on multiple counts of child molestation in the spring of 1989. He had drugged his daughter, put her on birth control pills when she turned thirteen, and violently sexually abused her until she reached the age of eighteen. By then, she was a suicidal drug addict.

SLAVISH DEDICATION TO PERFECTION

Until very recently, Hefner personally selected about four hundred cartoons for publication out of roughly two hundred thousand submitted annually. A careful reading of all Hefner biographies notes that the publisher himself chose every *Playboy* cartoon (including child cartoons). He would handpick each cartoon, rejecting others that did not suit his interest. Said Brady in *Hefner*:

> Hefner labored over the editing of the magazine and demanded such slavish dedication to perfection from his editors and contributors that he made Captain Ahab appear benign. Every item that finally saw print in *Playboy*, from the color of the lower eyelash of Little Annie Fanny to a misplaced semicolon in an

article on abortion was agonized over by Hefner.... Words, colors, cartoons, and photos were all given the special brand of Hefner diagnostic approval or condemnation, and *Playboy* was not printed until he felt it was perfect in every aspect.[4]

On 30 December 1984 the *Washington Post* (which has long maintained a friendly on-going relationship with *Playboy*) issued a massive article celebrating Hefner's glamorous success. The reporter noted that the publisher still screened cartoons and selected the monthly Playmate himself. Hefner's private vision of sexuality would be seen in his selection of magazine cartoons. On the evidence, Hefner enjoyed publishing photographs and cartoons of children being sexually assaulted by adults. No information is available on his possession and use of child pornography films and videos produced by others.

NO FREEDOM OF SPEECH INSIDE THE COVERS

Pedophiles exist in every line of work—as do thieves, wife batterers, and rapists. It should not therefore be surprising to find these felons among the staff, writers, and/or publishers of *Playboy*, *Penthouse*, and *Hustler*. Hefner had carefully designed his 1954 cartoon suggesting incest between a young boy and his older sister. Said Brady:

> An inordinate amount of time, for example, was spent on editing the "Party Jokes" page.... Though only ten or twelve jokes were published each month, Hefner insisted that his editors submit hundreds of jokes to him as a selection, which he would then carefully rewrite and reedit.... Hefner developed a "policy" covering what kind of jokes were acceptable to him (e.g. no military, animal, or salesman-farmer's daughter jokes), and this regimen had to be followed slavishly, under threat of dismissal for the editor responsible for compiling the selection each month.[5]

On the evidence, any pornographic "joke," letter, cartoon, photo, or article about children, women, or men could have been cancelled by Hefner. Despite his rhetoric about his writers being "free" to publish and say what they wished, Hefner censored material in his magazine that challenged his personal views. Everything had to be approved by Hefner and must fit his view of sex, drugs, or whatever— under threat of dismissal.

Love of religion, joyful chastity, happy, "straight," conventional marriage, arguments condemning pornography or advocating women's alimony rights, right-to-life, or protection of child innocence, or blaming the sexual revolution for venereal disease epidemics—these positions would be censored from *Playboy*. His biographies are rife with data on Hefner's control of "every single comma."

The publisher was then responsible for the nude, ten-year-old Brooke Shields—oiled and posed naked—with make up and suggestive props in his *Playboy* Press publication, *Sugar and Spice*. On record as saying that he wished he could have sex with Chastity ("You know who I'd like to have? Chastity!") the ten-year-old daughter of Cher,[6] biographer Miller suggests Hefner had sex (statutory rape) with a young friend of sixteen-year-old Christie Hefner's:

> Hefner had not had much contact with his children since his divorce from Millie in 1959, but when Christie was sixteen, he hosted a Sweet Sixteen party for her at the Mansion . . . [and] ten of her school friends. . . making love . . . bouncing a friend of his daughter on the round bed . . . the temptation proved too much.[7]

Miller—typical of Hefner's clan—dismisses the significance of Hefner's "fatherly" sex act with a youngster whom Dad hosted at his daughter's birthday party. The acceptance of and pleasure taken in child sexual abuse would begin at the top, with Hefner, and trickle down to those he selected as cartoonists, photographers, editors, copy editors, and general staff. From here, their views would move outward to the general society—to the decision-makers and the male generation that Hefner claims would express his own "message and spirit."

WINNING THE YOUNG

Hefner's strategy was to win the young. After explaining that each magazine is planned to the last dot, Brady quotes Hefner:

> *Playboy* was . . . capturing a younger audience: 25 percent of all copies were sold on college campuses. . . . The *Esquire* Girls are gone. . . . Vargas and Petty: the sophisticated cartoons are gone too. . . . And I'm quite certain that *Esquire's* editors planned it that way—the pattern is too well established at this point for it not to have been.[8]

And Weyr cites one *Playboy* staff member saying,
"Readers turn over constantly and must be replenished from
below, from the pool of the young.... [*Playboy* must] become
film played on the tube of the mind."9 *Playboy*'s "Child
Magnets" would certainly attract the young. Regarding the
pattern of child sex abuse cartoons and "Child Magnets,"
what Hefner said about *Esquire* would fit his own publication
as well: "I'm quite certain that [*Playboy*'s] editors planned it
that way—the pattern is too well established at this point for
it not to have been."

FORTY YEARS OF "ACCEPTING ITS MESSAGE AS THEIR OWN"

For almost forty years, American decision-makers have
followed the cult of Kinsey/Hefner, "accepting its message
and spirit as their own" and "educating" their readers and
society "mentally and morally" in Kinseyan sexuality.

Statistically, most cartoonists are male. Therefore,
Playboy's 100 percent male composition of all cartoonists is
not unusual. Some small number of *Playboy* cartoonists
portrayed children in harmless behavior. However, even
apparently innocent stories printed in between the covers of
explicit sex and other sexual and violent material are tainted
with the same brush. In any case, the majority of porn
magazine children are defined and treated in ways detrimen-
tal to child welfare. This reveals that the publishers are either
unaware of and thus disinterested in children's well-being, or
they purposefully endanger children.

Having to describe something of the character of the
Playboy director, it is important to analyze the manner in
which the magazines portray children's heroes, the special
characters belonging to the child's world.

THE CULTURE OF CHILDHOOD

In the *Reisman Report,* we found many soft porn
magazine characters taken from the "culture of childhood"—
children's literature, films and such (illustrations, photos, and
cartoons). Of 6,004 magazine scenes showing child images
under eighteen years, 871 (15 percent) included recognizable
childhood heroes, such as holiday symbols, comic book
characters and heroes, biblical figures, special television and
film "stars" (Brooke Shields, Jerry Lewis, Bill Cosby, etc.),
as well as animated, heroic characters.

Child heroes in a sex magazine are important. Superman, Batman, and Boy Blue would accomplish the most critical step in all communication efforts—to capture the child's attention. Once his or her attention is captured, the child is involved in the scene. Finally, the child would identify with and view the heroes' actions with approval. The process can be seen in the five-step model below of Child Magnets (DIAPR):

1. Draw the child's attention to the scene.
2. Involve/Identify the child in the scene.
3. Accept/Approve of the hero/heroines' actions.
4. Process/Store "heroic" sex-scene in memory.
5. Recommend imitation of "hero."

Relying on current psychological theory (e.g., associational, learning, and modelling theories), the idea is that once drawn into the "play," the child's identification and involvement leads to subconscious acceptance and approval of the scene events. Certain events would trigger the child's subconscious memory, causing the play's message to replay for years to come, and the actors' behavior modeled. This is something generations of parents have observed and recent law enforcement agencies are discovering. Again, why does society in general, and the media in particular, continue to deny this time- and lab-proven fact?

WHAT OF FANTASY HEROES WHO SEXUALLY ABUSE?

Of the 2,016 cartoons involving children in these magazines, 319 (16 percent) involved some "character from the culture of childhood." Drs. Wambolt and Negley's comment on children's fantasy heroes: that pictures or cartoons of sexualized children, or fantasy heroes sexually using children, could dangerously confuse, stimulate, and distress children.[10]

In the *Reisman Report*, Drs. Wambolt and Negley warned that heroes in cartoons and illustrations would become the child's role models:

> Developmentally, sexual exploration is normal for adolescents. . . . Many adolescents do not feel free to learn about sexuality from their parents, and use peer discussion and media to teach themselves. If these adolescents view confusing pictures of "sexualized

children" or cartoons about adult men, often fantasy heroes (especially Darth Vader) sexually using children, their dual developmental drives of becoming sexual as well as nurturant adults may blend, blur and be confused.[11]

As noted, *Playboy*, *Penthouse*, and *Hustler* (especially as these magazines are often found in the home) educate children about adult-child sex rather like the NCPCA *Spiderman* comic, which gave "tips on how to prevent sexual abuse."

Hard-core pornographers have traditionally created stories using fairy tales, Snow White, Santa Claus, Cinderella, the Wizard of Oz, and the like. The majority of these cartoon stories involve the hero(es) in some sort of sexual situation, often with the child. Just as the NCPCA used cartoons to teach children to reject advances from adults for sex, these porn magazine characters teach children that they should accept and enjoy sex with adults.

REPLENISHING FROM BELOW

Looking at the ideas expressed by *Playboy*, *Penthouse*, and *Hustler* (hereafter referred to as PPH) child cartoonists, *Playboy's* John Dempsey typically laughs at prostituted children. Consider the following Dempsey cartoon:

> SCENE: A nude, little blonde child, perhaps seven years, with budding breasts, still overlarge for her small face (large, wide eyes and pony-tailed hair). The child sits on an unmade hospital bed with naked adult females (one black, three white) and two males. The fully clothed doctor is talking to the "john's" wife, saying "When I gave your husband the go-ahead to have sex after his heart attack I didn't expect . . . "(August 1976, John Dempsey)

This "joke," as well as the following by Marty Murphy, and all others from *Playboy*, would have been either commissioned or approved of by Hugh Hefner:

> SCENE: Four males sit on a park bench; a "grandfather," a "father," "a teenage boy" and a little boy of about five. Each casually looks at four dressed, females strolling by together. In his "thinking bubble" grandad "imagines" the five-year-old girl—naked. Father imagines the pre-teen girl—naked. The teenage boy imagines both children, mother and grandmother—naked. The little boy imagines

himself playing with the little girl's dog. (Marty
Murphy, June 1971)

This "joke" about the "normality of pedophilia" was
ordered or approved by Hefner.

WHERE DID THE CARTOONIST PLACE THE CHILD?

Decades ago few parents expressed serious concern
about the safety of their child's immediate environment. Very
cautious parents warned their youngsters to be wary of taking
candy from strangers and took care not to allow their children
to stray into unknown or unsafe neighborhoods. Careful
parents in dangerous neighborhoods counseled children to
come straight home from school, not stopping anywhere
along the way.

As the sexual environment has changed, sexual threats
to children in both their public and private space have
increased. The havens of safety—streams, woods, and parks—
grow ever tighter around our children. Many parents now
escort their children by foot or car to church, scouts, school,
etc. Once inside, parents are often troubled, wondering whether
the minister, scoutmaster, or math teacher are trustworthy.
Parents' concerns about sex criminals (pedophiles and
pederasts) molesting their children is not unwarranted. This
apprehension reaches deeply into the home, so much so that
even young baby-sitters and close relatives become suspect,
instilling millions of children and their parents with a sense of
distrust and foreboding.

Based upon our concern for the likely locales of child
abuse, we examined the sites of child harassment in the sex
magazine culture of PPH. How often were children's places
of safety violated, used for adult humor, or for adult action?
We especially looked at how much activity took place within
or just outside the home, in the child's bedroom, or the adult's
bedroom. For example, the Murphy cartoon scene took place
outside (in the park) and the Dempsey cartoon scene took
place inside (in an adult's bedroom).

Any consistent scenes about children being harmlessly
assaulted in their own world would provide readers with very
dangerous sexual ideas. Drawings of sex with children in their
little bedrooms, or kidnapping children from a back yard,

meant that these sites would long remain in the unconscious memory of the juvenile and adult consumers.

CARTOONS VERSUS VISUAL SETTINGS

We found twenty-five areas in which the child was generally placed. The three magazines were very similar. The physical settings of the child cartoon scenes were primarily in the child's home, doorway, or yard. Visuals—photographs of children—in all three magazines overwhelmingly took place in an abstract background.

The differences between cartoons and visuals were striking. In first place for visual photos were 1,836 scenes in an abstract setting, followed by 482 in home, bedroom, or yard. For example, the January 1976 *Hustler* printed a photograph of a small, nude boy of about seven years—his sex organ plainly visible, with a nude adult woman, presumably symbolizing his mother. The woman and boy embrace in a diffused, hazily lit background. Typical of the 482 non-abstract photos, in August 1983, *Hustler* posed a young girl, nude, near a swing, allegedly in her backyard.

In contrast, first place for cartoons were 626 home/bedroom/yard scenes, followed by 172 depicted on streets and sidewalks.

Playboy (June 1973) posed two youngsters, one at the doorstep and one just inside the front door. Both were being sexually assaulted by their foster parents. And, in January 1979, *Playboy* posed a small, four-year-old girl next to her nude, prostitute mother, on the street. (The child was selling prophylactics.) The subconscious mind is hard at work when dealing with child sexual abuse imagery. It is a fine line between titillating the reader and admitting that one is viewing child pornography.

Playboy has been very careful to use child imagery with disclaimers. In her research for the University of Salford in England on *Playboy* cartoons, 1970-1979, Dr. Gail Dines-Levy found that males see the cartoons as truisms about women and not as "cartoons." And, she found denial among all her subjects of even the most blatant adult-child sexual abuse scenes. Dines-Levy tape-recorded the remarks of twenty-one subjects: seven males, seven females, and seven "feminist" females. The fourteen "non-feminist" men and women read the cartoons and the depictions of women as if they were real and not as if they were cartoons. There was no mention made of the concocted nature of the images, that these were not real women nor real situations. When they saw cartoons with child images—females with hair bows, pigtails, children's clothing, referred to as children by the captions and with children's bodies, but exaggerated breasts—the subjects said these were not children. And when they saw a cartoon with a child being sexually used by a preacher, the women felt the image was insulting to the clergy. In a picture of a secretary, with child symbols (hair bows, pigtails, socks) being sexually used by her employer, the readers worried that the man who stumbled in on the boss's assault might be penalized for his intrusion. No one commented that this was a "child-woman," graphically compromised.

The seven "feminist" subjects objected to the demeaning image of the women in the cartoons. They spoke of the cartoons as concoctions of men for men—but they also did not show any offense at the images of the children in sex acts with adults.[12]

In her research on *Playboy*, Dr. Dines-Levy found 43.2 percent of the children in the sexual scenes were being sexually used.

The fact that real youngsters were photographed nude in abstract backgrounds suggests the need to disorient the reader with a sense of unreality or fantasy surrounding his or her view of a sexualized child.

On the other hand, as a cartoon is, by its very nature, "fantasy," the reader already was situated in an imaginary world. This meant the child abuse itself could, and did, more closely resemble "reality." The child's home, doorway, or yard was most commonly cartooned, and children were often sexually involved or abused there. In fact, most sexual assaults of children do take place close to the child victims' everyday environments: close to or in their homes, in their own backyards, or in the home of a close friend, for instance.

WHERE THE CHILDREN ARE

Of twenty-five possible settings, the following nine appeared in rank order of most to least often in child cartoons:

Cartoons	Number of Appearances
1. Home/doorway/yard	626
2. Streets and sidewalks	172
3. Country/nature/beach and other	153
4. Bed/bedroom/hotel room	132
5. Unspecified	125
6. Medical setting	100
7. Playground/park	86
8. School building or grounds	79
9. Store	72

Photographs and Illustrations	
1. Unspecified or other	1,836
2. Home/doorway/yard	482
3. Country/nature/beach	412
4. Bed/bedroom/hotel room	290
5. Other cultural/national milieu	162
6. Streets, sidewalks, alley	134
7. Playground/sports area/park	118
8. Bizarre, fantastic or unreal	117
9. School building or grounds	99

TWO OUTDOOR SCENES

Examples of children being victimized in outdoor scenes are represented in two "Chester the Molester" cartoons by Dwaine Tinsley published by *Hustler*. In the first cartoon, an adolescent girl jumps up, shocked, from a park commode. "Chester the Molester" had hidden inside the commode hole. The reader sees Chester's soiled face raised up through the toilet seat, beneath the youngster (August, 1984).

Another scene was the subject of a 7 May 1984 Senate Oversight Hearing, which attempted to halt the Justice Department investigation. Sen. Arlen Specter (R-Pa) and Sen. Howard Metzenbaum (D-Oh) opposed the Reisman study claiming it was a waste of money. (What was unknown at the time was that Sen. Metzenbaum had recently been a paid *Penthouse* interviewee.) Sen. Specter asked to see a cartoon showing a crime being committed against a child. He was given a copy of a "Chester the Molester" cartoon. The *Hustler* scene shows an adolescent girl, standing with her legs wide apart and reaching up to catch a beach ball. Chester is underwater. He wears goggles and a snorkel. His arm is outstretched before him and his fingers are wriggling through the water as he reaches up toward the innocent girl's crotch (September 1976).

Although the title left no room for doubt as to the planned assault by the "hero" (Chester), the senator felt compelled to explain away the obvious depiction of criminal intent:

> I have never seen an actual picture of a crime being committed against a child. . . . You are seeing a different picture than I am. . . . He is moving toward her. There is not a touching here.

Why would Sen. Specter pretend to the press and public that "Chester the Molester" was an innocent cartoon? Why did he obscure the name of the monthly cartoon feature? "Molester" is a recognized term for the crime of child abuse. To reasonable persons "Chester the Molester" is a man who molests children. This, and most other Chester cartoons, show "a crime being committed against a child." Were this a photograph of a man engaged in such an act, it would be evidence of criminal intent.

In fact, both scenes were in the press a few years later as true crimes. A child really was assaulted in a park outhouse exactly as depicted in the first cartoon. And, reports of children assaulted by underwater molesters in local pools have also been received. Moreover, Dwaine Tinsley, Chester's creator, now sits in prison, convicted of felony counts of child sexual abuse. These cartoons and this report were part of the evidence that convicted him.

Chapter 10

SOFT PORN'S CHILD MAGNETS

Recently, due to the recognition of alcohol problems among children, the Washington State Medical Association banned advertisements linking alcohol consumption with "athletic prowess or professional or social achievements of any kind." Moreover, as reported in the *Washington Post*, the medical association also "ban[ned] use of themes or objects, such as toys, attractive to children."

This move to ban what we would call "child magnets" from all alcohol advertisement, stems, says Christine Lubinski of the National Council on Alcoholism and Drug Dependence, from a need to protect children. Why? Lubinski says, "Advertising is encouraging young people to move from non-alcoholic beverages to wine coolers" (*Washington Post*, 27 January 1991).

In the same way that child themes, such as athletes and toys are used as child magnets for the alcohol industry, these themes have been exploited by the sex industry for the same purpose. Children are drawn to pictures of other children and especially to colorful cartoons and illustrations. Examining the 683 magazines, the research team not only identified 6,004 images that included children, but thousands of additional images which qualified as "child magnets." Child magnets are images of identifiably special appeal to the average boy or girl: three dimensional pop-ups and cut outs, fairy tales, space ships, cowboys and Indians, dolls, brides, Mickey Mouse figures, and other likely "toys." When there was no child included, these "themes . . . attractive to children" were coded as child magnets without children.

When viewed from this "child's perspective," at least 30 percent of *Playboy*, 40 percent of *Penthouse*, and 50 percent of *Hustler*'s imagery overall were child magnets.

THE *PLAYBOY* COLORING BOOK

Among the used magazines obtained for the research project was a January 1963 *Playboy*. One of the staff noted a pull-out called: "The *Playboy* Coloring Book," a fourteen page coloring book to be crayoned by the consumer. Several pages had indeed been colored-in by a small child, probably barely reading age. The child had either been instructed by an older person about the proper colors, or had somehow followed the instructions given in the text for each page. One page had drawings of three young women. Each was colored in by the child. The instructions read:

> These are extra playmates. Every playboy should have several to spare. That is because variety is the spice of life. Make one of the girls a redhead . . . a blonde . . . a brunette. It does not matter which is which. The girls' hair colors are interchangeable. So are the girls.

The youngster's coloring, drawn by a small, unsteady hand ran outside the lines of the "girls'" bodies and hair. The coloring book gave further instruction to small and big consumers, teaching them about the fun of home pornography viewing for boys and girls. The text offered several methods to get girls drunk and to seduce them (similar to the directions for deflowering the virgin earlier). Finally, it counseled the reader that to have sex with a virgin you have to lie to her—promise marriage. Lying is not a problem, instructed *Playboy*. Just don't show up at the church. Leave the bride, in her white wedding dress, in front of the church with no groom in sight.

The child (or adult) consumer is told to blacken the entire page with the waiting bride and the church. After coloring it black, he is to tear out the page and throw it (the bride and the church) away. Once the playboy got his virgin, the wedding promise was void. With legal breach of promise long gone, the state does not even suggest the deceived victim is due reparations for a contract violation. Her rights were abandoned along with the law.

SANTA CLAUS AS A CHILD MAGNET

The Washington State Medical Association would agree that normal children are attracted less to photographs of naked women than to pop-ups, coloring books, and cartoons of Spiderman, Superman, or Santa Claus. Our research found these expensive, three-dimensional cut outs and pop-ups only in *Playboy*. The three-dimensional pictures frequently displayed very sadistic sex (e.g., an illustration of a woman's mouth shown engaging in [open the flap] graphic, spitting, splattering, oral copulation; the bright red imprint of a man's hand on [open the flap] a woman's nude buttocks, etc.)

These child magnets visually excite and instruct adults and children in such sexual conduct, violence, marital relationships, adultery, and family life in general. Remember Philip Kotler's marketing direction to achieve their "mental and moral" aims, the magazine would use "subtle thematic advertising to overcome resistance." Using this marketing expertise, millions of men and boys would accept the sex industry and *Playboy*'s "message and spirit as their own."

PLAYBOY'S 329 SANTAS

Due to the significance of Santa Claus as a symbol of Christmas, religion, love, and benign and benevolent authority, the use of the "Santa-as-a-pervert" theme in this genre would poison thoughts about what Hefner called "all that jazz"—the sanctity of love and family life. Culturally, we know Santa as a critical figure for children and, despite commercial exploitation, a religious figure relating to children's innocence, happiness, goodness, and well-being.

A preliminary survey of all Santa photos, advertisements, illustrations, and cartoons in these magazines, December 1957 to December 1984, found 507 Santa Claus figures:

* 329 (65 percent) *Playboy* Santas
* 139 (27 percent) *Penthouse* Santas
* 39 (8 percent) *Hustler* Santas

Without exception, beyond his role as a jolly salesman of liquor or other material goods, benevolent altruism (a key historical meaning for Santa) was non-existent. How have children responded to seeing hundreds of Santas engaged in illicit—and explicit—sexual and violent activities?

For example, his pants down below his knees, Santa is shown graphically mounting his reindeer from behind for sex (*Playboy*, January 1979). Children also can study Santa cannibalizing a child, his sharpened teeth bloody red, calling for another human meal (*Playboy*, January 1977). Santa murdered a little boy (*Penthouse*, December 1977), the child s head and body blown away, red blood splattered everywhere. Since he was often drawn as a victim himself, children could see Santa's blood spurting out as he was bloodily crucified by a giant mouse trap (*Penthouse*, October 1976).

In the "Santa-as-a-pervert" theme, children are constantly cartooned as initiating, receiving, or observing sexual or violent activity with Santa Claus. Children sitting on Santa's lap were regularly either initiating or receiving some form of sex or violence with Santa. For example, one of the more brutal *Penthouse* cartoons was the violent rape of a little girl sitting on Santa's lap (*Penthouse*, December 1974) while he sang, "Santa Claus is coming . . . ," his pants down around his ankles. And in December 1988, *Penthouse* celebrated Christmas with a naked, headless Tiny Tim about to be eaten for Christmas dinner by his family. Tim is "cartooned" with his naked buttocks prominent on a large serving platter and his father is saying, "God Bless Tiny Tim."

SANTA IMAGE USED AS GATEWAY TO PORNOGRAPHY

Santa Claus may qualify as the gateway image for the artist's attack upon religious belief, morality, and children's innocence. Along this line of thought, children's love of Santa makes him one of the most critical child magnets of all. Children are enticed by images in erotica/pornographies. Santa draws the child's attention to the magazine pages and helps create what the *Playboy* spokesman called a "pool of the young," consumers and decision makers for tomorrow. Even the youngest child is emotionally invested in cartoons, illustrations, and photographs of Santa.

When artists humiliate Santa Claus, religious belief, morality, and benevolent, altruistic authority are also ridiculed. Research conducted in 1896 and replicated again in 1977, found Santa of grave import to children.[1] It is hardly a surprise that children said Santa made children happy. In 1985, the *New York Times* reported that 87 percent of ten-year-olds and over 90 percent of children under five believed in Santa. The importance of Santa to children indicates his place of special concern in any research on communication methods to children.

In analyzing the magazine scenes, two players emerged as most critical in photos and cartoons. We identified these two as "the principal child" and the "other character." In general when sexual activity involved girls, the other character was found to be an adult male. In December and January the other character was likely to be Santa.

Due to *Playboy*'s special appeal and accessibility to even very young children, the following preliminary analysis looks only at *Playboy* Santas.

There have been eight consistently *Playboy* Santa themes (rank ordered below). Number one is the activity in which Santa is seen most often. Number eight is the activity in which he is seen least often. Although altruistic, benevolent Santa images (unassociated with sex, drugs, alcohol, violence, morbidity or illegal behavior) were included as a theme, none were found in the 329 cartoons, photographs, and illustrations.

PLAYBOY CARTOONS, PHOTOGRAPHS, AND ADVERTISEMENTS 1957 - 1984

RANK ORDER	ACTIVITY	CASES
1.	SEXUAL, INCLUDING ORGY, ETC.	170
2.	BENEVOLENT IN LIQUOR ADVERTS	81
3	DRUGS/ALCOHOL SALE ASSOCIATED	35
4.	VIOLENT	32
5.	SEXUALLY VIOLENT	6
6.	OTHER ILLEGAL	3
7.	MORBID	3
8.	STRICTLY BENEVOLENT/ALTRUISTIC	0
TOTAL SANTA IMAGE ACTIVITIES		329

The rank order of the above themes should concern the Washington State Medical Association. Santa Claus has been packaged by *Playboy* as 1) sexually active, 2) associated with alcohol and other drug consumption, and 3) associated with violence. When we examine the largest category—"sexual, including orgy, etc."—Santa is hyper-sexual and providing Christmas gifts in exchange for sexual services from women and girls. They gladly prostitute themselves for gifts and Santa joyfully bribes them accordingly.

Mrs. Claus is sometimes mentioned. As the "Mrs" may have meaning in children's visions of Santa, the specter of adultery is part of Santa's sex instruction. For, chimney to chimney, Santa engages in coitus, even while Mrs. Claus is having sex with Santa's little elves.

In December 1986, *Playboy* designed an expensive Santa child magnet fold-out. It was a centerfold illustration of Mrs. Claus, attractive to all children and especially appealing to teenage boys. "Mrs. Claus" (who would be subconsciously associated with the boys' mothers) was drawn naked and engaged in sex with one of Santa's very little elf helpers. A smiling teddy bear, a happy "child's moon," eight other tiny, little elves, and the readers, all peeped down at the bizarre and illicit full color sexual scene.

SANTA'S SEXUAL CONDUCT

RANK ORDER	SANTA APPEARS AS:	CASES
1.	ADULTERER OR ASSOCIATED WITH ORGY, ETC.	91
2.	OBSERVER/RECIPIENT OF SEX (ADULT)	17
3.	ASSOCIATED WITH SEX "OBJECT"	11
4.	SEX OBJECT IN SANTA CLOTHES	9
4.	PARTICIPATING/OBSERVING SEX WITH MINORS	9
5.	SEX-BUYING (JOHN-TRICK)	6
6.	AS PIMP OR PROCURER	5
7.	SEX WITH ANIMALS	4
7.	SANTA AS OUT-OF-WEDLOCK FATHER	4
8.	SANTA AS HOMOSEXUAL	3
8.	SANTA AS EXHIBITIONIST (FLASHER)	3
8.	OBSERVER/RECIPIENT OF SEX (CHILD)	3
8.	NAIVELY INVOLVED IN SEX ACTIVITY	3
9.	SEXUALIZED TOY SANTA	2
SANTA IN SEXUAL ACTIVITY TOTAL		170

HOW *PLAYBOY* KILLED SANTA CLAUS

Since erotica/pornography educates millions of youth each year, parents, teachers, clergy, therapists, police, and others who work with children need to question themselves and their charges regarding children's exposure to these pornographies. It is not possible as yet to identify the role pornographies play in each person's individual life. But, we know something happens to children exposed to a systematic sexualization of themselves, of violence, and of their few heroes, especially their religious heroes.

Santa Claus, fairy tales, and nursery rhymes have been primary to the symbolic world of a child's imagination. Such intuitive, affectionate, and emotional childhood experiences are imaginative rehearsal plays to prepare the child for adulthood. Santa stands apart for children as a critical hero in the larger world of fairy tales and religious heroes. Because of this high level of trust and affection, the treatment of Santa images across all three magazines as an exploitative, violent adulterer and murdering pedophile is hardly trivial for the emotional life of those children exposed.

It was as important for the sex industry to carefully plot strategies to attract children to the magazine as it has been for cigarette and liquor industries to plan their appeals to children. It is so difficult for non-manipulators to believe in mind control designs, that it is useful to provide some such information at this time. Briefly, certain orthodox techniques are employed to change the values and morals of unsuspecting young and old consumers (e.g., "conditioning" or "brain-washing"). Among other illicit and pathogenic activities, the values-changing program teaches consumers to tolerate and eventually accept the magazine's ideas of child sexual abuse and even violent and murderous assault on children.

DELIBERATE VISUAL PACING AFFECTS CHILDREN

In line with classical conditioning techniques, consumers receiving this violent and sexual Santa stimuli would be incapable of separating such jokes from the female genital and breast displays featured in the same issue. Weyr quoted Arthur Kretchmer, a *Playboy* executive:

> There is a care, a kind of compulsive delicacy . . . about the magazine. It is edited visually. . . . The magazine is visually paced. And pacing is the favorite word about this magazine. It has an internal rhythm, which I don't think the reader recognizes. But subconsciously he does grasp the enhancing value. We orchestrate the magazine so its features complement each other. . . . Redundancy is our biggest single enemy. We don't like there to be two cartoons in the same issue that might have a [similar] joke.[2]

As Hefner said earlier in discussing the kinds of materials included and excluded in *Esquire*, *Playboy* plans its mix of child sex cartoons, illustrations of violent animals or events, and sexually explicit female genitals. As in *Esquire*, said Hefner, it "had to be" planned. The 507 ads, cartoons, photos, and illustrations of Santa in these three magazines from 1957 to 1985 were planned to show the traditionally benevolent figure in sexual, violent scenes or drug/alcohol advertisements. The hundreds of exploitative or vindictive Santas "had to be" planned. And, their carrying out of nefarious activities within a framework of serious articles by prominent leaders also had to be planned. Lending authenticity to this brutality by allowing their works to be published by PPH are Jack Anderson, Masters and Johnson, Dr. Bill Cosby, "Dr. Ruth," Jane Fonda, Sen. Howard Metzenbaum, Jimmy Carter, Martin Luther King, Jr., and others.

An additional "environmental mix" issue involved surrounding the 6,004 images of children with roughly 14,000 crime and violence scenes and 49,000 images of sexual parts. Weyr quoted *Playboy* executive Arthur Kretchmer again:

> You touch every base. You do a light piece. You do a heavy piece. You do a girl [*sic*] pictorial. You do something else. You do a travel piece one month and a piece on the environment some other month. . . . We've yanked things because two artists will have drawn in a similar style, used the same colors, or drawn the same subject. If that happens, one piece comes right out. We don't want repetition.[3]

Playboy "yanked things" because two artists used the same color or subject. It is true that two jokes about prostituted and raped children never appeared in the same month. No two jokes about violence to children appeared in the same month. While several cartoons might show Santa in some kind of adultery, only one Santa cartoon at Christmas would have him sexually associated in a child scene.

Therefore, the magazine editors were well aware of the kind of child images they presented. "Redundancy is our biggest single enemy," said a *Playboy* spokesman. Based on the admissions by Kretchmer, the use of child pornography cartoons and photos was orchestrated, year after year, as was the sexual exploitation of rape cartoons and photos. This same orchestrated program of repetition was true of drug promotion jokes, anti-religion jokes, and murder, castration, and impotence jokes. The musical harmony Kretchmer spoke of in fairy tales, the "internal rhythm," was *Playboy*'s pied piper flute leading children from their parents and their past and into an unknown and traumatic *Playboy* world.

ABUSING CHILDREN IN FAIRY TALES

Beyond Santa Claus and "where the children are" (the home, school, playground, etc.) other cartoon and visual themes were examined. These themes, including fairy tales, were important since they revealed the shocking increase of sexual photos mixed with other brutal images. Fairy tales are close to the hearts of children. We welcome fairy tales as adults because they stir our memories of warmth, love, and childish trust. Hence, the fairy tale played a very important role in conditioning readers to accept the child as sexual. The change from fairy tale cartoon stories to photo stories was telling. Cartoons were the frequent art form used to display fairy tales; 209 (10 percent) of all child cartoons focused upon these fairy tale fantasies.

Having been around for fifteen years longer than even *Penthouse*, *Playboy* had the most, 125 (60 percent), of PPH overall fairy tale cartoons. Ten percent of *Playboy* child cartoons were fairy tales. *Penthouse* contributed thirty-two (15 percent) to the pool of overall fairy tales; but a slightly higher percentage—12 percent—of child cartoons were fairy stories. *Hustler* contributed fifty-two (25 percent) fairy tales, but only 9 percent of their own child cartoons were fairy tales. In sharp contrast, photographic fairy tales appeared only 2 percent of the time, with thirty-one of these in *Playboy*, eight in *Penthouse*, and forty in *Hustler*. The way it worked out, *Playboy* would set up the fairy tale cartoon first (e.g., Cinderella having sex with the prince or Dorothy raped by her Oz companions), leaving *Hustler* free to put the fairy tale into a sexually violent photo story.

PORNOGRAPHIC ENCHANTMENT

In fourteen years "soft porn" cartoons of children progressed in levels of violence: In 1954 *Playboy* boy scouts solicited sex from adult prostitutes and were refused. Twelve years later, in 1968, a *Playboy* "*Wizard of Oz* Straw Man" hinted that he wanted to have sex with flat-chested Dorothy. Ten years after that first attempted assault, in 1978, *Playboy*'s Dorothy has been given larger breasts—and she is cavalierly gang-raped by the Straw Man, the Lion, and the Tin Man.

Then four years after that, in 1982, *Hustler* photographs a "real" Dorothy—with shaved genitalia—happily engaged in graphic, close up coitus, including oral and anal sodomy with and drinking the urine of her three beast and object co-adventurers.

Further sexual violence conditioning techniques are found. In 1969 *Playboy* has children raped by a policeman on the school bus, and later that year, a child has sex with an adult while an uptight mother asks about love. And as early as 1967, a little girl scout is supposed to have sex with a cookie-buying adult male customer. These "jokes" preceded the entry of *Penthouse* into the soft porn world by months, or even years. How soft porn abuses children is a gauge of the level of atrocities against women. Children were increasingly brutalized because images of adult women had long passed the point of human sexuality and had plunged these women into an ongoing, artistic agenda of malice, revulsion, terror, and desperation.

Remember, these artistic lies and hatreds fed the imaginations of the Ted Bundys of society—long before the availability of "hard core" porn.

So, although *Penthouse* participated in and promoted adult-child sex scenes, it did not initiate the sexual exploitation of children. *Playboy* showed boys as sexually precocious in 1954, late adolescent girls as sexually precocious in the early 1960s, and little girls as sexually precocious by the late 1960s.

But, *Penthouse* was not on the newsstands until 1969. Now, subtle and blatant uses of adult women in bestiality, anal and oral sodomy, masturbation, sadism, scatology (feces, urine), necrophilia (sex with the dead), Satanism, and the like are all currently standard fare in all "skin," soft porn magazines. *Playboy* artists presented seventy-three exploitative fairy tale cartoons, *Penthouse* twenty-one, and *Hustler* thirty-nine, with Little Red Riding Hood, Cinderella, and Snow White appearing more often than any other single tale. In addition, Hansel and Gretel and Goldilocks each appeared in *Playboy* on several occasions.

CHILD PORNOGRAPHY BY MAL OF THE *WASHINGTON POST*

Mal is an editorial cartoonist for the *Washington Post*.

He draws small creatures engaged in various silly and sometimes sadistic activities. However, while Mal does not tend to evidence strong political views on his *Washington Post* editorial page, he does use his artistry to show children as appropriate sexual targets for gang rape and sodomy in PPH. Mal portends to be so taboo, so "ahead" of the rest of society, that his beliefs would not easily lend themselves to realistic drawings. In March 1976, Mal cast Alice in Wonderland in a blatant oral sodomy scene:

> SCENE: Alice in Wonderland stands on an empty "stage" (no background), looking up toward the right hand corner of the cartoon frame, she is addressing her annoyance at a wide, grinning mouth with teeth, which leers down at her. Alice is dressed and appears like a little girl. The sketch is black and white—typically Mal. She complains to the mouth: "Oral sex! Is that all you Cheshire cats are interested in?"

We are asked to consider if Alice is denouncing the cat's desire for oral sex with her, or if she is angry at the cat's disinterest in additional straight or other sex acts. In any case, Mal's special pleading shows children as sex objects, suggests sodomy with children (one can only see the "mouth," which could be the mouth of the reader, and so on), and bestiality—in 1976. In February 1974, another half-nude Alice by artist Ramonde has sex with an elf, after which she asks: "That was magic?" Ramonde's Alice has exposed, *Playboy*-exaggerated breasts.

For Christmas 1986, Mal cast the fairy tale story of Goldilocks:

> SCENE: Mal has Goldilocks in bed. The three bears are examining Mamma bear's "vibrator" which is shaped like a dildo (a false phallus). Goldilocks can be seen through the open bedroom door, in bed, smiling broadly to herself. Mamma Bear is holding the phallic object before Papa and Baby and she says: "Never mind the porridge—who's been using my vibrator?"

Again, Mal lies about child sexual development. The artist claims a happy child will seek sex—using a phallic-shaped vibrator when she has the opportunity. The bestiality implications, and such, are best left for another book. Mal's consistent fairy tale message is that children pursue sex wherever they can get it—bestial, oral sodomy, whatever. Thus, of course, gang rape, says the artist to the receptive right hemisphere, is harmless for children, as is suggested in a December 1977 cartoon:

SCENE: Mal draws Snow White, smiling, trustfully asleep in her little bed. All seven dwarfs are standing alongside her bed while one dwarf calls for a vote: "All in favor of a gang bang, say, 'hi, ho!'"

Mal's "joke" is again of the massive rape of a child by trusted friends. Such gangs do rape children and women—increasingly, a fact certainly not unknown to Mal the artist/political cartoonist for one of America's most prominent newspapers.

In any case, the magazine promotion of Santa as stupid, sexual, or malevolent is important as 1) these cartoons would be viewed/read by children; and 2) some male readers may effectively identify with Santa, widely viewed as a father substitute or as a symbol of God, religion, and/or love.

Chapter 11

KINSEY'S INFANT DATA
BROUGHT ALIVE

Stepping away from the child in the fairy tales, it is reasonable to examine the way the magazine depicts the reality of child from birth. Elsewhere in this book it is documented that marriage and virginity are both demeaned by Kinsey in 1948 and 1953 and under attack since the first *Playboy* issue. Were Hefner truly "carrying the Kinsey torch," the magazine would also treat children as unharmed by and benefiting from sex with adults. (Recall Kinsey claimed that the tiniest tots could "learn the benefits" of sex from adults, given adequate opportunity.) With this in mind, a Kinseyan soft porn magazine should sexualize the smallest infants.

Playboy alone presented a minimum of 480 images of pregnancy—children as pre-born (fetus in utero)—to children two years of age. Together, 977 cartoons, photos, and illustrations in these three magazines had stories that included infants and children pre-born to two years (186 *Penthouse*, 311 *Hustler*). While the focus of most cartoons were contempt for pregnancy and children, in some, babies were described as sexual and sexually associated with an adult.

In nearly forty years, none of the 683 soft porn magazines printed any cartoons, photographs, or illustrations that suggested that birth could be a beautiful, joyful, and wondrous event. Never was it even hinted that all experiences pale before the birth of a child born of the love between a woman and a man. Never was a child displayed within a religious framework, as a "child of God," to be treasured, cherished, beloved, and protected. While the magazines had thirty-three cartoon scenes with angels (Cupids, cherubs), these representatives of God and heaven were seen engaged in sex, (including sodomy), or brutally shot.

Penthouse (August 1978) erotically illustrated a full-breasted, lactating woman, from her chin to waist, holding her naked infant with her hands, blood oozing down her neck and from the infant's lips and body. The most egregious example, however, of sexualizing the newborn may be in the September 1977 *Hustler*:

> SCENE: A hospital-viewing window for newborns—a neonate has jumped up from his hospital bed, laughingly grabbing onto the hair of his attending nurse as he plunges his oversized phallus into her mouth. The father, looking into the viewing window says to his friend, "That's my boy!"

In celebration of Valentines Day, the magazines often published angels copulating. This is especially troubling since Valentine cards given annually by children in the schoolroom resemble the "angels" pictured copulating in these periodicals. Although there had been objection from critics, insisting that our research should ignore these angels as images of children, the entire history of western art with its role of the cherub/angel as child counters such critical nonsense.

Note this *Playboy* cartoon from the 1970s (in February, of course):

> SCENE: A full color, two-page cartoon cameo collection for Valentines Day—all of the images of children are sexually compromised, with Little Boy Blue holding a whip, about to torture a naked little girl (with *Playboy*'s exaggerated breasts). The blonde child is bound and gagged and stands in high heels, garters, and black stockings. Nearby, nine little angels are romping, two of them engaged in sex.

MISREPRESENTING INFANT SEXUALITY

The December 1974 *Playboy* story "Getting Off" follows a full-page, full-color rendering of an infant. Still in diapers, the baby has broken his rattle, and with his hand deep in his diaper he has seized his reproductive organs while a depressed adult expression settles over his face.[1]

Either due to the artist's ignorance of child development or out of sheer malice, the "Getting Off" illustrator and his publisher provide false visual information regarding an infant's capacity and desire for sexual stimulation. The illustrator draws the infant as a bloated child under one year of age. Yet, by his conduct the author suggests the infant had attained the motor skills of a much older child. The image is all the more repugnant because of the brutalization of the infant's face, distorted to resemble that of a heavy lidded, debauched old man. This is not the happy, little boy toddler who finds his little penis in the same manner that he discovers his nostrils and the inside of his ears, and who runs about naked, holding on and shrieking with laughter.

Such sexualized illustrations are treacherous for the imaginations, belief systems, and behavior of sexually vulnerable adults or youths who have infants available to them! Increasingly hospital emergency wards give accounts of infants who are in agony from venereal diseases and brutal lacerations and perforations of the throat, vagina, and anus, confirming the susceptibility of the public not only to "child sexuality" propaganda, but even to "infant sexuality" propaganda. Variations of this libelous illustration are found in *Hustler* and in "legitimate" sex history books. "Getting Off" further legitimizes Kinsey's myths of "infant sexuality."

This visual "data point" speaks rather accurately of four decades of Kinseyan mythology distributed by the *Playboy* ethic. Again, the fact that this infant is exhibited so savagely in the Christmas issue should be classified with the anti-child, anti-religious, and anti-family pattern of the magazine and its imitators.

TEENAGE SEX AND PREGNANCY

The majority of pregnant females in these three magazines—PPH—were defined as single mothers-to-be. That is, roughly two-thirds of these images were out-of-wedlock, unwanted babies. The out-of-wedlock jokes in PPH are often cast in terms of a pregnant teenage girl who "hadn't planned to go this steady" or of employees made pregnant by their bosses at the Christmas party.

In looking at child sex in cartoons, it was found that the real interest was in children in sex scenes with adults. These occurred nearly one thousand times. On the other hand, children appeared sexually with older youth only sixty times and with "each other" in peer sex roughly half as often as with older youth. Moreover, parents shocked at youthful coitus in 1971 became more accepting of peer sex and incestuous participation themselves in 1977. Again, in the June 1971 *Playboy*:

> SCENE: A young couple is nude, on the living room couch, as the parents of the girl enter the room. The boy, holding his pants up so that we do not see his phallus, signals the two-fingered "peace" sign to mom and dad, saying: "Peace." (A John Dempsey cartoon)

Six years later, in January 1977:

> SCENE: Mom and dad have burst into the living room where two youngsters are having sex on the couch. Mother, ugly and bizarre, is shouting to the girl: "Charlene! You promised to wait until we got slip covers." (A Brian Savage cartoon)

Or, as mentioned, pregnancy commonly occurs to a secretary, maid, or other working girl impregnated by her boss. (She had not anticipated single motherhood as a Christmas bonus.) The publications regularly laughed about the fact that the young woman was tricked, manipulated, and probably even drugged and raped by her boss, boyfriend, etc. And it laughed at the mother—teenage or adult—because she had to assume responsibility for the infant.

The spirit of these educative "jokes" centered as much upon the father's nonplused rejection of his baby as upon the ridiculed mother's foolish plight. While the young mother was often clearly the victim of sexual abuse, the cartoonist found his humor in her tragedy, suggesting she was stupid to trust a man's promises of love and marriage.

While jokes and cartoons, which ridiculed pregnancy, were a staple, there were few actual photographs of pregnancy. As noted, in the 373 *Playboy* issues and 1,849 child scenes, only 50 visuals (29 in-wedlock and 21 out-of wedlock) portrayed pregnancy or birth, while at best, 2 scenes touched on venereal disease. Out of 1,196 child cartoons, most of which involved some sexual scene or conduct, VD was mentioned only eight times in *Playboy*.

However, as skittish as *Playboy* was about VD, the nasty disease was never mentioned in 265 *Penthouse* cartoons, and got two comments out of 555 *Hustler* cartoons. These same figures were reflected in adult sexual humor as well. Venereal disease just didn't exist in the sexual fantasy land—promiscuity did, of course—but no VD.

Since *Playboy* and its imitators are documentably teaching youth and adults about "love," "sex," values, responsibilities, problems, and joys, the absence of any visible sign of joyful birth or horrific venereal disease in the midst of coitus (anal, oral, multiple copulations) sends a powerful message and spirit to impressionable young readers and viewers. This view of costless, painless, "recreational" sex would "have an impact that nobody feels." The price for male-female relationships to survive has been costly and disastrous.

NUDE AND PREGNANT

Playboy balanced its twenty-nine apparent in-wedlock visuals with twenty-one out-of-wedlock visuals. *Penthouse* carried almost the same number of visuals as did *Playboy* (thirteen and twenty-two). The maximum for highest number of pregnant visuals was carried by *Hustler*, whose use of nude pregnant women is part of its otherwise sexually explicit format. An entire series of pornographic magazines exploits graphic, sexually explicit pictures of pregnant women and lactating mothers. These photos do not celebrate nurturant motherhood and birth. On the contrary, they are seen as a violation and exploitation of the entire concept of procreation, motherhood, sanctity of life, privacy, and family.

ABORTION AND DEFORMATION HUMOR

When abortion was involved in a cartoon, state of marriage was generally vague. Abortion turned up in twenty-five cartoon cases, mainly in *Hustler*, using full color, "bloody" displays.

A major—and alarming—finding was the unique category of "child as a thing." That is, objects were "born" to a human mother and father. A nurse carried out a huge "10-pound tongue" (*Playboy*, November 1974) to a shocked father in the delivery room, saying: "Congratulations. It's a 10-pound tongue. " Such "newborns" were said by the magazines to be the natural offspring of human parents. The humor ran along the line that perfectly normal persons (such as the adult or juvenile reader) could be expected—should they give birth—to parent bizarre life forms and freaks of varied kinds.

However, the "freaks" were born largely into formal marriages—those our research team coded as "in wedlock." A man who did what the magazines had warned him not to do (married) found himself awaiting news of the successful birth only to find his child is deformed, or a dildo, or feces, or a wooden doll, or another object.

Penthouse presented several jokes about children born without arms with hooks for hands awaiting dad in the delivery room (Penthouse, January 1978). Disguised as good-natured humor, "jokes" about birth defects and the physically impaired move the boundaries of brutality toward children and the disabled to ever lower levels.

Again, remember that cartoons of birth and children are "Child Magnets." They draw the child's attention to the story, and the images. While each adult or child consumer would process these magnets differently, all have some similar response. How do cartoons about deformed children impact a child—at a given age? How would such "jokes" impact upon a deformed child or his family?

Some have compared the sex magazine's description of children as "freaks" to racist propaganda of Jews or blacks as "freaks" (i.e., non-human). The idea here is that these notions of "freaks"—deformed children, Jews, blacks—serve the purposes of those promoting such a view. This argument takes on greater power if we consider these child images to be actual sex industry propaganda.

Remember, children are *never* shown as asexually charming, lovely, and treasured—in any pornographies. Contempt for children is in keeping with the belief that the primary use for women is as depositories for intermittent male sexual release and violence. Loved children undermine the power of the sex industry to control men. Hence, children are the natural enemies of the sex industry, as are wives and mothers.

The following identify some of these categories of child as subhuman or otherwise despised:

*Child as an anthropomorphic object, demon-like creature, deformed, monster, birth defect, etc:

Playboy-30 children
Penthouse-10 children
Hustler-42 children

*Child mysteriously deformed in some unique manner:
Playboy-52 children
Penthouse-38 children
Hustler-59 children
*Combined deformations:
Playboy-Of 3,045, 82 (3 percent)
Penthouse-Of 1,180, 48 (4 percent)
Hustler-Of 1,779, 101 (6 percent)

Any unbiased study of these magazines would confirm these cartoon findings as the adult findings have similarly been confirmed by American, British, and New Zealand studies. It was vitally important to analyze the way in which the magazines described "what" was born of human parents. As might be expected, this category comprised 6 percent of *Hustler*'s child images. Descriptions of birth as producing bizarre and deformed creatures would have serious implications for forty years of youthful consumers' view of birth and marriage.

Playboy's 3 percent and *Penthouse*'s 4 percent are not the result of chance. Any examination of women's magazines would not uncover images of deformed children—unless this were a heart-rending report on the results of a poisonous medication or some other tragedy. It seems all sex industry materials consistently describe birth as a traumatic and totally undesirable activity.

Again, classification of deformed birth objects as "children" came under attack by our research opponents, who preferred to ignore roughly two dozen newborns described as a ten-pound tongue, a vibrator, or a doll. However, the job of this research was not to please some special political, economic, or business interest, but to objectively record the products "born of human parents." Recording the way in which a child was portrayed by these magazines required a candid analysis of the way in which birth was described.

The political positions of pornographers under study should be mentioned here. *Playboy*'s political position is revealed in its traditional and public funding of legal campaigns, beginning with efforts to end alimony and to legalize abortion-on-demand. The pornographers' political positions on birth and abortion is expressed in the magazine art—its own sex education vehicle.

Playboy has used its influence to cripple alimony laws

and to undermine public policy on protective custody of children. The publications *would* be expected to display children and marital responsibility in concert with its political and economic agenda.

Certainly, men who properly support their wives and children have less discretionary funds to expend on sexual toys, drugs, trips, and trivia. Men who are "unencumbered" by wives and family have more funds for the sex industry, its magazines, and other products. As noted in the brief look at the economic history of sex industry, this is at least an eight to ten billion dollar business in the U.S.—one which is closely allied with organized crime and sales of marijuana growing units.[2] As with all major enterprises, the sex industry fights for laws and social values that will serve its interests.

DEATH AND DYING—BEYOND ABORTION

One gets a sense of the violence toward children by noting that beyond their sexual abuse, there were numbers of lifeless bodies found in child cartoons and visuals—293 of the 6,004 child scenes. Fully 293 (4 percent) carried at least one lifeless body. Of these 197 (67 percent) were found in *Hustler,* 62 (21 percent) in *Playboy,* and 34 (12 percent) in *Penthouse.*

Moreover, 73 percent of *Hustler*'s dead bodies included dead children, 45 percent of *Playboy*'s dead bodies were children, and 47 percent of *Penthouse* dead were children. One of the earliest "jokes" about dead children was found in a 1956 *Playboy* cartoon spoofing the heroic William Tell. Tell shot his arrow through an apple on a little boy's head. Strewn about the ground are half a dozen little boys with arrows through their hearts. The "joke" apparently was that William Tell was a poor shot and kept killing boys until he finally pierced the apple. The deaths of the boys were a strike against this treasured child's tale.

Hustler's dead included a bloody murder of a boy and girl by gun fire, following a graphic description of the youngsters' sexual tryst. Lifeless adults appeared in the child stories forty-five times in *Hustler,* twenty-seven times in *Playboy,* and thirteen times in *Penthouse.*

RITUALISTIC ABUSE AND MURDER

One of the child categories we looked at was murder.

Playboy was identified in 43 child scenes involving murder (the William Tell joke would be one), *Penthouse,* 19 scenes, and *Hustler,* 114 scenes! The accuracy of the research continues to be reflected in the consistency of these numbers across the three magazines. Looking at the forty-three murder scenes in *Playboy*, one finds "virginity" as a key to several killings. *Playboy* found much humor in cartoons of very young girls who were ritualistically sacrificed. One such young girl is placed on a sacrificial alter, while another, waiting her turn to die, comments, "Takes some of the incentive out of being a virgin, doesn't it?" (March 1968).

The laughing exploitation of ritualistic sacrifice of virgins (traditionally underage) led to some disturbing questions, quite removed from the "child images." Psychiatrist Linnea Smith addressed these images in personal correspondence dated 11 April 1988:

> Public and professional concern is growing regarding ritualistic abuse cases. Bizarre and sadistic rituals, acted out as part of a cult, satanic church, coven, or other occult organization include systematic emotional, physical, and sexual abuse of infants, children, and adults. Linking religious, pseudo-religious, or supernatural symbols and ceremonies with the abuse of victims often involves wearing robes or costumes, drinking blood and urine, smearing feces, animal and human mutilation, multi-perpetrator, multi-victim sexual abuse, torture, and homicide. These cartoons from *Playboy* magazine glamorizing and trivializing this type of activity for entertainment are unacceptable.

Beyond the March 1968 "virgin sacrifice" scene, which involved youths, note other *Playboy* examples of "glamorizing and trivializing" adult satanic sacrifice:

SCENE: A well dressed, middle class couple sits, drinking martinis, as the husband says to the wife, "This witches' coven you've joined—is it here in Stanford? I don't want to worry about you down in the city at all hours" (March 1972).

SCENE: A group of hooded men are praying to a devil leader who holds up a knife over the sacrificial pyre. He is about to sacrifice a chicken. One member asks the other "How do you like our Wednesday-night get-togethers?" (October 1972).

SCENE: A buxom woman lies on the sacrificial pyre when the chief of the tribe says, "Are you guys nuts? The gods would never be this angry" (December 1972).

SCENE: A nude, young woman lies on the sacrificial alter giggling, as are the eight male coven members surrounding the alter. The coven leader is asking "All right, who slipped me the rubber knife?" (October 1978).

SCENE: A nude, young woman lies on the sacrificial alter surrounded by the male coven members who are drinking and waving the sacrificial knife about. One of the hooded men asks the naked victim, "Was it good for you, too?" (November 1980).

Consider this material in concert with the review of Robert Mapplethorpe's photographs depicting child pornography, homosexuality, and "demon" symbols and the federal funding going to Andres Serrano to create "art works composed from human body parts and decapitated heads of animals exhibited in glass vats."[3]

Those who believe in demons may literally see demons at work here. The Mapplethorpe and Serrano "art" symbolizes a breakthrough opportunity for thousands of new "artists" to gain attention, popularity, and income. Art gallery and museum pornography will be increasingly more visible. Some who disdain the doctrine of demons may still, as libertarian Rollo May has said, understand the demonic power represented.[4] In any case as our country is reeling from a recent "ritual sacrifice find" in Mexico among other shocking discoveries, symptomatic of criminal demon worship, we would do well to pay heed to the pornographer's exploitation of Satanism.

Recent reports on ritualistic sacrifice and cases of devil worship throughout the nation suggest that this humor is less than funny. PPH supports the child pornography industry, including satanic pornography, in a myriad of ways. Initially, legal employment of naked models for commercial sex ventures establishes an employment standard. This then swings the focus to "age" limits rather than prohibitions against sex commerce.

Next, the larger sex industry has established a full-scale publicity, legal, public policy, "buddy" network and a structure within which all of these players assist one another.

Assistance includes providing good publicity and hiding damaging information, providing sources for models, and coordinating political bribery for legal and other services. Moreover, in creating social acceptance for deviance, "adult" pornography creates laws, policies, and a network of well placed professionals who hamstring prosecution against their industry or its members. In this way, the adult pornographer makes it almost impossible for law enforcement to police any part of the industry, even the juvenile prostitution operation.

SUMMARY STATISTICS

Playboy, *Penthouse* and *Hustler* December 1953 to
December 1984

TOTAL CHILD SCENES:	6,004
PHOTOGRAPHS:	2,971 (49 PERCENT)
CARTOONS:	2,016 (34 PERCENT)
ILLUSTRATIONS:	1,017 (17 PERCENT)

SEX OF PRINCIPAL CHILD	SEX OF OTHER CHARACTER
	(Where Depicted)
47 PERCENT FEMALE	49 PERCENT MALE
32 PERCENT MALE	35 PERCENT FEMALE
21 PERCENT BOTH/OTHER	16 PERCENT BOTH/OTHER

AGE OF PRINCIPAL CHILD	AGE OF OTHER CHARACTER
16 PERCENT UNBORN-2 YEARS	78 PERCENT ADULTS
39 PERCENT 3-11 YEARS	7 PERCENT 3-11 YEARS
26 PERCENT 12-17 YEARS	7 PERCENT 12-17 YEARS
14 PERCENT PSEUDO-CHILD	6 PERCENT UNSPECIFIED
5 PERCENT UNSPECIFIED	2 PERCENT UNBORN-2 YEAR

RACE OF PRINCIPAL CHILD	RACE OF OTHER CHARACTER
85 PERCENT CAUCASIAN	85 PERCENT CAUCASIAN
3 PERCENT BLACK	3 PERCENT BLACK
12 PERCENT OTHER MINORITY	12 PERCENT OTHER MINORITY

* 1,675 child images associated with nudity
* 1,225 child images associated with genital acts
* 989 child images associated with adult sex acts
* 792 adults portrayed as pseudo-children

* 592 child images associated with force
* 267 child images associated sex w/animals/objects
* 29 percent nude/genital displays (visuals only)
* 21 percent visually exposed/sexualized
* 20 percent genital activity involved
* 16 percent sexual encounter with an adult
* 10 percent force used in scene
* 10 percent killing/maiming/murdering
* 6 percent internal genital exposure (visuals only)
* 4 percent with animals and objects

PART III: Where Are We Headed?

Chapter 12

WHATEVER HAPPENED TO CHILDHOOD?

Webster defines "to educate" as "to develop and cultivate mentally and morally."

The way a nation educates its children—formally and informally—determines that nation's future. A photograph from the cover of the *Washingtonian* visually summarizes our current dilemma. Those who argue that sex industry magazines do not "condition" readers would generally agree that these magazines do "educate" their readers. By the definition noted at the beginning of this chapter, juvenile and adult consumers of magazine articles, essays, jokes, reviews and photographs are "developed and cultivated mentally and morally." For nearly four decades *Playboy* has done precisely this.

In May 1976, the *Washingtonian* rhetorically asked: "Whatever Happened to Childhood?" The two attractive children on the magazine cover are seen as siblings around six years of age. The youngsters are playing "house," practicing for the grown-up world. One would conclude, based on the *Washingtonian*'s constituency, that the children are the prototype of the reader's progeny.

Taking in the modern leather and chrome chair, the rich foliage, and the generally well-groomed appearance of the children, their clothing, and the family dog, this picture is meant to represent a well-to-do, educated, and "up-scale" household. The cover has even more meaning, due to the nature of the *Washingtonian* readership. This magazine reaches the movers and shakers of society, the legislators, congressmen, senators, staffers, lobbyists, and the various individuals who shape the laws and public policies of our country.

What is said about the children tells us something of the *Washingtonian* parents. The small boy sits in father's big chair reading papa's *Playboy* magazine. His little sister (imitating mama?) looks somewhat apprehensively over her "man's" shoulder, following his perusal of the magazine pictures. He seems to be smiling. She appears dejected, forlorn. Her man has carelessly rejected her for paper doll fantasies. And this scenario, this drama, imitated by the children, is reenacted daily, monthly, yearly in American homes. Can we see these fantasies as encouraging distance and disappointment between real moms and dads, as laying fertile ground for divorce? What would you think?

Responsible adults would ask, what do our children "do" after they study the nude models—the "mommies"—posing in these magazines? In particular, what could this little girl (mommie) do to attract the attention of her unresponsive husband?

The *Washingtonian* chooses to ignore that obvious question. If the siblings are playing "house," what is the next scene they will play? Children practice adulthood by careful imitation of adult activity. As with adolescent sex offenders, youngsters commonly imitate what they see in films, video, television, and still photos. That means that, if they can, many will light the brand of cigarettes, drink the beer, eat the candy or food, wear the clothes, and do the sex acts—as shown.

JOHNNY JUST WANTS TO SEE HOW IT FEELS

The following is a typical scenario cited by M. O'Brien and W. Brea in *Preventing Sexual Abuse*, of what they call "The Naive Experimenter (Type 1)":

> Johnny is a 13-year-old boy who had been asked to baby-sit a neighbor girl, age 5, named Nicky, [He] . . . discovered a *Playboy* magazine hidden under the couch and Johnny found the explicit photographs arousing. While helping Nicky change into her pajamas he wanted to see what it was like to kiss and touch her in the way depicted in the

The *Washingtonian* cover May 1976

photographs. After a short time he felt guilty and
stopped. Later that week Nicky told her mother, and
Johnny was arrested for criminal conduct.[1]

Here, the baby-sitter, Johnny, was angrily reported to
the police by the very parents who supplied the stimulus for
Johnny's crime against their own child. Since Johnny, a
thirteen-year-old minor was asked into their home, his parents could have sued Nicky's parents for the crime of child
sexual abuse against Johnny! Certainly the boy was badly
damaged by this exposure to *Playboy*—an exposure that
branded him criminally. One wonders about the long term
effects of this abuse on both child victims—Johnny and
Nicky—and of Johnny's future—having been classified as a
sex criminal. (However, it is also true that a juvenile's crimes
are largely cancelled once he becomes an adult. Even homicide is no longer a crime of record once a child reaches
eighteen years of age.)

Later in this chapter we will discuss the growing number
of sex crimes committed by our children. For now, just bear
in mind that in 1988, hundreds of adolescent sex offenders
were identified in Michigan, one of the few states to collect
and release such data. The average offender was a boy barely
in his teens with the youngest offender age seven. Most
victims were little girls, ten-years-old or younger and most of
the abuses involved penetration. This violence has become
the modern version of: "You show me, I'll show you."

Burgess and Clark (1984) found that 62 percent of
children entrapped in child sex rings had been shown "adult
pornography."[2] Other researchers   (e.g., Battaglia, 1983;
Burgess, 1984; Keating, 1970; Linedecker, 1981; and Lanning,
1984) described popular sex magazines (*Playboy, Penthouse*
etc.) as tools to entrap youngsters into sex, child pornography,
and child prostitution. Most readers of this book will, on
reflection, recall some such small personal trauma in their
own lives.

ADOLESCENT PORNOGRAPHY USE

While people hide their own crimes in an interview,
youthful attitudes on pornography are reflected in *Teenage
Sexuality*, by psychologist Aaron Hass. Hass interviewed
over six hundred boys and girls, ages fifteen to eighteen about

their sexual attitudes and behaviors.[3] As shocking as Hass' 1979 findings were, and despite the increase in juvenile sex crimes, his research on youth and pornography has not been up-dated. Personal conversations with Pamela Swain, the past director of research of the Office of Juvenile Justice and Delinquency Prevention (OJJDP), confirmed that OJJDP was no longer interested in serious studies of pornography's effects on children.

What is the data connecting children's (or adults') use of pornography to their sex crimes against younger children?[4]

Despite the fantasy of pornography as an "adult right," children testify they are serious consumers. Hass says that children "learn how to do it" from pornography, that "she discover[s] what he looks like" from pornography (as does he) and he believes he knows "what she really enjoys" from pornography. Says Hass:

> Almost all teenagers have seen or read some form of pornography. . . . Pornography provides teenagers with a sexual education. Many adolescents turn to movies, pictures, and articles to find out exactly how to have sexual relations.[5]

So, over a decade ago, before the spread of pornographic home videos, Hass reported almost 100 percent of the boys and over 90 percent of the girls had "looked at sexy books or magazines . . . almost 60 percent of the boys and over 40 percent of the girls had seen a sexual movie." It should come as no surprise that the youngsters "report being aroused by reading material or explicit photographs."

BOYS ARE AROUSED—NOT "ROMANTIC"

Hass reported that boys were aroused and placed themselves into the pornographic action. Girls tried to create "romantic" stories to justify the action—and their own arousal. Youngsters, like older folks, study and "learn" from sex magazines and films, believing much of the sex information to be factual. Although many youngsters disliked brutalized, sadosexual stories and pictures, said Hass, they accepted and incorporated much of it into their own lives. In these "early" years, children consistently named *Playboy* as their key sex information source:

15-Year-Old Boy: It's interesting to read about

problems and solutions in the "*Playboy* Advisor."
You really learn a lot.

17-Year-Old Girl: Sometimes my partner and I look
at *Playboy* during sex because we find it enjoyable.

15-Year-Old Girl: I looked at *Playboy* a couple of
times because I was in the mood to masturbate.

16-Year-Old Girl: [M]y dad [kept] *Playboy* buried
under his socks.

17-Year-Old Girl: Curiosity was the reason, I guess.
I also got in the mood where I felt like doing something I wouldn't normally do. I don't exactly enjoy
looking at sexy pictures (*Playboy*) but some of the
articles are pretty interesting and informative.[6]

Many youngsters mentioned pornography magazines
and films in general, but not *Playboy* specifically. It would be
assumed that in 1979 all these adolescents had viewed *Playboy* and probably *Penthouse*. *Hustler* was new (1974) and still
relatively hidden. In 1979 youngsters found *Playboy* the most
authoritative sex education among the spectrum of
pornographies.

YOUNGSTERS THINK MAGAZINES GIVE "REAL FACTS"

In the heyday of widespread venereal disease (including
the homosexually incubated "AIDS" virus), *Playboy*, et al.,
avidly promoted—and continues to promote—anal and oral
sodomy along with promiscuous, multiple partner sex. As late
as its May 1989 issue *Playboy* was describing wildly promiscuous teenage—and younger—sex as joyous and
unproblematic, with the misleading notion that "everybody's
doing it."

Yet, it is clear from the statements of the Hass child
subjects that they imitated the media sex acts shown for the
children and assumed these to be normal, common, and
harmless:

I like to read the articles to see what other people are
doing sexually—so I know if I'm right. . . . Also the
articles about what girls enjoy from guys helps
me. . . . It gave me an idea of what to expect when I
eventually have sexual intercourse.

[I like] to see what other people do sexually.

They help! You can read about other people, problems, and solutions. Magazines and books are great.
They give you experience.

From what I remember, I enjoyed looking at the
magazines.

I wanted to learn real facts . . . where things are, how
they're done, and how it feels.

It helps to visualize what sex can be like.

It helps me to understand boys better.

I like to find out what guys like so I read the articles.

I wanted to see what was interesting to men, what
turned them on.

[I read] so I could see what girls looked like.[7]

THEY LEARN WHAT "SEX CAN BE LIKE"

Let us attend to the words of our youngsters about their
special trust and vulnerability to soft porn. Adults allow soft
porn to be advertised and sold. Reasonable children conclude
that adults would not permit toxic media (i.e., harmful, fatal
media) to reach and to teach them. After all, great, famous
Americans appear as interviewees. Youngsters conclude these
are reliable guides for sex. Youth are, by nature, naive,
impressionable and seeking affirmation that they are normal:

I compare my body. . . . I like to read about how other
people feel. . . . I like to read about "other methods"
and I also like to know that I'm normal. . . . I feel better
about my boyfriend and the sexual experiences we
have had. . . . It makes me feel better to know that
somebody else might have had the same sexual
experiences or feelings I have.

The comments reflect what young people do with the
material:

It makes you feel good to the point that you want to
masturbate. . . . They turn me on . . . to be with my
boyfriend . . . to get horny and to get to the point where

I would be able to have an orgasm through masturbation.... [It] turns me on ... [and gave me] ideas for my fantasies.... [It] got me going.... I often look at those pictures when I'm masturbating.... I liked the images it formed in my mind when I masturbated. I learned a lot.... [It] educated me about the different ways of performing sex and ways of pleasing your partner.[8]

HE'S "BUMMED OUT" AND SHE'S "A LITTLE JEALOUS"

Pornographic material creates anxiety and hostility in most normal people—especially vulnerable, developing youth. Many youngsters admitted these angry feelings to Hass:

I knew that none of them could be mine, so I was bummed out.... I'm a little jealous that I'm not as good-looking as some of the girls in the pictures. ... The pictures ... give men a model lady to which their wives could never live up to.... [T]hey're kind of boring and some are gross.[9]

Did Hass ask the six hundred juveniles if any had committed a sexual crime? If so what crime? Who? What were the ages of their victims? No interviewee is reported as volunteering this information. People do not properly report their crimes to psychologists doing sex surveys. Out of six hundred youths, statistically some number of them, roughly 120 (1 in 5) would have been a sex crime victim and some sex offenders. Anecdotal reports, interviews, and crime records support appalling findings on juvenile sex offenders. Many of my clients revealed experiencing early abuse by older juveniles, including rapes, sodomy, and urination and defecation on the victim by older boys.

MICHIGAN REPORTS WHAT HAS HAPPENED TO CHILDHOOD

So, "whatever happened to childhood?" What happens after the millions of child readers put down daddy's sex magazine? The noted Michigan report on "Adolescent Sex Offenders—Kids Abusing Kids" addresses the cases where children are exposed to stressful sexual situations. In January 1988, the Michigan Adolescent Sexual Abuser Project (MSDSP) released a comprehensive study on "Sexual Offenses by Youth in Michigan."

In 1986, 681 adolescent sex offenders were identified in Michigan. The average age of the offender was fourteen. His victim was likely to be a seven-year-old girl. Over 56 percent of the reported cases involved penetration.[10] John Whitehead in *The Stealing of America* (1983) reminded readers: Between 1950 and 1979 the rate of serious crime committed by children increased 11,000% "including crimes such as forcible rape."[11]

The Michigan study found 93 percent of offenders were trusted (i.e., male relatives, acquaintances, friends or baby-sitters of the victims), while 3,790 of these were relatives and immediate family members. Have American boys always criminally assaulted younger children? No. If so, the numbers of victims and offenders would have had to hold constant for generations.

This is simply not the case. The latest estimates of child sexual abuse identify "about a third of the women and a tenth of the men in North America are sexually victimized before their mid-teens."[12]

Statistically speaking, this shocking number of child victims activates an equally shocking increase in numbers of offenders and a branching out of sex criminals to the wider population. That is, if girls next door have been pictured as "wanting it," then what is expected of the boys next door? Police reports across the nation confirm that massive numbers of juvenile sexual abusers are being "created."

Identical sex crimes by so many boys strongly suggests that millions of boys are receiving identical sex crime instructions. If boys of every race, religion, and economic status are sexually abusing children (and they are), then "boys" in general are sharing some common pool of sexual training, a "boys" culture—or, a guidebook for sexual abuse. Drs. John Gagnon and William Simon, both Kinseyans and supporters of the *Playboy* and pornography experience write:

> The major users of pictorial erotica are adolescent males. . . . *Playboy* is an explicitly sexual document . . . nearly a national institution. . . . [It] has taken for itself the role of legitimizing not sexual behavior, but . . . sexual conduct. It is the equivalent of the Boy Scout Manual . . . creating . . . scripts for the playing out of sexual dramas . . . providing masturbatory

fantasy . . . [and] a social context inside of which sexual desires may be thought of and in some measure acted out.[13]

Gagnon and Simon think the sexual conduct *Playboy* teaches boys is harmless. However, *Playboy* and all soft porn teach trickery, deceit, seduction, oral, anal, and vaginal rape, gang rape, bestiality, homosexuality, sex mutilation, and even sexual murder. Most Americans feel these behaviors are not harmless and ought not to be in a sexual Boy Scout Manual. This conduct was not considered conventional among youth until it was "in some measure acted out" by millions of young offenders.

TRAINING HARRY AND JOE

One can see the beginning of a nationally shared, boy's culture of sexual abuse in the *Esquire* comic strip, "Boy Talk" (November 1984). Harry and Joe, about twelve-years-old, lay on the floor with their soft porn. Each boy has his magazine opened to the centerfold. Their ritual begins:

Joe says, "This one is my girlfriend."

Harry replies, "O.K. This one's mine."

"Ready?" Both begin to kiss their "girlfriend's" pictures.

"Hey! Look, Harry, you slobbered," complains Joe. [Documenting the imitation and training process]

Harry says, "That's how you're supposed to do it, dope."

"Yeah, but it wrecks the picture. And besides, girls hate spit. I'm wipin' it off."

Harry and Joe begin a loud and angry fight, because Joe accidently tore Harry's magazine while trying to wipe the saliva off Harry's "girlfriend's" picture.

"Hey! You TORE my girlfriend! This means WAR!"

The boys are violently assaulting one another when Harry's mother calls for them to stop. Harry says,

"Looks like we gotta play with our dumb trucks again."

We know the things we give our time and emotions to as youngsters will shape our entire future. "Boy's Talk" struck a nerve because so many boys recall similar experiences—similar intense passion for and even acting on paper doll centerfolds. But, what *Esquire* did not say, and what few want to admit, is that when the boys tire of ruining the exciting pictures with saliva, some Joes and Harrys try to examine and explore someone resembling these pictures. Adult women are scary and generally unavailable. But, little sisters, cousins, and neighbors have similar body parts to practice on and are accessible.

Following the Bundy confession of use and addiction to pornography at twelve years of age (the ages of the *Esquire* boys), a reporter asked two alleged child abuse specialists whether parents should worry if they "find *Hustler* magazine in Johnny's drawer." The experts claimed there is "very little scientific evidence" for concern. Sadly, parents were told even *Hustler* was harmless and should remain in Johnny's drawer. One expects some day to see such poorly supported expert advice cited in a major malpractice suit.

CHILDREN LEARN FROM THE ADULT MODEL

Official data on juvenile sex criminals provides a low estimate of actual levels of offense. Juveniles have easy access to small children—they are still one of them. A boy's easiest access is usually to his own family members—younger siblings. When they learn of incestuous abuse by their son, parents generally try to halt the assault without reporting the crimes to the authorities. Therefore few assaults by brothers on younger sisters or brothers would be recorded—unless the attacks were particularly sadistic or so physically damaging as to result in pregnancy or to require a physician's report.

Indeed, in *Behavior Today*, forensic psychologist, Dr. Charles Patrick Ewing, predicts "homicides committed by juveniles under the age of 18 will rise to epidemic proportions (20 August 1990)." With the record numbers of children victimizing and being victimized, it should come as no surprise that the latest vital statistics (1988) document that juveniles are attempting suicides in numbers of over eighty a day, eight of these youngsters succeeding.[14]

The Michigan report on juvenile crime reflects the national crime scene. Both reports on the harms of early sexual abuse and incest sharply differ from Kinsey's 1948 and 1953 claims. Kinsey insisted that during the 1930s through the 1950s, child sex offenders rarely attempted penetration. The team documented that child sexual abuse seldom went further than exhibitionism and, sometimes, fondling. The team reported no use of children in prostitution or pornography. They had no record of juvenile or child sex rings, or of children being the chief victims of serial-rape murderers—as is known today. Either 1) their data was wildly false—avoiding the tragic truths about child abuse to weaken protective laws and legitimize child sexual exploitation, or 2) sexual violence against children has dramatically increased since the Kinsey Reports helped initiate the sexual revolution, or 3) both are true.

CHILDREN PREFER PRETTIER PICTURES

All sexually explicit images and stories involving humans teach children how to sexually abuse younger children—for smaller children are the only "objects" realistically available to any child.

Children are increasingly reported as sexually battering smaller children. Police often dismiss pornography as irrelevant—although the FBI has found pornography involved in most child sex abuse cases and in almost all youthful deaths that occur as a result of masturbatory asphyxiation (strangulation). Since the press often censors the mention of pornography even when it appears in the police record, cases such as that of the recent murder of a baby by a twelve-year-old give special pause. On 31 January 1989 the *Boston Herald* reported:

> A 12-year-old Salisbury boy accused of killing a 23-
> month-old toddler may have to give a dental imprint
> to determine whether he also bit the infant.

One who has studied the role of pornography in violence to children would suspect that the little boy was either a sex abuse victim himself or exposed to pornography—or both. Biting is a common image in pornography. The biting of the toddler should be evidence, requiring a search for pornography in the boy's home and that of his tiny victim. Recall Johnny and his arrest for child sexual abuse when it was the victim's parents who exposed the boy to the tool that provoked the attack—pornography. As with Johnny, printed, audio, and video pornography is commonly a child's stimulus and instruction. After the New York Central Park "wilding" incident, talk show experts and columnists across the nation clucked their tongues, shook their collective heads, and asked, "Who taught them rape was fun?" Who indeed?

EIGHTY-NINE PERCENT OF JUVENILE SEX OFFENDERS USE PORN

Even those who find the facts, about children learning sex from pornography, generally refuse to accept the "street reality" of those facts. Dr. Judith Becker of Columbia University in New York denies proof of a relationship between pornography and sexual violence. Yet Dr. Becker, who served on the Attorney General's Commission on Pornography, reported that

> 89% of the 160 adolescent offenders whose average age was 15 reported that they use [sexually explicit] materials. 35% cited pornographic magazines, 26% pornographic videos, 15% TV and 13% books as the sexually explicit sources used most often. 67% said the material increased their sexual arousal. The number of sex crimes committed and the use of sexually explicit materials were not correlated according to Becker.[15]

Writing for the National Coalition on Television Violence, Thomas Radecki, M.D. pointed out that the average child is still not a pornography "user"—although almost all have been exposed. To state that 89 percent of these juvenile sex criminals "use" pornography as part of their life-style, and then to disregard the correlation between massive porn use and the youth's sex crimes, tells us as much about the biases and fears among adult researchers as it does about pornography-using juvenile offenders.

Just as worrisome as nearly 90 percent porn use among juvenile sex offenders, the Council for Children's Television and Media reported what the "average" American child was watching:

> The Junior League in New York did a study of children between the ages of 12 and 13 years. Here is some of what they found:

The average child viewed 12 movies in a typical month. These children reported that 34% of the movies they viewed were R-rated, for an average of slightly more than 4 "R" rated movies per month. . . . The majority of the movies they saw, a whopping 64% were on Cable or were rented and were not seen with an adult. . . . When asked what their favorite movie was, 20% of these children named not just an R-rated movie but 20% named an R-Slasher movie.

Children who have seen these movies are likely to have viewed them at least twice. For instance the 115 children who had seen *Nightmare on Elm Street* had seen it an average of four times.[16]

The percentage of youngsters who also sneak screenings of mom n' dad's X-rated videos to supplement R-rated films and *Nightmare* on TV is not known. Considering the millions of X-rated videos rented and sold to couples with families, are we not programming sexual violence among future generations? And will not some growing numbers of these youths form mutilating bandit hordes? It seems absurd to pretend this is not occurring. On 12 September 1984 during Senate Hearings on the "Effect of Pornography on Women and Children," Senator Jeremiah Denton (R-Ala) affirmed

the St. Petersburg, Florida, account of the 9-year-old boy who was convicted of first degree murder, aggravated child abuse, and three counts of sexual battery in connection with the torture death last September of an 8-month-old girl. . . . The brother of the 9-year old boy testified that, in sexually assaulting the infant with a pencil and coat hanger, they were imitating actions they had seen in their mother's sex magazine.

And, in early February 1991, the Department of Justice sent out a mailing that included a report of "a 10-year old boy . . . who learned to have sex by watching X-rated movies was arrested on charges he raped and sodomized an 8-year old girl and her 4-year old sister. . . . Medical tests showed evidence of sexual intercourse. . . . Whoever is responsible for letting the boy see the movies [police said] should be arrested for endangering the welfare of a child."

John Rabun, director of the Missing and Exploited

Children's Center in Washington, D.C., an investigative
organization funded by the Department of Justice, reported
that *Playboy* (as the most accessible, acceptable, and attractive of all pornographies—the "gateway pornography") is
typically used to sexually entrap a child. Testifying in the
1984 Senate Hearings on "Effect of Pornography on Women
and Children," Rabun said that of fourteen hundred cases of
suspected child exploitation

> all, that is 100 percent of the arrested pedophiles,
> child pornographers, pimps, what have you, all of
> these, in effect child molesters had in their possession
> at the time of arrest, adult pornography ranging from
> what is in the literature typically referred to as soft
> pornography such as *Playboy*, on up to harder, such
> as *Hustler*. . . .

Entrapment of the child, certified Rabun, proceeded
from showing children

> pictures in decent magazines . . . progressing to
> something in the form or fashion of *Playboy*, where
> you had partial or full nudity going on, up until
> something like *Penthouse* and *Hustler* . . . all of which
> was done over a long period of time.

As the most popular, public, and easily accessible of all
sadosexual materials, *Playboy* would naturally be used most
often to seduce children. Market research confirms academic
research and common sense—yes, *Playboy* is used by
children. The adolescent sex offender programs, scholarly
research, interviews with youngsters, and even magazine
"letters-to-the-editor" identify the use juveniles make of
these magazines to entrap peers and tots into humiliating,
dangerous, and now even AIDS-producing sex acts.

This brings us back to the two little *Washingtonian*
children who were examining daddy's April 1976 *Playboy*.
Marketers long ago did profit assessments which found that
the most important point-of-sale feature for a magazine is the
cover. This finding continues to be confirmed. The April 1976
cover that the children have before them, is created, as all are,
to capture the passing eye and newsstand dollar. It displayed
a pouting, petulant, half-nude "pseudo-child" (an adult dressed-
up to resemble a child). The *Playboy* model was dressed in a
similar manner as the age of the *Washingtonian* six-year-old-
girl who was peering over brother's shoulder at the magazine
pictures.

When the two siblings looked at this cover, they saw a peaches-n'-cream child-woman model in Mary-Jane shoes, a virginal white petticoat, and white tights. The cover model, however, had an ample bosom. A few blonde curls caught up in little girl hair clips decorated her bare breast and nipple provocatively. Child objects surrounded the model, objects very similar to those that the *Washingtonian* girl would probably find back in her own little-girl bedroom: dolls, stuffed animals, a stuffed, white (*Playboy*) bunny.

The pseudo-child is well known in the pornography industry. She is generally blonde but can be a brunette—even Oriental (seldom black). In "hard-core" films, the pseudo-child is posed eating lollipops or ice cream cones while engaging in oral and anal sodomy and intercourse with numerous adult male and female performers—or animals. The Attorney General's Commission on Pornography included a complete description of this routine pornography character:

> Pseudo child pornography or "teasers" involve women allegedly over the age of eighteen who are presented in such a way as to make them appear to be children or youths. Models used in such publications are chosen for their youthful appearance (e.g., in females, slim build and small breasts); and are presented with various accoutrements designed to enhance the illusion of immaturity (e.g., hair in ponytails or ringlets, toys, teddy bears, etc.). "Pseudo child pornography" is of concern since it may appeal to the same tastes and may evoke responses similar or identical to those elicited by true child pornography.

PETERSEN'S COUNTERATTACK

The October 1988 *Playboy* displayed this pseudo-child in its five-page article on what the magazine called, "The Reisman Lie Revisited." The editors reduced the April 1976 11-by-14 inch pseudo-child cover to 2 1/4-by-3 1/4 inches and placed it on the first page of the essay attacking my research. *Playboy* claimed the pouting pseudo-child and her toys were unrelated to childhood. In the "*Playboy* Advisor," James Petersen (recall his advice to a high-school girl to have her boyfriend "drill small holes" in a paddle in order to prolong the pain of their sadosexual affair) wrote:

> Reisman has invented a species called Pseudo-Child

and claims that 792 adults were portrayed as Pseudo-Children in *Playboy*. . . . Reisman claims that by dressing women as children, we get around the obvious child pornography laws.[17]

Playboy and Petersen continue to play fast and loose with the truth. It is Hefner's biographers who reveal his extensive collection of pornography films, which he and his guests view regularly. At least one writer points out Hefner's special affection for bestiality films. Any such "hard-core" collection includes pseudo-child porn, or adult women dressed as children. Moreover, real child pornography would generally be part of such a collection unless there is a special point made of its absence.

The pseudo-child is as much a staple character in pornography—as noted by the Attorney General's Commission—as is the nurse, the stewardess, the cheer-leader, the co-ed, the bored housewife, or any other of the key characters who populate these films. Reisman did not invent the pseudo-child. Petersen knows very well that the pornographers invented her. *Playboy*, as a pornographer, naturally created many pseudo-children and used them where it could.

CHILDREN, CRIME, AND VIOLENCE

Responding to an onslaught of sexual crimes against children committed by older youngsters and adults, in 1983 the Department of Justice Office of Juvenile Justice and Delinquency Prevention (OJJDP) had requested that I examine the major magazines that provided sex, sadism, and drug information to the nation. By 21 January 1984, when the research began its start-up, the New York Times had reported on what was then called "random, senseless killing," or "motiveless crimes." What the public did not know about this new kind of violence was that the victims were mainly children. Police on the sex-crime beat often observed that those who were entertained by seeing sex and violence linked, frequently became entertained by acting out both sex and violence:

> [A]fter a study of homicide reports spanning the last few decades, the officials assert that history offers nothing to compare with the spate of such murders that has occurred in the United States since the

beginning of the 1970's . . . as many as 4,000 Americans a year, at least half of them under the age of 18, are murdered this way....."Something's going on out there.... It's an epidemic."... [Robertson and Heck charged a link] to an increase in movies that depict sexual violence uncritically and may encourage it. "[I]n the past 20 years ... I think you'll find sex as the dominant factor in almost all the serial murders," said Captain Robbie Robertson of the Michigan State Police, who is regarded as one of the nation's foremost investigators of such crimes.

PORNOGRAPHY LOWERS THEIR CONTROLS AND "AWAY THEY GO"

In an interview with the *Detroit Free Press* (12 October 1980), John Preiesaik, Jackson State Prison clinical psychologist, maintained that most of the five hundred sex offenders in his program are "definitely influenced by pornography":

We had a guy here who stabbed a woman 23 times. I asked him why he stabbed her so often, more than was needed to kill her, and he told me, "That's the number of times I need to get an erection." They may sometimes have an orgasm during a violent act . . . They're fighting to control their impulses all the time—it takes an inordinate amount of energy . . . pornography lowers their controls, and away they go.

Back at OJJDP, Police Specialist Robert Heck and the OJJDP Assistant Deputy, James Wootton, were concerned about the "motive" in these new pornography-associated sex crimes. Were the offenders feeling "sexual" arousal when they tortured and murdered women and children? According to the *Washington Post* (20 February 1984):

In 1962 there were 644 U.S. murders, 6 percent with no known motive. By 1982 that had soared to 4,118, or 20 percent. "Get scared about that if you want to get scared about something," said Robert O. Heck, Justice Project Manager.

And *Life* magazine reported, in an August 1984 piece entitled "An American Tragedy:"

For years on end, many of them fed these emotions on horror movies, slice-and-dice pornography [which] filled them with murderous frenzy [so] the ritual drama of death and rebirth began.

"FEEDING THE EMOTIONS" ON PORNOGRAPHY

As noted, until the mid-1980s, the random serial rapist-murderer-mutilator was a rare breed in Western society. But recently, researchers examined forty-one such men in prison.[18] Fully 120 such vicious criminals were "captured or singled out by police ... during the last 20 years." OJJDP's Robert O. Heck and FBI specialists in the Behavioral Science Unit as well as scores of other law enforcement officials have grown quite confident of pornography's role in the serial rapist murderer's profile. This was the conclusion of an OJJDP workshop on a National Center for the Analysis of Violent Crime held at Sam Houston State University Criminal Justice Center, Huntsville, Tex., in conjunction with the FBI Behavioral Science Unit, July 11-15, 1983.

ANALYZING THE MAJOR PORNOGRAPHY MAGAZINES

OJJDP agreed it was past time to analyze the contents of the three most popular pornographies distributed nationwide—based on numbers of readers and their frequent presence as on-site evidence in sex crimes. In the last few years, as PPH consumers have taken their place among our nation's "creators," pornographic sadosexual ideas are found in every form of entertainment, art, and literature.

Men and women and boys and girls of every race, creed, color, socio-economic class, religion, political persuasion, and geographic and ethnic distribution have had their first visual exposure to sex through these magazines. Now, of course, cable porn, video porn, dial-a-porn, and other forms of pornography compete with *Playboy* to provide that "first" experience.

Moreover, sadosexual media like PPH have been a form of unique "male bonding." In fact, soft porn crosses every boundary historically known to divide men. Males of every age, race, creed, color, religion, profession, and economic and social status have empathized with, agreed to, and shared in the world view of visual soft porn.

Soft porn provides a world view that unites billions of males from youth to old age. Hefner's biographer Thomas Weyr called it a worldwide "sexual religion" that

> married religion and sex—serious moral concerns—
> with unbridled hedonism . . . [and] touched the lives
> of millions. . . . The [*Playboy*] Philosophy imputes
> deep moral purpose to his enterprises.[19]

FOURTEEN MILLION CHILDREN SUFFER FROM MENTAL DISORDERS?!

The mental health of our exposed youngsters is another barometer of soft porn fallout. Sociologist Dr. Marvin Wolfgang of the University of Pennsylvania insisted in 1970 that children are unharmed and could be helped by pornography:

> There is no substantial evidence that exposure to
> juveniles is necessarily harmful. There may even be
> beneficial effects if for no other reason than the
> encouragement of open discussion about sex
> between parents and children relatively early in
> young lives. . . . [W]e know that high percentages of
> adolescents now read and see pornography.[20]

Wolfgang suggested pornography exposure was causal. It would cause "effects" which he predicted would be "beneficial." After over twenty years of pornography causing "effects," we can now measure the effects on our youth's sexually related behavior. We witness an onslaught of licit and illicit drug use, sex offenses, unwed pregnancy, venereal disease, juvenile suicide, declining SAT scores, dropout rates, youthful gang violence, and the like. James Leckman of Yale University also released the results of a study on childhood (under eighteen) mental health. The report claims were printed in 7 May 1989 *Washington Post*:

> As many as 14 million American children suffer
> from some mental disorder, a problem that is costing
> society billions of dollars and depriving the nation of
> productive citizens. . . . The report said that a
> conservative estimate indicates 12 percent of
> America's children are mentally disturbed, that the
> true number could be as high as 22 percent. . . . "The
> likelihood is that the rate is increasing."

Academicians are notoriously libertarian, like Wolfgang of the University of Pennsylvania. The very scholars who are now asked to cure our social problems are the scholars who gave us the advice that caused the problems in the first place. By definition, these are not objective scholars.

Now, this segment of the academic community insists more government funding is required. According to the *Washington Post* article, they plan to "develop research and to train professionals to deal with mental illness of those under 18." The press says the academicians think that up to 22 percent of our youth are deranged because of "developmental impairments" caused by "slow education and learning!"

What are these sudden "developmental impairments," which eluded our (often) poverty-ridden, struggling parents and grandparents—our ancestors? Why should such a large number of youths suddenly be slow learners, and why should this cause "mental illness"? In a classic example of circular reasoning and denial, other "problems" offered by the credentialed academic committee are "emotional disturbances including anxiety and depression; and antisocial behavior." They note with some amazement that mental illness is often expressed in drug use and eating disorders! These are scholars denying that their own ongoing liberal efforts are a part of the problem. Relying on false—even fraudulent[21]—academic research, legislators enacted bad libertarian cures, which only made matters worse.

WHERE THE PROBLEM IS

A respected Yale child psychiatrist of my acquaintance has long consumed pornography, as have many of his psychiatry and psychology colleagues. They used it in college, as did most college boys, and later in adult life. While I must emphasize that though soft porn is not the single source of our nation's moral collapse, it is certainly a toxic substance poisoning the main sexual water line. The good doctors exemplify the problem facing our youth. Mom, dad, the doctors, politicians, and law enforcement professionals have all been drinking the same toxic sexual water.

As an example: the renowned psychiatrist F. Scott Peck, author of *People of the Lie* and *The Road Less Traveled*, was interviewed by *Playboy* in March of 1991. Speaking of the need for a spiritual life, Peck (a married man) reveals that he "likes" pornography and that he uses it. But, he thinks demeaning pornography, really violent stuff, is not good. One wonders, would Dr. Peck pose nude in a magazine for all the world to examine and measure him? I doubt he would agree to such a photo of himself. Why not? Is it because he would feel demeaned?

Soft porn has produced a monthly re-education and desensitization program for college-educated males. Most readers of the 1950s and 1960s eventually married and fathered little tykes. As the adult consumer was shaped, more so would his children be shaped. The *Washingtonian*'s little *Playboy* consumer whose little wife was ignored while he enjoyed naked paper dolls was a blueprint for increasingly lethal heterosexual hostility.

Chapter 13

WOMEN'S TESTIMONY ABOUT PORNOGRAPHY

As the numbers of "Ted Bundys" increase, some of them become our sons, husbands, and lovers. While only a small cadre of boys become Ted Bundys, a much larger group become rapists, molesters, and batterers. Such men are found among our teachers, dentists, doctors, pediatricians, novelists, dishwashers, producers, clergy, attorney generals, legislators, judges, and so forth. Incest victims—adults and children—report that mainstream pornographies are a consistent tool used to facilitate assaults. Terri Rosenthal, completing an autobiography of her own incestuous abuse, reports that her brothers used these magazines:

> My two step-brothers showed me *Playboy* and *Penthouse* when I was about 10-years-old and they were 14 or 15 years. They first explained how pretty the women were and then insisted I take off my clothes like these ladies. I was threatened if I didn't and then was threatened after I did. They made me pose like the women in *Playboy* and then like the ones in the other magazines, and yes, they raped me—many times.[1]

Brothers (and step-brothers) grow up, marry, and have their own children. Too often, the cycle played out upon their little sisters (and often brothers) is similarly played out upon their own children. For example, in testimony before the Attorney General's Commission on Pornography, "Sharon" spoke of her dentist husband, who read *Playboy* and *Penthouse* when they married:

> He has molested ten of his patients. He does this by turning his nitrous oxide up to three times as much as is normal and safe. Then he asks the nurse to leave the room.... John has molested our daughter.... I saw

a man whom I cared for deteriorate over a period of eleven years. I saw pornography that is sold at a lot of the convenience stores come to dominate—the only real influence to that man's existence. I'm not talking about that kind of pornography that is sold in those kinky little sex shops. I am talking about magazines that are sold in local convenience stores. The pornography John collected, and was obsessed with was *Penthouse, Oui, Hustler, Playboy*.[2]

At the hearings, "Evelyn" testified about the fall-out of pornography in her marriage:

For more than thirty years I watched pornography destroy our marriage. . . . We live in a fairly small community in Wisconsin where pornographic material was not readily available during the first years of our marriage. The addiction began with *Playboy*, cheap paperbacks, obscene playing cards, and R-rated movies. It then progressed to movies of lesbians and prostitutes he secured through the mail. . . . He could have destroyed me as a person if it were not for the memories I have of myself and my life before I met him. . . . Masturbation took over our sex life. I know for a fact that pornography destroyed our marriage.[3]

KATHARINE HEPBURN SPEAKS OF WOMEN AND PORNOGRAPHY

Quickly looking to the "woman's magazine" for what women have said to women about sexual liberation, the *Ladies Home Journal* (January 1984) reported an interview with one of America's most highly esteemed and outspoken women, Katharine Hepburn:

"We women have deliberately stepped off any kind of pedestal," she says. . . . "The result is a mess, I think, and very hard on young women." We seem, she thinks, to have jumped from the pedestal into pornography. "If you judge by the movies, women are now merely sex objects. And promiscuity is a terrible mistake—some women don't seem to recognize that anything that's too easy to get is not desirable. If a girl holds herself at so little value that she will sleep with one man after another, *then other people will also hold her at very little value.*"

But, Hepburn was wrong. Women hadn't "jumped" nor had they "deliberately stepped off" a pedestal. In truth, pedestals were really reserved for the elite. Nonetheless, these women were driven off by the Kinseyans and pornographers. Once driven off the privileged pedestal by respected adult males, most boys, like those in the Glen Ridge High School and Central Park crimes, would hold woman and her children at little value. Recall Hefner's triumphant claim: "Before *Playboy* women were typecast either as Madonna or as whore. But [we showed men] nice girls like sex too" (*Playboy*, January 1989).

In October 1980, almost a decade before the Glen Ridge assault, Inspector Isaiah McKinnon, head of the Detroit Sex Crimes Unit, told the *Detroit Free Press* that the nation increasingly expects sex and violence from kids:

> As a society, I believe we're more accepting of violence, we're accepting things we weren't accepting before, 10 or 20 years ago. . . . There's also, for instance, a new, remorseless type of juvenile offender.

Remorseless offenders have no sense of guilt and often find humor in the most brutal of crimes. Is it a coincidence that one cannot find any vile, savage kind of "sex" crime against women and children that has not, at one time or another, been a "joke" in the pages of soft porn?

SEX EMPLOYMENT FOR OUR DAUGHTERS

On 17 October 1985 Miki Garcia, a former *Playboy* centerfold (Miss January 1973) and corporate executive for six years, testified before the Attorney General's Commission on Pornography. She stated:

> [T]his testimony, I believe, will put my life and those of my family's [*sic*] in danger. . . . Hugh Hefner suppresses the truth about his organization through his extensive connections in the media and political world. . . . In May of 1982 my suspicions were confirmed that some of the Playmates were involved in an international call girl ring which had ties to the *Playboy* mansion. Because of *Playboy* security's influence with the LAPD a major investigation of the Playmates was thwarted. . . . I have chosen to be identified because I want to break *Playboy*'s conspiracy to silence the Playmates. . . . Once a Playmate

loses her attractiveness, or is out of control with her drug abuse . . . she is suddenly dumped. Oftentimes the women do venture into other avenues of financial support, such as prostitution, starring in X-rated hard-core films, this type of thing. . . . By the way, a Playmate is a product. The term "Playmate" is a trademark of *Playboy*.

Garcia identified *Playboy* as gateway porn for "nice girls." From here they frequently entered into the worst kind of pornography and prostitution, experiencing drugs, abortions, rape, and even death because of their *Playboy* involvement.

[Answering a Commissioner's question] "Do you imply that the girls, while under contract or employed by—however you want to phrase that—*Playboy*, actively engaged in prostitution?" Ms. Garcia: "Yes."[4]

A reading of the Hefner biographies confirms the mysterious deaths of several *Playboy* bunnies.

Brenda McKillop, a former *Playboy* bunny, lived at the mansion and worked at the Playboy Club from 1973 to 1976. She spoke of her introduction to pornography:

My first association with *Playboy* began in childhood when I found *Playboy* as well as other pornographic magazines hidden around the house. I have since discovered that a great deal of pornography ends up in the hands of the children. This gave me a distorted image of sexuality. . . . I believe that the *Playboy* philosophy of pleasure-seeking lust influenced my father to make passes at other women and to ask a neighbor to swap wives. I believe my mother's battle with obesity caused her to feel jealous of the playgirls and jealous of her own daughter's body. I never questioned the morality of becoming a *Playboy* bunny because the magazine was accepted into the home.

Drug abuse is deeply interwoven into the *Playboy* lifestyle. I saw marijuana being used at Hefner's mansion on a regular basis, and cocaine as well. . . . I experienced everything from date rape, to physical abuse, to group sex, and finally to fantasizing homosexuality as I read *Playboy* magazines.[5]

McKillop's remarks echo those of women nationwide

who saw their mothers humiliated by these pictures, with dad sometimes choosing to have sex with his daughter as she began to resemble the Playmates more than mom did. The voices of pornography's living victims, their stories and their pain underpin this book. You will be spared the descriptions of the truly brutal photos, films, and videos of child sex abuse, which I have seen at FBI and law enforcement seminars. Nor will I describe the most violent of the stories I have listened to in interviews with child and adult survivors.

MOTHERS SELLING CHILDREN FOR "CRACK"

As pornography and prostitution grows and gains in consumer demand and legitimacy, unscrupulous parents and guardians are prepared to reap unbridled profit. Historically and cross-culturally, adults have sexually violated their children for amusement and income. Parents prostitute their babies for pornography, trading the pictures with other incestuous parents and guardians like baseball trading cards. It all depends upon the attitudes and conditions of the times. Infants are on record arriving in emergency wards with their internal organs ruptured, permanently destroyed, infected with oral, vaginal, and anal venereal disease passed on by fathers, older brothers, grandfathers, uncles, and mom's boyfriends.

In 1980 I was quoted in *Take Back the Night* regarding the selling of incest to America:

> I think the selling of incest is part of a process whereby a particular kind of pornographic imagery percolates through all the media before it has saturated them, and then a new level of degradation begins to become acceptable.

The May/June 1977 issue of *UCLA Alumni Monthly* magazine ran an article entitled "Help for the Child Abuser." One paragraph in particular caught my eye: "Adolescents have been the primary targets of sexual abuse, but there is a *recent sharp increase* in oral venereal disease among children under five years of age, who have been infected by their fathers, older brothers, or boyfriends of the mother."[6]

The nation was stunned several years ago by the horror story of little Lisa Steinberg, raped and murdered by her drug-using lawyer "adopted" dad. Few realize that the small child was also used in pornography, sold by her adoptive parents.

A Northern Virginia mother and her boyfriend were arrested in 1989 for sexually renting her three little boys, and for "first-degree rape" of her two and one-half-year-old daughter. One small son said a man "came in and had sex with all of us, including Mama" (*Washington Post*, 22 August 1989).

The next day (23 August 1989) a clipping in the *Washington Post* noted, "A New York couple was charged yesterday with sexually assaulting or torturing . . . raping, sodomizing, or beating nine of their [twelve] children, ranging in age from 4 months to 16 years." Police were digging for the "remains of the children said to have been buried."

The same day, the *Washington Times* reported on two men (one a "Big Brother" and a real estate agent in an affluent Virginia community) who were arranging to buy a young white boy for sexual abuse and homicide. The men planned to film their rape and torture of the boy as well as his murder, otherwise known as a "snuff" film. Both were later convicted of the murder plan. One of the would-be child-sex-murderers said of the innocent boy, "I want to strangle the kid, I want to hang the kid, I want to suffocate the kid." Sexually abusing moms and dads increasingly provide sex with ever younger children to ever-younger rapists-killers for their own pleasure and gain.

As noted, since the early 1980s, emergency wards began reporting new intakes—infants and small children with venereal disease. In less than one decade of PPH images, mothers moved from shock to tolerance of and participation in their child's sexual abuse. Now, in real life, we find mothers who initiate the cruelty. Writing of the above recent child sex abuse case, the judge convicted the participating mother, saying: "I just think that when a mother knowingly and intentionally makes a child available to someone for the types of offenses alleged here and sits and laughs while the action is being perpetrated" she seeks "to make that act succeed."

Recent talk of resurrecting the old-time orphanage has great merit. The orphanage had abuses, but the growing population of tortured children requires protection by some institution that will be held publicly accountable.

Again, despite the tendency to hide many of these crimes, these reports of historically unheard-of sexual atrocities against children are surfacing in the nation's press, coast-to-coast. One wonders how much longer the press, police, social workers, parents, teachers, and legislators will deny the role pornography plays in the violation of our children's right to life, liberty, and the pursuit of happiness?

Just as Hefner altered his past beliefs about sex and male-female relations after reading Kinsey, boys by the millions altered their past beliefs about sex and male-female relations after viewing *Playboy*. If *Playboy* changed American boys and men, it thus changed American women, children, and families as well.

It took nearly two thousand years for Judeo-Christian sexuality to discard both the Third World idea of women as witches and its misogynist sexual dogma that all females (small girls and women) were sexually ravenous and must either be controlled or eliminated.[7]

In fact, only recently have some of the Third World cultures begun to penalize "clitoridectomy," (the removal of a small girl's clitoris, often followed by sealing the vaginal lips with needle and thread). Based on a belief in uncontrolled female sexual desire, this form of genital mutilation still is widely practiced—especially amongst Arabs and Africans—to insure virginity prior to marriage and fidelity afterwards.

On the surface, *Playboy*'s notion of "nice girls like sex too" sounded like a harmless advance. But, it was advancing backwards. Biblically, sex was the blessing by which God's plan for his children was fulfilled. And, if God saw all, he saw one's nudity and one's excretory and sexual acts. Therefore, "nice" girls (godly girls in western nations) frequently "liked sex," but within marriage and under conditions of privacy and respect. Ironically then, the seemingly forward Kinsey/Hefner view of sex brought us full circle back to the primitive and anti-Western idea that all women were licentious and thus seeking to seduce and control men. This view inevitably targeted the girl-next-door as an object for use and assault.

WE TOOK GIRLS OFF THE STREET

One's mothers, sisters, nieces, cousins, daughters, grand-daughters, etc., are "nice girls." And they are "next door." There is danger when millions of boys and men using these magazines for masturbation fantasies in their rooms, bathrooms, and closets, think their kin or friend next door also likes sex and wants it specifically with them. Before *Playboy*, only prostitutes had been seen naked in pictures. Hefner bragged that *Playboy* was the first magazine to portray all females as panting, sexual adventurers—as willing to be displayed sexually. Said Hefner in the *Sunday Plain Dealer* interview:

> We humanized the pin-up picture... we took girls off the street: secretaries, clerks, college coeds, stewardesses. . . . Women's magazines wouldn't even run bikini pictures. . . . Nudity was unknown in the women's field. . . . What we were doing was really counter-culture at that time.

The Central Park boys and the Glen Ridge boys "took girls off the street." This fact—repeated across the nation—updates the *Playboy* "counter-culture" fantasy into the real world. Such play is increasingly interwoven in popular male culture. All of the professions noted by Hefner ("secretaries, clerks, college co-eds, stewardesses") have been among those millions of raped and sometimes murdered women who were taken "off the street." In the last few years, elementary school children and infants have been "taken off the playgrounds" to be raped and/or murdered.

As of this writing, four young college co-eds were sexually assaulted, murdered, and mutilated in Gainesville, Florida, according to the *Washington Times*. These grizzly rape/murder/mutilations are similar to the kind of stimuli broadcast weekly on television on such fare as "Friday the 13th," a youth cult series in which sexual arousal is commonly linked with homicide, mutilation, devil worship, and maniac heroes.

Another one of the scores of college co-eds taken off the street, raped repeatedly, photographed, and murdered was twenty-two-year-old Linda Gallery. (Her mother's story is found in the Appendix and on p. 17 of an AFA booklet: *Pornography: A Report*.) Photographing the torture of their victims (as in the Glen Ridge crime) is now routine in sex abuse cases. "Date rape" has become a common phrase, as has "acquaintance rape" and "boy-friend rape"—all terms that point to young women being sexually assaulted by trusted peers—the boy next door.

The theme that perhaps runs clearest throughout PPH is the training up of young, remorseless juvenile offenders, crossing the length and breadth of our land and all racial, economic, and religious lines. As the offenders get younger, their victims must also become younger. In a small item in the *Washington Post* (9 February 1991), seven boys from age eight to thirteen were arrested. "The group is alleged to have dragged the victim into her bedroom and raped her, officials said."

As noted, scores of children are now taken off streets and playgrounds. Little ten-year-old Rosie Gordon was abducted as she rode her bike on a Burke, Virginia street in July 1989. She was raped and murdered.

An eleven-year-old girl in the affluent suburb outside Washington, D.C., was abducted as she was walking to her elementary school. The child was not killed. But, like Rosie, she was driven to a rural area, raped, and sodomized (*Washington Times*, 25 August 1989).

Nor are little boys exempt from rape and murder. They too seem like sexual prey to many men and boys. The television film *Adam* told of the abduction of Adam Walsh from a department store by two homosexual rapist-killers. The child was brutally raped and then decapitated. From this heinous crime came the Center for Missing and Exploited Children in Washington, DC. Indeed, SLAM (Society League Against Molesters), was formed by the grandmother of a four-year-old girl. The child was abducted from her own yard, tortured, raped unmercifully, and then brutally murdered. Again, the killer was a sex offender out on parole. In a 7 June 1989 rape/mutilation report from the *Washington Times*, "[A seven-year-old] boy was riding his red bicycle through the residential wilderness when . . . he was grabbed from behind by a man who wrapped a rope tightly around his neck and dragged him into a brushy area along the creek." This little boy was stabbed and raped, his penis "cut off up to his abdomen" by a child sex offender out on parole. The parolee, Earl Shriner, began his recorded violent attacks on younger children when he was fifteen-years-old.

In *Oakes v. the Commonwealth of Massachusetts*, the child pornography case before the United States Supreme Court, the step-father who photographed his fourteen-year-

old step-daughter,   said he wanted to make her "big for
Playboy."[8]

Such use of *Playboy* and its models for child and adult
pornography are now conventional. And, the taking of women,
girls, and boys off the streets, playgrounds, bike paths, and
parks for rape and murder is no longer uncommon.

Chapter 14

REGAINING A LOST CIVILIZATION

In our Justice Department study of the three major sadosexual magazines, well over nine thousand images were originally identified as presenting images of people under eighteen years of age. Our research guidelines narrowed these numbers down to the 6,004 analyzed for our final report. It was empirically obvious that numbers of nude juveniles, as young as thirteen or fourteen years of age, were made-up to appear to be "of age." However, without sufficient proof, we seldom counted these youngsters as minors.

It is clear that only through the cooperation of influential, highly placed decision-makers that a nation like ours could permit our youth to become fodder for commercial sex merchants. There must be legislators, judges, mayors, police, police chiefs, and others whose interests are served by child prostitution/pornography. It is the author's view that while society permits sex commerce to be legal, no child should be permitted to be involved prior to age twenty-one—the age one must be to purchase liquor.

In 1974, the government lost the carte blanche to act in the stead of missing or negligent parents. No longer could children be placed in protective custody when they were found on the streets at inappropriate hours or in inappropriate places. By accepting the idea that children are "free agents" unless they are committing an act that is criminal for adults, we handed over millions of youth into the hands of pornographers, pimps, drug dealers and eventually rape, addictions, diseases (including AIDS), and death.

Momentarily stepping out of my role as a scholar and into the role of a child protection advocate, let me emphatically urge the public to demand that our children finally be protected from sex exploiters. We must immediately find and house our runaways in permanent, secure harbors where these children are fed, clothed, educated, medically cared for, counseled, and maintained until age eighteen—like (as they say) in the "old days" of protective custody. It is true that there were terrible abuses in orphanages and juvenile homes in "the old days." However, institutional violations of American children cannot be compared to the brutality of the street—the suicidal/homicidal situation to which they are currently exposed. We must get our children off the streets and into custody until these youngsters are able to enter society as reasonably secure and protected youth. Where it is possible to return children safely to their homes, this can be done with care and sensitivity.

FREUD, KINSEY AND HEFNER

The "Etiology of Epidemic Child Sexual Abuse" is the theoretical framework for this book and provides us with a look at the origin of today's child holocaust. Let me briefly review Freud's theory of "infant sexuality" or "polymorphous perversity."

While Freud strongly disapproved of adult sexual use of children, his ideas and writing (i.e., the claim that the child desired sex with the parent) provided Kinsey a "scientific" forum to say adults can have sex with children. Following the outrageous Table 34 "findings" on his twenty-four-hour orgasm "tests" of infants and boys,[1] Kinsey justified his tests and his results by citing Freud:

> These data on the sexual activities of younger males provide an important substantiation of the Freudian view of sexuality as . . . present . . . from earliest infancy, although it gives no support to . . . a sexually latent or dormant period in the later adolescent years, except as such inactivity results from parental and social repressions of the growing child.[2]

Dr. Jeffrey Masson showed that Freud betrayed his patients—real incest victims who had come to him for help. Freud's claims of children's "seductive" nature were a sham. Freud opened the door for "polymorphous perversity" and Kinsey walked through. Kinsey opened the door for child sexual abuse and the pornographers and sex educators have promoted this ever since.

ABSTINENCE TO AIDS: THE KINSEY/HEFNER CONNECTION

This Judeo-Christian nation has witnessed a major shift in the last forty years from valuing a delayed sexuality and exclusive monogamy, to valuing an early sexuality and extraordinary sexual experience. The fallout could be seen as one in which we moved from abstinence to AIDS.

The epidemic of childhood mental illness in our country implicates up to fourteen million young victims. The emergence of Ted Bundy-type serial rapist-killers reveals a cadre of boys who grew up with *Playboy* and such. While "open pornography" was *supposed* to free us from sexual repression, it imprisoned millions in sexual obsession. Indeed, we have instead an unprecedented generation of addicts of every type, rapists, murderers, and madmen.

We agree with *Playboy*'s claim that this generation is "their own." The Central Park boys who were convicted of savaging a young women jogger, the Glen Ridge High boys who were convicted of savaging an innocent young girl, and the elementary school boys who raped a classmate are examples of America's "changed sexuality." The 1988 Michigan data on juvenile sex offenders reflects an increasingly toxic sadosexuality pattern within this new American male generation.

The charge here is that *Playboy* and its imitators in magazine, film, television, dial-a-porn, advertisements, and other media are sadosexual training manuals for juveniles. The charge is that these materials teach and have long taught young and old that "the girl next door" can be used in perverse, harmful ways for films and fun—even if she or he is a small child, and that "no" means "yes." The charge is that sex materials in the home often lead to sexual abuse of children by kin and/or to a broad range of other emotional and physical problems.

Playboy's testimony that "we took girls off the street" reveals its sexualization of ordinary girls and women, making all children into sex objects for the taking. It is argued the sexualization of everyone is reflected in the numbers of women and children—kidnaped, raped, and murdered—"off the street." As changing college males change society, as our college boys absorb sadosexual imagery, our nation becomes increasingly sexually violent.

Hefner's "free sex" model began to dominate male-female relations. Women felt used and vulnerable. One decade after *Playboy*'s opening issue, disillusioned and bitter wives, most college educated, founded the "women's liberation" movement. With even the Madonna seen as a whore, Katharine Hepburn observed that women had fallen "from the pedestal into pornography." As a result, men held her "at very little value."

Women and wives increasingly became "surrogate centerfolds." Comparing themselves to massive photographic and cosmetic fakery, they were more and more ashamed of their bodies, their age, and their wrinkles. Millions of virginal men climbed into their marriage beds after years of masturbating to Hefner's paper dolls. Alarmingly, having lived in between the covers of porn magazines for decades, these men insisted they knew women. They expected antics, novelties, sexual gymnastics, and ageless, cosmetic "perfection" from wives and girlfriends. Suddenly men were the experts on women's sexuality.

It is hardly surprising to find *Woman's Day* reporting that most women they surveyed want pornography outlawed, believing it has caused them real harm. They see pornography as making women and children second class citizens. Feminists have argued that the propaganda of pornography interferes with women's freedom of movement and their equal access to streets, buildings, schools, entertainment centers, etc. Pornographic sexual attitudes, say feminists, put women's and children's very lives at risk and discriminates against their rights as Americans.

THE FATHER OF IT ALL

Kinsey was the "father of sex education," and mentor for the "new" Hefner, popularizer of modern pornography. Today's sex education, kindergarten-to-college, is Kinseyan and *Playboy* disseminated, the Kinseyan model of pornography. If the pornographic re-education of American males has led to the current epidemic of heterosexual hostility, then Kinsey and team are to be thanked.

PLAYBOY AND ITS IMITATORS

The impact of *Playboy* can not be overstated. Scores of ancient societies were based on religious sexuality cults with sacred prostitution and sexual/blood sacrifice as part of their beliefs. Hefner may be said to have popularized America's first sexuality religion, now taught as "science" in the nation's public, private, and parochial schools nationwide.

Ironically, *Playboy*'s key enemies were 1950s college males, for most believed in Judeo-Christian "female sexuality" values—chastity, monogamy, and marital fidelity. The magazine sought and gained control over Joe College by obtaining control of his sexual identity. The sex industry scrambled to eliminate the tradition of lifelong marriage because marriage and fidelity undermined its power.

Wives, too, were natural, financial, and spiritual enemies of *Playboy*, so *Playboy* had to destroy the power of wives. Soon Joe College was collecting naked paper dolls. Increasingly, with lessening embarrassment, he began to rely on masturbation and paper dolls, putting off a serious commitment to seeking and pleasing a spouse. The sex industry triggered male and female misunderstanding, a spiraling divorce rate, as well as scores of adult and childhood disorders.

Instead of admitting that Kinseyan ideology and pornography were toxic material, health and sexuality professionals developed new methods to further bamboozle millions into becoming their patients. Indeed, many sexuality health professionals began using and creating pornography in their own practices to allegedly help cure the very psychosexual dysfunctions they helped create.

HIGH ON PORN

As "America's Number One Drug Promoter" for roughly thirty years, *Playboy* made a popular cocktail of sex, children, drugs, and athletes. Millions of youngsters drank it in, along with *Playboy*'s "All-American" team. Once drugs were seen as "recreational," steroids and "blood doping" became a necessary component to increase athletic performance. In this way, it is agreed among leaders in the athletic world that American sports and American athletes have been nearly destroyed.

Income from subscriptions, point-of-sale, and advertising provide vast resources for the sex industry to lobby politically for its sex-and-drug interests. Freedom committees, financially supported by *Playboy* and *Penthouse* via its

"Media Coalition," have been directly involved in suppressing and subverting public knowledge on pornography harm—including works such as this book.

As sex is, after all, an eight to ten billion dollar-a-year industry, censoring the opposition is possible through pressure on publishers, broadcasters, and through lobbying friends on Capitol Hill, in the Department of Justice, the Senate, Congress, and within the academic research community.

DESTROYING CHILDHOOD

The July 7, 1989 statement that roughly 12 to 22 percent of our youth are mentally ill should be taken with deadly concern. A health profession that admits the tragic status of youth, gets an *F* for its youth programs. The 22 percent does not necessarily include masses of youngsters who have been beaten, sexually abused, and neglected, but who have never sought or obtained mental health treatment.

After examining the status of our youth, we note that naturally curious children will do what children are supposed to do—they imitate the adult models around them. This includes those in real life as well as those models on television, in films, advertisements, and now, albeit less so, in books. The people imitated are those available—therefore "good" characters and "bad" characters become role models. Excitement also teaches behavior. The visual material in pornography is largely believed, "swallowed" by the intuitive, right hemisphere of the brain. Subsequently, one would expect juvenile sexual disorders to climb and 89 percent of juvenile offenders are recorded as using pornography as a tool for their crimes.

Add to these grisly numbers the roughly one thousand men and boys who die annually from masturbation strangulation (autoerotic asphyxiation). The young victims are almost always found using "soft core" pornography.

These data are more than "probable cause." They are enough to suggest "beyond a reasonable doubt" that women and children are differentially harmed by all public forms of female and child commercial sex and nude displays. We may not like "the message and spirit," but these are the data.

CHILDLIKE IMAGES AND CHILD MAGNETS

Children learn from comics. For this reason, the comic

character Spiderman was used by a child protection agency to teach children how to avoid sexual assault. So, when juvenile sex offenders use soft porn, they use its cartoons. It stands to reason that if one in four young girls and one in seven young boys are sexually abused, and if juveniles are assaulting younger children, soft porn's cartoon and visual "messages" are implicated in sex crimes against children.

This would especially be the case since soft porn employs scores of "Child Magnets" to attract children (e.g., coloring books, airplane models, pop-ups, Santa Claus images, child culture heroes, and fairy tales). In 1954, children first were *associated with* adult sex. By the 1960s, children were *associated directly in* sex with adults. By the 1970s, the children were being *gang raped* by adults. Our research also found that only little boys were originally shown in sexually implicit scenes with women. It took over a decade before *Playboy* joked about little girls being sexually assaulted by adult males and trusted adults.

The magazines' preferred age of child exploitation was between three and eleven years of age, also the most prevalent age of victims of sex abuse reported in real life. All three magazines display a strong death orientation, beyond children, a hatred of all the values regularly associated with life. Soft porn expresses a fear and horror of marriage, birth, religious and spiritual commitment, nonsexual relations, patriotism, care for the helpless, the elderly, and the handicapped, and sanctity of life.

CLEANING UP OUR PORNOGRAPHIC POLLUTION

A few years ago I worked with a clergyman who taught self-defense to victims of sexual assault. We were sharing horror stories one day when he shook his fist, saying:

> Were the current rate of rape and murder of our women and children due to a conquering army, our men would engage in hand-to-hand combat against that enemy. [Growing angrier, he asked,] How could we have come so far from the honor and esteem due to our mothers, our wives? What of our children? How can we continue to pretend that the mental poison of pornography doesn't increasingly tell men and boys to rape and murder our women and

children? Unless men end this . . . hate "entertainment," ban it, destroy it, and fight to the death to defend our women and our children, who will defeat our unseen, unprecedented, internal enemy?

This clergyman agreed that while Hefner may be immodest, he was correct when he said: "*Playboy* is the magazine that changed America." When my friend asks: "How could we have come so far from the honor and esteem due to our mothers, our wives? . . . How can we continue to pretend that the poison of pornography does not increasingly direct our men and boys to rape and murder our women and children?" would Hefner reply, because "*Playboy* is the magazine that changed America?" Would he brag that two generations of American youth have accepted the message and spirit of *Playboy* as their own?

ONLY MEN CAN WIN THE PORN BATTLE

Just as men and boys have been the soft porn targets, only men and boys can rid us of these toxins. A message and spirit that once was too appealing to resist has left a heritage too devastating to ignore. Women can organize. Women can expose the atrocities, and speak, encourage, and vote. But the battle will not be won until American men have gone to war not just against soft porn media but against a world view that degrades and victimizes women and children.

Much has already been done. More will be accomplished as American men increasingly take up the fight against all sex industry profiteers. War strategy has been mapped out. Organizations are in place. Procedures have been established, political channels have been opened, and significant steps have been taken to provide constructive opportunity for Americans to eliminate sadosexual pollution. Efforts have been made that will help define, contain, and eventually erase the sadosexual media from television, convenience stores, video rental outlets, retail bookstores, libraries, art museums, and the air waves.

As was the experience of my minister friend, this is a time for constructive and directed anger. The anger will be focused, confronting those whose lies have polluted our emotional environment, endangered our public health, and undermined our economic strength. The lie has too long deceived our people, creating a huge consumer base for the

Playboy myth while blinding users to the carnage of women and child victims. The lie is that the *Playboy* philosophy provided men and boys a rite of passage into the world of male sexuality—a safe way to calm doubts about their own maleness and prepare them for maximized sexuality.

Given the facts, men will realize that "soft" pornography is really "hard" abuse, scarring the emotions and bodies of women, children, and men. The damage is being done by sadosexual material accessible to children and adults—*Playboy* and its satellites. The damage is being done by the Kinseyan world view that all women and children desire sex, both homosexual and heterosexual, under almost any circumstances.

It is time for men to become angry at what the "soft" sex industry has done to them and their families. There are no untouched consumers of commercial sex. As shown earlier, one's high arousal to commercial sex is a result of the brain's reaction to stressful visual data, images, and text that produce a mixture of shame, lust, guilt, anger, and fear, and trigger the "high" of erotica/pornography. No human brain can casually balance provocative nude women with cartoons, text, and photo essays of orgies, violence, adultery, adult-child sex, homosexuality, sadism, and bestiality.

As we discussed, the consumer's confusion of sexual or genital arousal with his youthful or immature adult sense of guilt and fear intensifies his stress—and thus his sense of what he thinks is sexual arousal. Many men who seek to be more intimate and responsive to their wives are victimized by these confusing signals in soft porn. They do not know why the arousal from magazines, films, and videos often seems more predictable and exciting than their arousal in the marriage bed. By exploiting men's fears of impotence and their fears of female rejection and offering naked paper doll stimulants, the sex industry would rob men of their manhood to create dependency on all forms of pornography.

The sex industry lies will be exposed in part when men understand its hold on their lives. Men who are free of pornography's allure will more easily discern and confront Kinseyism and the *Playboy* myth in the work place, in entertainment, in art, and in the schools. The playboy world is one of control and dominance—not of equality and mutual respect.   Porn kings do not walk as friends and equals alongside our nation's men. Thinking, compassionate men will reject the sex merchants' cheap and stressful wares and men and women freed from the grip of pornographic illusions will begin the long struggle toward true emotional and spiritual intimacy.

Pornographers have undermined women's trust in lifelong marriage, in a faithful mate, in love forever. They have robbed her of her right to withhold sexual intercourse until the commitments are in place to nurture the goals of marriage and family. Premarital sexual purity and marital fidelity are not the final measure of a person's worth. But a woman has the right to be associated with those womanly values. And a society that is influenced by such female sexuality is better served than one controlled by "recreational" male sexuality. Every woman has the right to assume she will not have to compete with or share the marriage bed with fantasies of Miss November.

AN OVERHAUL OF SEX OFFENDER LAWS

Both the popular press and politicians are beginning to sense a moral and social change in the wind. "Accountability" and "ethics" are the new watchwords in government and science. For example, states with an under-twenty-one drinking age lose federal highway funds; airlines prohibit smoking on domestic flights; television sponsors have withdrawn support from scores of financially rewarding but jaded television programs; and youngsters in some school districts can leave an unsuccessful school to join one with a better academic record.

Responsibility for one's actions, long a Judeo-Christian notion, is also being felt by pornographers, sex offenders, and other social outcasts.

The idea of accountability is now taking hold in the area of criminal justice. By rejecting the forty-year-old sex-offender clemency model motivated by Kinsey, legislators are overhauling sex offense laws. California reenacted capital punishment after a twenty-three year hiatus.

Citizens organized into lobby groups are demanding that elected officials reflect the will of the people. If this continues, fewer rapists and child sex offenders will be paroled to rape and murder again. The 1 January 1990 front page of the *New York Times* announced that in the state of Washington, the rape and genital mutilation of a seven-year-old boy by a paroled sex-offender had triggered a governor's "task force on sexual predators." According to the *Times*, the impact of this trend toward tougher laws is most dramatic in Washington state, which had been considered a national model in treatment of rapists and molesters. After a series of brutal offenses by parolees who had completed years of intensive state-sponsored counseling and therapy, Washington officials are overhauling sex-offender laws:

> [They] recommend life sentences for violent rape and molestation of children. The Governor's panel stated, "The research demonstrates that most child sex offenders will continue their abuses for many years and rarely are cured" . . . [and recommended that] "all convicted sexual offenders register with the county in which they reside after leaving prison."

The governor of Washington state, the model for sex offender counseling programs, recently signed a bill creating the nation's most comprehensive and toughest system to deal with sex crimes. It was to give "longer prison terms for indefinite civil commitment of the most violent predators and expand treatment programs for offenders and victims," according to the *Washington Post* (8 March 1990).

In South Carolina, the get-tough policy of a formal liberal police chief has brought "law and order to the city's public housing developments, which have been murder-free for five years" (*Washington Times*, 28 February 1990). In New Mexico and Texas, both attorneys general and legislative candidates have advocated abolishing parole to restore "the lost link between crime and punishment" where more than three-fourths of prison admissions were parole or probation violators (*Washington Times*, 23 February 1990). And in liberal California, 83 percent of state residents now favor capital punishment. A 28 March 1990 *Washington Post* article reports that voters there have just removed capital punishment foes from the state Supreme Court resulting in reinstatement of the death penalty.

Kinsey Institute team members (Wardell Pomeroy, Gagnon, Paul Gebhard, et al) claimed that child molesters seldom commit rape.[3] They said pornography does not motivate sex crimes. And they explained that drug addicts rarely figure in sex crimes. But science and real life continue to prove the fallacies of the Kinsey team and the discipled sex therapists. It is past time for accountability for the Kinsey team. It is time for American citizens to create a national victims' rights movement to redress our grievances against the Kinsey model and the sex industry. After burying hundreds of thousands of innocent victims, our society is beginning to discover that lenient sex laws (even those relating to consenting adult activity—such as anal sodomy) act upon society in unanticipated ways. Apparently in concert with other social changes, liberal sex laws free many men and boys from critical inhibitions that had worked in the past to restrain their sexual violence toward women and children.

OF GOD, GOOD, POLITICS, AND EPICURUS

The sex industry presents the nation with a clear contest between good and evil. Most Americans intuit "evil" in both pornography and other sadosexual mass entertainment. Many Americans have also dimly suspected "evil" in the school sex education programs that we hoped would save us. I have said that it is evil to put women and children at risk from sexually exploitative media (both in entertainment and education) and that this undermines the survival of the civil society. Our laws are in place, "to ensure domestic tranquility." Yet, our media have become almost entirely irresponsible and out of control—despite the causative role they play in domestic bloodshed.

In speaking of the massive violence in our streets, George Will wrote in a recent column, "You do not talk long with cops before they mention movies that are desensitizing young people by glorifying casual brutality. . . . Cops lead lives rich in instructive anecdotes, enough anecdotes to justify generalizations. Cops know that business is booming for . . . bulletproof vests for children."

A mother just organized a new group: "MOMS," Mothers of Murdered Sons. Her boy was killed for his jacket. The lad who killed him was obsessed with the movie *Scarface*. The mom, owner of an advertising company, wants advertisers to stop sending out messages like "Just Do It" and she wants Hollywood and the music industry to cease promoting and teaching violence, says a *Washington Post* article (10 February 1991).

It would be unacceptable to leave the subject of sadosexual violence without briefly noting the role of religion and God in pornography.

In December 1989, the *Atlantic Monthly* published an article by political theorist Glenn Tinder titled "Can We Be Good Without God?"[4] Tinder argued that the Old and New Testaments are political and that God is "deeply engaged in the affairs of the world." Without spirituality—without belief in a God who demands that public leaders obey His laws—politics become demoralized, he says. What follows is government that supports "group interest and personal ambition . . . power and privilege." Those who do not fear that a higher power will judge and punish their acts, will serve only their own selfish interests. Tinder has an important argument to make:

> It will be my purpose in this essay to try to connect the severed realms of the spiritual and the political. In view of the fervent secularism of many Americans today, some will assume this to be the opening salvo of a fundamentalist attack on "pluralism." Ironically, as I will argue, many of the undoubted virtues of pluralism—respect for the individual and a belief in the essential equality of all human beings, to cite just two—have strong roots in the union of the spiritual and political achieved in the vision of Christianity. The question that secularists have to answer is whether these values can survive without these particular roots. In short, can we be good without God?

Once carefully explaining the Judaic roots of Christianity, Tinder thereafter speaks as a serious Christian on the volatile issue of evil and "sin:"

> Christian doctrine so offends people today as the stress on sin. It is morbid and self-destructive, supposedly, to depreciate ourselves in this way. Yet the Christian view is not implausible. The twentieth century, not to speak of earlier ages . . . has displayed human evil in extravagant forms.

Tinder cautions: "Sin is ironic. Its intention is self-exaltation, its result is self-debasement," and referencing history, he asserts humans always worship and exalt something—a man, a class, a nation, or an idea such as "science." He asks why it is logical to exalt those things that have consistently failed, while rejecting God—when following His laws initially permitted us to erect what we now have of a civil life?

Honing in on the clash between other social philosophies and Western Christianity, Tinder shows the shared principle of communism and fascism—a principle clearly manifested in pornography: "that a single individual does not necessarily matter." As a clear example of inequality—humans demeaned to the level of objects purchased for use—we begin to see the inherent fascism of pornography when Tinder says:

> When equality falls...liberty, too, is likely to vanish; it becomes a heavy personal and social burden when no God justifies and sanctifies the individual in spite of all personal deficiencies and failures.... [T]o what extent are we now living on [Judeo-Christian] moral savings accumulated over many centuries but no longer being replenished?

While candidly noting that "Christians have accepted, and sometimes actively supported, slavery, poverty, and almost every other common social evil," Tinder cites such acts as reflective of poor faith and the fallibility of human beings. He issues a call for Judeo-Christian believers to faithfully participate in the political arena. "Political goodness" calls for maintaining responsible hope, which, he says, "without God—is doubtful."

> Epicurus called for withdrawal from public life and political activity; he argued that everything essential to one's humanity . . . can be found in the private sphere. . . . The absorption of Americans in the pleasures of buying and consuming, of mass entertainment and sports, suggests an Epicurean response to our historical trials. . . . Being good politically means not only valuing the things that are truly valuable but also having the strength to defend those things when they are everywhere being attacked and abandoned.

Tinder concludes by citing the heroism of German pastor and theologian, Dietrich Bonhoeffer, who opposed Hitler, he says, returning to sure death in Germany in order to fight in the resistance. When he was killed by the Gestapo, Bonhoeffer composed a prayer in prison: "Give me the hope that will deliver me from fear and faintheartedness." Asked Tinder of his readers: "If we turn away from transcendence, from God, what will deliver us from a politically fatal fear and faintheartedness?"

It is the thesis of this book that the evils of illicit drug use and pornography constitute the most important political issue in our current history. Tinder asks: "If we turn away from . . . God" can we be delivered from "a politically fatal fear and faintheartedness?"

He charges that in a pluralistic society, the voices of those who believe in the fundamental values that built this nation must be strong, loud, and clearly heard. The Judeo-Christian laws, which formed the country, are in place to make explicit the people's beliefs and commitments.

Disdaining the elitist Epicureans, more and more Judeo-Christian believers are taking public office on school and library boards and at the local, state, and federal levels in an organized, united, and aggressive manner. Folks of every denomination are reminding their pastors and co-religionists of their civic duty to resist evil. Some broadcast facilities have recently been purchased by serious Christians while other broadcasters are responding to call-ins, letters-to-the-editor, articles, boycotts of products, and the like. There are organizations, many of which are listed in the Appendix, which fight for Judeo-Christian values and beliefs. The Appendix includes tear sheets for three "action" booklets on mass media (pornography and television). These may be obtained from the American Family Association, a non-denominational, Judeo-Christian organization.

The public needs to identify the places where good laws are no longer in place, where they have been eroded or removed while their guardians looked elsewhere. These include the elimination of "protective custody," the lowering of the age of consent, thus restrictive statutory rape laws, the paroling of rapists and murderers, legalization of AIDS-productive sodomy, nude bars and strip joints, tolerance of blasphemy, and excessive violence on television and the distribution of sexually explicit and fraudulent Kinseyan data in schools. The public needs to ascertain who is responsible for abusing the public trust in these and other cases, to follow through properly on any possible breach of law or ethics, and to be diligent that their will be done.

An informed and knowledgeable public does not need to tolerate drugs, school sex mis-education, pornography, and the like. It is the American way for communities to determine their health standards by united action. Remember the amazing events of 1989 in the communist countries of the world Ours is a tradition worth preserving. Change is possible for evil or for good.

Tinder said, "The foundations of political decency are an issue I will raise, not settle. . . . Can we be good without God?"

Appendix One

WHY ORGANIZE?

(The following is excerpted from the American Family Association booklet, "A Guide to What One Person Can Do About Pornography," available from AFA by writing to P.O. Drawer 2440, Tupelo, Mississippi 38803. Sincere appreciation is extended to AFA for allowing the author to reprint the material.)

In the first place, an organization provides a highly desirable and efficient means of gathering and distributing information and materials.

In the second place, organizational machinery provides for cohesiveness and unity of action by the entire group. Ten organized members striving towards one goal will accomplish far more than one hundred inspired but disorganized. Organizational influence provides a tremendous economy of time in mobilizing a group for action.

In the third place, organization provides for tremendous clout and influence. In an organization that is well integrated and harmonious, the leaders can speak confidently of representing the views of dozens, hundreds of thousands of members.

RECRUITMENT

Where do you find prospective members?

1. Churches.

2. Other organizations. Visit other organizations and ask for an opportunity to express your concerns. Examples: Christian Business Men's Association, Civitan Club, Women's groups, Kiwanis Club, the Ministerial Association, etc.

3. *AFA Journal.* Request the AFA Journal printout for your area/areas by sending AFA the applicable zip codes.

4. Advertising. Purchase advertisement in the local newspaper and on area radio stations concerning meetings and special events.

5. Inform media that carry community announcement formats of events.

6. Visit prominent business people, community leaders, and city/county officials.

7. Visit physicians and other medical/psychological field personnel that may have opportunity to be exposed to sex abuse victims.

How do you recruit?

1. Inform prospects. When visiting the prospects, it is helpful

to offer brief informative materials. Keep in mind the following precepts:

  a. Share the problem.
  b. Use accurate, current information.
  c. Share your vision of the solution.
  d. Explain how they can become involved.
  e. Make your request (what you want them to do).
  f. Follow with an appropriate letter.

 2. Establish a mailing list.

 3. Publish newsletter and develop brochure. Keep it simple and current. Include address and phone.

 4. Establish professional image. Print organization stationery and envelopes.

 5. Advertise. As funds allow, consider purchasing billboard space or doing other promotional efforts.

 6. Schedule rallies. Hold a major meeting yearly using it to push for new members. Schedule speakers that will be informed and draw crowds.

CONVENIENCE/VIDEO STORES

In a kind manner ask the manager or owner to discontinue the sale of pornographic material. Approach the subject using facts and statistics to enforce your arguments. Many are surprised that it often takes just one nice request to get a store to remove their pornography.

The DEAR MANAGER CARD. Print up some of these pocket sized cards to leave with the manager or clerk when asking that the pornography be removed.

Dear Manager,
  I noticed that you sell (rent) pornographic magazines (videos). I believe that pornography is harmful to our community and does not belong in the family marketplace. I respectfully request that you stop offering these materials. Should you continue to sell these materials I cannot in good conscience patronize your store, and must encourage my friends, acquaintances, fellow church members and others not to shop here. Should you decide to remove the pornographic material, please call me at the number listed below. I will at that time resume shopping in your store and will encourage my friends to do the same.
  Signed
  Phone Number

On the other side of the cards print some general information or statistics. For example:

DID YOU KNOW . . .

* A study of habitual sex-offenders at a penitentiary noted that 38% of the rapists used "soft-core" porn to arouse and incite themselves before the rape. Another 19% used "hard-core" porn immediately prior to committing the offense . . .

* A study by the Michigan state police department showed that 41% of the 38,000 sexual assault cases on file involved some use of porn immediately prior to or during the act . . .

* One in four females and will be sexually molested in her lifetime . . .

1. *Contact manager.* Leave the DEAR MANAGER CARD with the manager of a family store that sells pornography in your community.

2. *Write letters.* Follow up with a letter to the business owner.

3. *Check laws.* Approach your city officials concerning any ordinances that may apply to the material in question. Ask your city/county prosecuting attorney to investigate and enforce your local or state obscenity law.

4. *Encourage officials.* Simultaneously, approach your local officials such as mayor, councilmen, supervisors at a public meeting. Ask them to support the enforcement of these codes. Ask that the proper officers be instructed to investigate and enforce the existing ordinances in your local area. This should be done in a tactful and well prepared presentation, again avoiding a moral/religious angle. You may need to ask for a law to be passed if none exists.

5. *Build support.* Get as many people as possible to write and call the officials from their voting area prior to the meeting. Try to fill the room with people and inform the news media prior to the appearance.

6. *Boycott.* After all other attempts have failed, organize a boycott of the business. Share your experience with your pastor and church leaders asking for their support. Provide factual material concerning its harm and accurate information about its availability in your community. Encourage each individual to inform the manager/owner of the business of their participation in the boycott. Regularly report the status of the boycott and continue to encourage it for however long it takes to obtain a positive response from the business.

7. *Picket.* Organize a picket.

SEXUALLY ORIENTED BUSINESS

Local communities have the ability to regulate the secondary effects brought about by sexually oriented business. Secondary effects may include increased crime rates, declining property values and a lower quality of life in the area surrounding a sexually oriented business (e.g., "adults only" pornographic outlets, massage parlors, topless or nude bars or businesses, houses of prostitution).

Contact the American Family Association regarding two recent United States Supreme Court decisions that have eliminated much of the confusion in this area: *Renton v .Playtime Theatres, Inc.*, and *Arcara v .Cloud Books, Inc.* On the basis of these two decisions, local governments clearly have the ability to regulate sexually oriented businesses in an effort to control the adverse secondary effects. In addition, lower courts have stated that governments may constitutionally restrict the behavior of wholly or partially nude employees.

One of the most comprehensive regulatory schemes restricting sexually oriented businesses has been enacted by the City of Dallas. Recently, the Fifth Circuit found that the ordinance regulated only the secondary effects and was designed to maintain the quality of urban life. This ordinance can serve as a model for other communities that wish to regulate the adverse effects of sexually oriented businesses.

More extensive information about the local regulation of sexually oriented businesses is available through AFA (and assistance in drafting such ordinances.)

In addition, there are several other actions you may take:

1. Visit your city hall and county courthouse to learn about the various laws and ordinances that may be applicable (e.g., local or state nuisance laws; zoning laws; fire codes; health codes; traffic hazards; business permits.

2. Check with city or county tax assessor to see who pays the taxes and who owns the property or building.

3. Picket/boycott the business or other highly visible businesses that he or she may own.

CABLE TV PORNOGRAPHY

1. Document cases of video porn.

* Tape segments of the channel over a period of several days, preferably night programs.

* Note date, time, and channel number on which the movies were shown.

* Copy short clips of some of the worst scenes.

2. Show a small group of pro-family leaders the tape. Arrange a meeting with the local cable franchise owner and show the tape. Request a commitment from the cable system not to carry the channel. Take the tapes with your notes to your state District Attorney, city or county prosecutor and ask that a Grand Jury view the tapes for possible violations of local ordinances or state obscenity laws.

3. Plan a mass meeting in which a larger group or community leaders participate. All community ministers, business and civic leaders should be invited. Arrange a separate room for viewing the material, allowing men and women to view the material separately. WARN the people BEFORE the viewing that the material is extremely explicit! DO NOT INSIST they view it they prefer not to. Arrange a viewing for council members prior to the discussion and ask them not to grant a cable franchise to the company.

4. Schedule a Sunday asking pastors to address the issue from the pulpit and encourage their congregations to express objections to the cable franchise. Utilize the post card method again, informing the local franchise that a boycott may be called and members may drop their cable subscriptions if the decision is made to carry the pornographic channel. Issue local press releases to call attention to the movement.

5. Schedule a major community-wide rally at a central, neutral site such as a public library or community building. Invite appropriate speakers and highly publicize the meeting within the community.

6. Schedule a Cable Cancellation Sunday. Ministers should again be called upon to address the problem from the pulpits and ask congregations to complete a cancellation order to their cable service (during the service). These notices are legal documents. If the cable company refuses to disconnect the service (as they often do,) the subscriber should refuse to pay any future bills.

7. Picket the cable company.

The steps outlined above may be applied toward an existing porn channel with minor variations. However, it is far easier to prevent its entering your community than to remove it.

BROADCAST MEDIA

The FCC is empowered to investigate and regulate broadcast channels against suspected obscene or indecent materials in whatever format it may be aired over our nation's radio frequencies and TV channels. Recently in response to public pressure upon politicians and thus transmitted to the bureaucracy of the FCC, this organization has begun vocalizing their intent to investigate and prosecute alleged violations. To date, very little if any positive or effective action is to be seen as a result of citizen complaints turned in to the FCC. With your help, this can be changed.

1. Approach the station manager explaining your concern with the program and follow up with a letter.

2. Repeat this process with the station owner/owners.

3. Initiate a letter-writing and/or telephone campaign to the station.

4. Monitor the program and note the advertisers.

MONITORING TV PROGRAMS WITH A VCR

* Use a VCR to record the program for five days.

* Note the local advertisers and the total amount of time each advertiser appears.

* Note the advertiser with the most time on the program.

* Arrange an interview with this local advertiser. Take a portable VCR and show him the edited tape.

* Point out your objections. BE SPECIFIC.

* Request that he STOP SPONSORING the program. Emphasize the seriousness of your request by informing the advertiser that a 4-step process may follow: a letter-writing and/or television campaign, a boycott, a picket, and finally, a formal complaint to the Federal Communications Commission (FCC) along with a copy of the tape with the worst parts of the program. (See Appendix 2 for address).

UNSOLICITED PORN THROUGH THE U.S. MAIL

1. Copy all materials including the envelope and turn over the original to the U.S. Attorney in your area.

2. File a complaint alleging violations of federal law. Note the date received, the date submitted to the U.S. Attorney, and a brief summary of his words and actions.

3. If the material is addressed to a minor (under the age of 18), the U.S. Attorney will have a stronger case.

In addition to the above, ask your Postmaster for Form 2150 (Title 30 U.S. Code, Section 3008) and Form 2201 (Title 39 U.S. Code, Section 3010). Complete these and return them to your Post Office. This will require your name to be removed from the mailing list of the company sending the materials. They could be penalized by law should they not remove your name.

DIAL-A-PORN

Dial-a-porn is the name given to recorded or live television sex messages on a pay-per-call basis. These numbers are widely circulated in porn magazines and have been verbally passed around many school systems by young people. Some very high phone bills have been incurred by parents because their children acquired and used the numbers.

1. After the fact.

   a. Make copies of the phone bill.

   b. Note if the calls were made by a minor.

   c. Contact your United States Attorney. Give him the original billing and notes and ask him to investigate.

   d. Call your state Public Service Commission. Speak directly to your Commissioner and ask him to get the phone charges dismissed (if you don't want to take the prosecuting route). He may or may not be able to do so under existing state laws. If not ask that he arrange to let you pay the phone company over a period of months.

   e. Follow up with a letter involving a copy of the phone bill and notes.

2. Prevent the problem.

   a. On the federal level, a law was recently enacted that would amend 47 U.S.C. Section 223 to prohibit all indecent or obscene telephone messages.

   b. Complain to the phone company.

   c. Petition your state utility public service commission to enact a statewide tariff (ruling) for your local phone service which would require the local or statewide phone carrier to block all dial-a-porn calls originating from residential and commercial phones. Insist that there be no charge for blocking these calls.

WORKING WITH YOUR PROSECUTOR

The sale, display, and distribution of pornographic material can be totally prohibited if it meets the legal definition of obscenity. While "pornography" is a generic term, "obscenity" is identified by a three-part test which was given by the United States Supreme Court in the 1973 case of *Miller v California*; 1) the average person, applying contemporary adult community standards, would find that the work, taken as a whole, appeals to the prurient (lustful, erotic, shameful or morbid) interest; 2) the average person, applying contemporary adult community standards, would find that the work depicts or describes, in a patently offensive way, ultimate sexual acts, normal or perverted, actual or simulated, and masturbation, excretory functions, lewd exhibition of the genitals and sado-masochristic sexual abuse; 3) the work, taken as a whole, lacks serious literary, artistic, political or scientific value as determined by an "average" person.

Most states have statutes incorporating the *Miller* definition of obscenity, thus making it a crime to distribute obscene material, as well as various forms of civil legislation, such as public nuisance abatement, declaratory judgments, and injunction actions, to control the distribution of such materials.

The open display of materials harmful to minors and the use of children in any kind of sexual performance are prohibited in many states. These child pornography laws have been given approval by the United States Supreme Court. A number of states also have laws that prohibit the private possession of child pornography.

There are federal laws which can be used to control the distribution of obscene material, prohibiting the interstate transportation of obscene material, the use of common carriers to distribute obscene material, and the importation of obscene material into this country from other countries. These laws make it a felony to transport, ship, or send obscene matter across any state or U.S. border; or in the U.S. mails; or by common carrier, such as bus, train, plane, trucking company, and UPS, even within a state. (Title 18, U.S. Code Sections 1461, 1462, 1465.)

Federal laws also control the content of radio and television broadcasts, and prohibit any obscene, indecent or profane language, or conduct by means of the broadcast media. All are enforcable regardless of whether a state has an effective local obscenity statute.

FINDING APPLICABLE LAWS

For city/county ordinances contact: City Clerk, County Attorney, City Attorney County Prosecutor, City Prosecutor. These offices can be located in the phone directory or by contacting city hall, or the County Courthouse.

For State ordinances contact: State Attorney General's office, Secretary of State's office. These may be located by dialing information for your state capitol.

For Federal statutes contact the U.S. Attorney's office.

When researching applicable laws, always request the statute number and a copy of all statutes in each of the applicable areas.

APPROACHING YOUR PROSECUTOR

1. Approach your official as a representative of an organization. Many prosecutors are elected (or appointed by an elected official) so the more votes you represent the more you are apt have his attention.

2. Establish a friendly relationship with the official if at all possible.

3. Have with you a copy or statute number of all statutes that may apply for their easy reference. Present factual information and resources for their assistance.

4. Be persistent. Prosecution of obscenity is not a priority across our country.

5. Always conduct yourself as a concerned citizen working within the law.

WHAT IF A PROSECUTOR IS UNCOOPERATIVE?

1. Where laws are not being enforced (a. and b. below), it may be necessary for a private citizen to file an affidavit to secure an arrest of a pornography dealer.

> a. Where you suspect materials to be obscene, have someone with a witness rent/purchase some of the material that has been found obscene in another area of the country.
>
> > (1) Obtain a receipt with the date, time, and title on it. Note these if your receipt doesn't have them.
> >
> > (2) Make a copy of the receipt before turning it over to the authorities.
>
> b. Take the material to your officials and ask that they uphold the law.
>
> c. If they will not act, attempt to file a complaint yourself. You may have to find a "friendly judge" who will allow you to swear out a complaint by signing an affidavit. The complaint will go to law enforcement officials
>
> and an arrest will be made. You will be required to appear in court to testify. Should you decide to use this method, be aware there is always the possibility of a personal lawsuit.

2. Another option would be to take material to your state District Attorney, asking him to review the tape and ask for a Grand Jury to review it. If the Grand Jury views it and returns an indictment then the case will be heard in court.

3. The Prosecutor's position is a public office. He is not free to act upon his personal preferences but is to professionally carry out the responsibilities outlined by the appropriate charter for his office. Public pressure can be focused upon the appropriate offices through the various means of letter writing, picketing, etc. It may be necessary to check campaign contributions which are, according to state law, a part of public record. (You may check at your county or city clerk's office for a copy of the political contribution

records). Remember to respect the official's privacy. Address all action to his public office rather than personal residence.

HOW TO WRITE AN EFFECTIVE LETTER

The following general letter writing guidelines are adapted from Citizens For Decency Through Law.

1. The content of the letter should be written in your own words. Form letters, petitions, and pre-printed postcards have their place but do not carry as much weight as your own letter.

2. Typed letters are good, but handwritten letters are very acceptable if they are legible. If it's hard to read, they won't!

3. Clearly identify the issue about which you are writing. Cover only one topic. Keep the letter to one page if at all possible.

4. Be polite. Be firm but courteous.

5. Clearly state the action you would like the reader to take.

6. Get your facts straight. Give at least one reason for your request.

7. Ask the recipients to state their view on the subject and what action they intend to take.

8. Send a thank-you or follow-up letter, whichever is appropriate.

WRITING COMPANIES

1. Word the letter as if you were talking to your next door neighbor or close friend. Grammar is not nearly as important as your message.

2. A letter neatly written on a notebook tablet sheet is just as effective as a letter written on the most expensive stationary.

3. Keep your letters short and simple, one page if possible. Be pleasant but firm.

4. Don't approach your subject from a religious perspective. By doing so you will give opportunity for the opposition to say that you are trying to impose your particular religion or morals on others.

WRITING ELECTED OFFICIALS

Congressmen value your opinion since you are a voter and they want to keep your vote. In one survey ranking 20 different factors influencing congressional opinion, a spontaneous letter from a home-state constituent ranked number one! Following a spontaneous personal letter was a personal telephone call, a post card, and near the bottom a form letter.

1. Be firm but polite in stating your view.

2. Address one subject.

3. Commend them on issues or actions when you can.

4. Refer to bills and resolutions by NUMBER whenever possible.

5. Time your letter to arrive mid-week when the mail deliveries are lower.

6. Be factual and accurate.

7. Be neat and legible.

8. Include your name and address on the letter and ask for a response. If appropriate, send a copy to the local newspaper "letter to the editor" section.

WRITING LETTERS TO THE EDITOR

1. Remember the editor has the advantage and often can edit in such a way as to twist or slant your words to his bias.

2. Check your information and sources for accuracy.

3. When writing to any media, it is always good to have someone edit a document for grammatical and spelling errors in addition to content and composition.

ORGANIZING AN EFFECTIVE PICKET

It does not require a great number to picket effectively, in fact, two or three people in a well-planned picket can effectively get pornography removed. In listing the following steps it is assumed that personal visits, letters, telephone calls, or other applicable means have already been employed with no results.

1. In determining the picket date, consideration must be balanced in the following areas: availability of picketers, timing, highest traffic time of the establishment being picketed, safety, and preparation.

2. Once the date and time have been established, the proper local officials need to be contacted concerning a parade/demonstration permit. Picketing is the exercise of two constitutional rights: "freedom of speech" and "peaceable assembly". Denial of a permit without a definitive reason should be in writing and carefully considered before accepting.

RULES FOR PICKETING

a. Picketers must remain on public property at all times.

b. Never impede/block traffic; vehicles or pedestrians.

c. Refer the media to the media spokesperson.

d. Use only approved signs.

e. Customers should not be debated or engaged in conversation.

f. If the manager or his representative asks you to leave; do so immediately! The chairperson will call the police to enforce your right to picket. Resume picketing only when they arrive.

g. Should you encounter other picketers supporting the business, picket in a peaceful manner if possible; otherwise peacefully leave and let the picket chairperson call the police to supervise.

h. Always conduct yourself in a Christ-like manner, remembering your testimony in the community.

3. AFA recommends that the literature be generally anti-porn in nature. Avoid material that promotes other causes, local organizations, etc. so that the focus will remain centered on the immediate issue.

4. Wording of picket signs should be brief and general in nature. Lettering should be large, clear, and neat to enhance reading from a distance. One sign per picketer is ideal. In some areas, signs must be carried at all times.

UTILIZING THE MEDIA

DEALING WITH FRIENDLY PRESS

1. Establish a friendly personal relationship with media personnel. Make them aware of who you are, the organization you represent, and your availability.

2. Always inform them concerning any events. If it is printed media, try to determine what format they prefer for press notices.

3. Remember they have several items of interest and perhaps a large area to cover so don't be disappointed if they do not show the same amount of enthusiasm or priority toward your news as you would prefer.

WITH HOSTILE PRESS

1. Always remain tactful and courteous in any encounters with the media whether on camera, in print, or privately.

2. Act, don't react! Your opposition will attack you, your motives, or whatever they can to draw attention away from them to you or secondary issues. Ignore them and focus on the issue.

3. Avoid, if at all possible, any type of edited formats when dealing with TV or radio. Regarding print media, remember that the ability to edit has a tremendous advantage in story presentation.

4. Avoid talk show formats on secular TV or radio. If you feel you must appear, give preference to live programs and use a spokesperson who has media experience.

5. Avoid debate formats.

THE NEWS INTERVIEW

If you are to get media coverage then you will of necessity need to grant on-the-spot interviews with the news team.

1. Know your subject. Answer their questions as accurately and briefly as possible. Designate a media spokesperson to represent your group and insist that only he/she is authorized to speak for your organization.

2. Be prepared with a concise statement that you want to project to the audience. The media will not always be content with a prepared statement but this is especially helpful to those unaccustomed to dealing with the media.

3. Maintain control. Tactfully but firmly dismiss yourself. Avoid giving them time to pick at your answers or information.

4. Don't be discouraged if you "blow it" in an interview. There will be other opportunities if you remain in the battle. Experience will quickly teach you how to use the media to your advantage.

THE PRESS RELEASE

A news release is often the first impression the media will have concerning your organization or event.

1. Essential elements. A well written release will contain: date, name of organization, complete address, contact person, and phone number of contact person.

2. A concise statement incorporating all necessary and relevant information to the event or organization. It should be neat, type-written, double-spaced, and checked for grammar and spelling. The statement should be written to allow reporters to lift phrases easily from the written text.

3. The release should be as early as possible prior to the event. No later than five days prior to the event is a good rule of thumb.

Note: Anticipate argument from the media regarding censorship charges, freedom of speech, right to privacy, etc. For recommended responses to these arguments contact AFA and request the booklet titled *Pornography: What One Person Can Do*.

Appendix Two

ADDRESSES

(The following material is excerpted from the American Family Association, "A Guide to What One Person Can Do About Pornography," available from AFA by writing P.O. Drawer 2440, Tupelo, Mississippi 38803. In addition, an address directory, providing addresses for television sponsors, government officials, law enforcement agencies, and pornography promotors, is available by contacting AFA.)

PRESIDENT
The White House
Washington, DC 20500

YOUR U.S. CONGRESSMAN
House of Representatives
Washington, DC 20515

YOUR U.S. SENATOR
U.S. Senate
Washington, DC 20510

U.S. JUSTICE DEPARTMENT
10th & Constitution NW
Washington, DC 20530

FEDERAL COMMUNICATIONS COMMISSION (FCC)
1919 M Street NW
Washington, DC 20554

TELEVISION NETWORK ADDRESSES
ABC
Chrm. Thomas S. Murphy
Capital Cities/ABC, Inc.
24 East 51st Street
New York, NY 10022
Phone 212-421-9595

NBC
Chrm. John F. Welch, Jr.
General Electric

Fairfield, CT 06431
Phone 203-373-2211

CBS
Chrm. Laurence A. Tisch
CBS, Inc.
51 West 52nd Street
New York, NY 10019
Phone 212-975-4321

MOTEL/HOTEL PORN MOVIE OUTLETS

Holiday Inns is the largest distributor of in-room porno-
graphic movies in the world. Holiday Inns carries porn movies in
all their corporately owned motels and in many of the locally
owned motels.
Chrm. Michael Rose
Holiday Corporation
1023 Cherry Road
Memphis, TN 38117
Phone 901-762-8950.
To register your complaint, call 1-800-465-4329

PORN MAGAZINES RETAILERS

In the past few years, more than 20,000 stores have decided
that they care more about the families in their communities than the
money porn brings in. However, the stores listed below have
decided the money porn magazines bring in is more important than
the families in their communities. At the time of publication, these
are the leading retailers of porn magazines:
Chrm. Karl Eller, Circle K Corporation, 1601 North Seventh
Street, Phoenix, AZ 85006, phone 602/437-0600. The toll-free
number is 1-800-237-5674.
Chrm. D.B. Haseopes, Cumberland Farms Stores, 777 Dedham
Street, Canton, MA 02021, phone 617/828-4900.
Chrm. Charles Nirenberg, Dairy Mart/Lawson Convenience
Stores, 240 South Road, Enfield, CT 06082, phone 203/741-3611.
Chrm. Bernard M. Fauber, Kmart Corporations, 3100 West
Big Beaver Road, Troy, MI 48084, phone 313/643-1000. (Kmart
sells porn magazines in their Waldenbooks bookstores.)
Pres. V.H. Van Horn, National Convenience Stores (Stop 'n
Go Stores), 100 Waugh Drive, Houston, TX 77007, phone 713/
863-2000.

Chrm. Dillard Munford, Munford, Incorporated (Majik Market Convenience Stores), P.O. Box 7701, Station C, Atlanta, GA 30357, phone 404/352-6641.

Chrm. David M. Roderick, USX Corporation (Starvin' Marvin, Ecol and Value Convenience Stores), 600 Grant Street, Pittsburgh, PA 15230, phone 412/433-1121.

PORNOGRAPHIC MAGAZINE ADVERTISERS

These two companies are the largest supporters of porn magazines with advertising dollars. Both of these companies annually sink millions of advertising dollars into supporting pornographic magazines. In fact, without the money given them by these advertisers, *Playboy* and *Penthouse* would probably go out of business.

Philip Morris/General Foods, Pres. John A. Murphy, 120 Park Avenue, New York, NY 10017, Phone 212-880-5000. PRODUCTS: Alpha Bits cereal, Baker's chocolate, Batter'n Bake cooking mix, Beaux Villages cheese, Birds Eye foods, Brim coffee, Calumet baking powder, Cheyenne corn cereal, Citrus 7 soft drink, Cocoa Pebbles cereal, Cool Whip whipped cream, Country Time lemonade, Crispy Critters cereal, Crispy Seasons, Crystal Light powdered drink mix, Diet Sun drink mix, Dover Farms whipped topping, Dream Whip whipped cream substitute, Frosted Rice cereal, Fruit'n Fibre cereal, Fruity Pebbles cereal, General Foods International Coffees, Good Seasons salad dressing, Grape-Nuts cereal, Great Loaf meatloaf mix, High Life Genuine Draft beer, Honey-Comb cereal, Jell-O desserts, Jell-O Fruit & Cream bars, Juice Up concentrate, Kool-Aid Koolers, Kool-Aid soft drink, Like caffeine-free cola, Lite beer, Log Cabin syrup, Louis Rich meats, Lowenbrau beer, Max-pax coffee, Maxim coffee, Maxwell House coffee, Meister Brau beer, Mellow Roast coffee, Miller beer, Milwaukee's Best beer, Minute Rice, Oscar Mayer meats, Oven Fry, Pebbles cereal, Post cereals, Postum cereal, Sanka coffee, Shake'n Bake meat coating mix, Sinex, Smurf-Berry Crunch cereal, Stove Top stuffing mix, Stuffin' Burgers, Sugar Crisp cereal, Super Sugar Crisp Cereal, Tang orange drink, Yuban coffee, CIGARETTES: Alpine, Benson & Hedges, Cambridge, Marlboro, Merit, Multifilter, Parliament, Philip Morris, Players, Saratoga, Virginia Slims.

RJR Nabisco, Chrm. J. Tylee Wilson, 1100 Reynolds Blvd., Winston-Salem, NC 27102, phone 919-773-2000. PRODUCTS: A.1. Steak Sauce, Almost Home cookies, American Classic crackers, American Harvest crackers, Baby Ruth candy, Baker's Blend margarine, Beech-Nut gum, Better Cheddar crackers, Blue Bonnet margarine, Breath Savers, Brer RAbbit molasses, Bubble Gum chewing gum, Bubble Yum chewing gum, Bugs Bunny cookies,

Butcher Bones dog food, Butterfinger candy, Care-Free chewing gum, Charleston chew candy, Chicken in a Biskit, Chips Ahoy cookies, Chit Chat crackers, Chun King oriental foods, College Inn food products, Coronation specialty foods, Corn Champs snacks, Country Crackers, Cream of Wheat cereal, Crunchy Trio snack thins, Davis baking powder, Del Monte foods, Duet fudge and peanut butter patties, Fig Newtons, Fleischmann's Egg Beaters, Fleischmann's margarine, Giggles Fudge cookies, Grey Poupon Dijon mustard, Hawaiian Punch Fruit drink, Island Blends fruit drink, Junior Mints, Life Savers candy, Milk Bone pet food, Milk-Mate chocolate syrup, Morton's frozen foods, Mr. Salty snack food, My*T*Fine pudding and pie filling, Musk aftershave, Nabisco foods, Ortega chiles, Patio Mexican foods, Planters peanuts, Potato 'n Sesame snack thins, Premium Saltines crackers, Replay gum, Ritz crackers, Royal pudding, Sea Land freight service, Sesame crackers, Shredded Wheat cereal, Spoon Size cereal, Team cereal, Triscuit snack crackers, Wheat Thins crackers, Wheatworth crackers, Vermont Maid maple syrup. CIGARETTES: Camel, Century, Doral II, More, More Lights 100s, Now, Salem, Vantage, Winston. Other tabacco products: Carter Hall, Days Work, George Washington, Madeira Gold, Prince Albert, Royal Comfort pipe tobacco, Work Horse chewing tobacco.

Other organizations dealing with pornography:

Morality in Media
475 Riverside Drive
New York, NY 10115
212-870-3222

Citizens for Decency Through Law
2845 East Camelback Road, Suite 740
Phoenix, AZ 85016
602-381-1322

National Coalition Against Porn
800 Compton Road, Suite 9248
Cincinnati, OH 45231
513-521-1985

Concerned Women for America
370 L'Enfant Promenade, SW, Suite 800
Washington, DC 20024
202-488-7000

Appendix Three

SEXUAL ABUSE OF INFANT
DAUGHTER TRIGGERED BY PORNOGRAPHY

(The following material is excerpted from the American Family Association booklet, "A Guide to What One Person Can Do About Pornography," available fro m AFA by writing P.O. Drawer 2440, Tupelo, Mississippi 38803.)

By an abused wife and mother

Author's name withheld by AFA

"Pornography—I don't particularly care for it but I believe in freedom of the press and freedom of expression. I can live with or without it." These were the words I spoke to my new husband. Words that I would live to regret.

I was reared in an independent Baptist home where pornography was considered distasteful, bad, and illegal. My exposure to it was a gradual process over my teen years. The "R" rated drive-in movies and pornographic magazines at school were the extent of my exposure. But with its acceptance by peers I eventually adopted an attitude of being "straddle of the fence." I didn't personally care for it but I condoned it so I would fit in with the crowd. This was the attitude I conveyed to my new husband.

Early in our marriage there wasn't any pornographic influence that I'm aware of. My husband was a kind and gentle man. He is a past president of a local chapter of United Way, an ex-Little League coach, and he has worked with handicapped children. He seemed to be well adjusted, normal, and happy. Our relationship was very loving, good, and happy.

After several months of marriage my husband brought home a VCR movie. He invited his daughter and son-in-law over for dinner and movies. The movies were pornographic. I could not believe that he was actually watching those with his daughter. I confronted him with my feelings.

His reply was, "We have been watching those kind of movies together for a long time. I'm proud my daughter watches them— she's learning how to keep her husband happy. Everybody does this, don't be such a drag."

I felt ashamed, embarrassed, and cheap. But I tolerated it to fit into my new family. I found reason to excuse myself to other parts of our home when the movies were being viewed.

After the movies my husband would often approach me sexually. I would discourage him because I felt he was excited by the trash that he had watched and not by our relationship. He would become angry and withdrawn. I was very uncomfortable with his aspect of our relationship and we began to grow distant from each other.

Then I became pregnant. About seven months into the pregnancy he asked me, "How would you feel about me having sex with a couple of friends while you watch, you know, like in the movies?"

I was shocked and replied, "Absolutely not!"

He tried to laugh it off as a joke but deep in my heart I knew that he was serious.

Our baby was born, a beautiful little girl. I was so proud of her and wanted to share her infancy with her father. He had become a very cold person and did not seem very excited about the birth of our daughter. The pornographic movie watching increased and he was buying books on sex with animals and family members. I tried to shut out of my mind what he was doing, but it was always with me like a bad cloud hanging over my head.

Two weeks after our daughter's first birthday my worst fears came to be. I discovered my husband naked in the family room with my daughter's little hands wrapped around his penis masturbating. I felt angry, betrayed, confused, and sick. I removed the baby from the room and begged him to go for help. He lay there on the floor masturbating and screamed at me, "You are so stupid. Everybody does this, I was not hurting the baby. It is fun and exciting, just like in the movies. You are so stupid and boring!"

My daughter and I slept in the guest room that night but much to my dismay the same incident was repeated the next morning. Only this time he became very violent. He slapped me across the face and said, "Maybe you are more into pain; after all, the girl in the movie I watched yesterday was into pain."

Child sexual abuse continued on court ordered visitation during the divorce.

Now distance separates my daughter and me from her father. I have often thought back to my statement on pornography. Sitting astraddle of the fence caused my child and me physical and emotional pain beyond description. Yes, there were other problems in the marriage, but I feel that the pornographic materials that he enjoyed contributed greatly to his attitude and actions. It has taken great amounts of energy to work through the trauma that we experienced. I am deeply ashamed of the attitude that I had adopted.

My daughter and I now live in a small town. Recently I discovered that a local video shop had pornographic movies. I thought of the children who might be abused by what someone learned in those movies. I thought of my little girl and our broken home. I could not sit "astraddle of the fence" anymore. I made one phone call to a city official and the owner was asked to remove the movies. He willingly did so. Never again will I be silent on an issue that made me feel the way pornography did.

Chapter One

1. C. Everett Koop, M.D., *American Medical News*, (10 October 1986).

2. See Focus on the Family transcript of Ted Bundy speaking to Dr. James Dobson at the Florida State Prison, 23 January 1989.

3. Ibid.

4. Ibid.

5. See Franklin Mark Osanka and Sara Lee Johann, *Sourcebook on Pornography* (Lexington Books: Lexington, Massachusetts, 1989), 18-19. The authors report that the study "found that youths between the ages of 12 and 17 were pornography's prime purchasers."

6. Koop, *American Medical News* (10 October 1986).

7. Additional evidence of a coming avalanche of sexual violence and its causes is noted in "The Mind of a Rapist," *Newsweek*, (20 July 1990).

8. See the *Attorney General's Report on Pornography* (July 1986). While this book focuses on the personal tragedy wrought by pornography, the Attorney General's Report also addresses the association between the pornography industry (e.g., magazines, videos, films, theaters, etc.) and organized crime. See also the American Family Association (AFA) publication titled *Pornography—A Report: An In-Depth Look at the Effects of Pornography* and other AFA reference documents on citizen action. Review pp. 19-24 for some of more than forty cases in which only *Playboy* would have been readily available to the criminal.

9. *Playboy* (January 1989).

10. Ibid.

11. *Reisman Report*. See chapter on "Child Sexual Abuse." Institute for Media Education, Arlington, VA (1989).

12. Report to the Michigan Legislature "Sexual Offenses by Youth in Michigan" (Safer Society Resources of Michigan: Detroit, 1988), Executive Summary.

13. Aaron Hass, *Teenage Sexuality* (Macmillan: New York, 1979), 153-161.

14. John Gagnon and William Simon, *Sexual Scene* (Transaction, Inc.: USA, 1970), 8.

15. Neil Malamuth, "Rape Proclivity Among Males," *Journal of Social Issues*, 37, (1981) 138-157. See also Neil Malamuth and James Check, "The Effect of Mass Media Exposure on Acceptance of Violence Against Women," *Journal of Research and Personality*, 15, (1981) 436-446. Also, see Osanka, *Sourcebook on Pornography*.

16. "What Sex Offenders Say About Pornography," *Readers Digest* (July 1971), 56.

17. Ibid.

Chapter Two

1. David Mura, *A Male Grief: Notes on Pornography and Addiction* (Milkweed Editions: Minneapolis, 1987), 3.

2. Ibid., 5.

3. Ibid., 21.

4. Ibid., 3.

5. Isadore Rosenfeld, *Second Opinion* (Bantam Books: New York, 1981), 173.

6. Roy Pinchot, ed., *The Human Body: The Brain* (Torstar Books: New York, 1984), 122-123.

7. Ibid., 98-99.

8. Ibid., 98.

9. David Scott, ed., *Symposium on Media Violence and Pornogra-*

raphy (Media Action Group, Inc.: Toronto, 1984), 142.

10. Ibid., 143.

11. Drs. Despopoulos and Silbernagl, *Color Atlas of Physiology* (Yearbook Medical Publishers, Inc.: Chicago, IL, 1981), 10, 240.

12. Jo Durden-Smith and Diane deSimone, *Sex and the Brain* (Warner Books: New York, 1983), 85.

13. Ibid., 61.

14. Ibid., 81.

15. Ibid., 87, 89.

Chapter Three

1. Paul Robinson, *The Modernization of Sex* (Harper and Row: New York, 1976), 64-66.

2. Max Lerner, "In His Own Words, Hugh Hefner Remains in the Romantic Vanguard," *New York Post* (6 July 1989), 25.

3. Hugh Hefner, *Playboy* (January 1989), 5.

4. Russell Miller, *Bunny* (Holt, Rinehart and Wilson: New York, 1984), 235.

5. Note Paul Gebhard's comments about penis ridicule in *Playboy* cartoons as quoted by Thomas Weyr in *Reaching for Paradise* (Times Books: New York, 1978): "Any cartoon with an impotence theme would distress an impotent male to some extent and perhaps plant the seed of worry in another man's mind. . . ." (p. 218) "After Kinsey," says Weyr, "the dildo industry [was] booming. . . . Without Kinsey [and his followers] Masters and Johnson, the dildo manufacturer would never have been in business." (p. 212)

6. Frank Brady, *Hefner* (Ballantine Books: New York, 1975), 79-80.

7. See discussion of *Playboy* pres-sure on a political figure in Stephen Byer's *Hefner's Gonna Kill Me When He Reads This* (Allen-Bennett: Chicago, 1972) and note Patrick Anderson, *High in America: The True Story Behind NORML and the Politics of Marijuana* (Viking Press: New York, 1981) for information on both Playboy's informal political connections via the National Organization for the Reform of Marijuana Laws (NORML). Also, review the "Letters to the Editor" and "Forum" in *Playboy* for friendly letters from a broad spectrum of congressmen and senators to *Playboy* regarding issues addressed in the magazine. Examine also the *Playboy* Foundation lists of political activism gifts, and note the January 1979 *Playboy* for public funding activities.

8. *Brady*, Hefner, 79.

9. See *Male* volume (especially pp. 325-326 where the text states that "alert" boys masturbate early and "inept" boys do so later). Robinson sums up Kinsey's arguments in *The Modernization of Sex* saying Kinsey insisted "the more one indulged one's passions in adolescence, the richer one's adult experience," (pp. 59, 61).

10. Phyllis and Eberhard Kronhausen, *Sex Histories of American College Men* (Ballantine Books: New York, 1960), 20.

11. Ibid., 254-256.

12. See Hugh Hefner's "*Playboy* Philosophy" for his discussion of *Playboy* as a bridge until marriage.

13. Robinson, *The Modernization of Sex*, 49.

14. Ibid., 51.

15. Weyr, *Reaching for Paradise*, 221-222.

16. Margaret Mead, *Men: The Vari-*

ety and Meaning of Their Sexual Experience, ed. A.M. Krich(Dell Publishing, Inc: New York, 1954), 23.

17. Ibid.

18. Weyr, *Reaching for Paradise*, 222.

19. See"Teenagers and Sex," *Parents* (January 1987); "Teenage Pregnancy in Developed Countries," Alan Guttmacher Institute, Vol. 17, No. 2 (March/April 1985).

Chapter Four

1. See Hugh Hefner interview with Paul Krassner, "An Impolite Interview with Hugh Hefner," *The Realist* (May 1961).

2. Rollo May, *Love and Will* (Dell: New York, 1969), 57-58.

3. Russell Miller, *Bunny* (Holt, Rinehart and Wilson: New York, 1984), 23.

4. Thomas Weyr, *Reaching for Paradise* (Times Books: New York, 1978), 195-196.

5. Ibid., 197-198.

6. Ibid., 11.

7. Ibid., 197. Note that oral sex, even between husband and wife, was still illegal in many states.

8. See Rene Guyon, *The Ethics of Sex Acts* (Octagon Books: New York, 1948).

9. Weyr, *Reaching for Paradise*, 24.

10. Miller, *Bunny*, 23-24.

11. Hugh Hefner, *Playboy* (December 1987), 41-44.

12. Ibid. See also Weyr, *Reaching for Paradise*, 197.

13. Weyr, *Reaching for Paradise*, 11.

14. Miller, *Bunny*, 46.

15. Frank Brady, *Hefner* (Ballantine Books: New York, 1975), 174-175.

16. Ibid., 172-173.

17. Ibid., 177.

18. Patrick Anderson, *High in America: The True Story Behind NORML and the Politics of Marijuana* (Viking Press: New York, 1981), 137.

19. Ibid.

20. Gay Talese, *Thy Neighbor's Wife* (Doubleday: New York, 1980), as quoted in Dr. Patrick Carnes, *The Sexual Addiction* (CompCare Publications: Minneapolis, 1983, 1.

21. Dr. Patrick Carnes, *The Sexual Addiction* (CompCare Publications: Minneapolis, 1983), ix, x.

22. Ibid., 10.

23. Erich Fromm, *To Have or To Be*, (Harper and Row: New York, 1976), 108.

24. Ibid., 182.

25. Ibid. See also p. 173.

26. See Jeffrey M. Masson, *The Assault on Truth* (Penguin Books: New York, 1985). See also Alexandra Mark and Vernon H. Mark, *The Pied Pipers of Sex* (Haven Books: Plainfield, NJ, 1981).

27. Bernard Barber, *An Analysis of the Kinsey Reports*, ed. Donald T. Geddes (Mentor Books: New York, 1954), 50-61. See also Lionel Trilling in the same collection, p. 220.

28. Ibid., 61.

29. Ibid.

Chapter Five

1. Reported 10 October 1988 on "The Reporters," Fox TV.

2. Frank Brady, *Hefner* (Ballantine Books: New York, 1975), 124-125. Alcoholics Anonymous calls such hourly "maintenance drinking" a "problem."

3. Ibid., 190-191.

4. Rollo May, *Love and Will* (Dell: New York, 1969), 37, 40, 54, 56.

5. During my lectures and work-

shops, I identify the castration and impotence humor of *Playboy*, et al, and provide evidence that, were these jokes published by a women's magazine, men would quickly see the attempt to castrate and unman them. It is much harder for them to acknowledge that type of attack from groups of other men. But the underlying attempt of depraved groups of men to destroy other, peaceful men is part of our historical record of war. Pornography is war with new weapons. The target of men's dominance is as it always has been—other men. Women and children are of course severely harmed, but they are merely tools to that end of men controlling and destroying other men.

6. As quoted in Abraham Maslow and Pitraim Sorokin, *New Knowledge in Human Values* (Gateway: Chicago, 1971), 154.

7. Ibid., 6-9.

8. Ibid., 122.

9. Ibid., 153.

10. "Erotica" is supposed to be the celebration of "Eros," the Greek god of love. It is not therefore possible to be exploitative and erotic at the same time since one does not exploit the person(s) one loves. I am sad to say that when sexuality becomes entertainment in any society, even non-exploitative erotic art becomes pornography when it is publicly displayed. That is, when a public is extremely prejudiced toward blacks, even

an honorable painting of a nude black male is interpreted as anti-black pornography. Widespread pornography closes the avenues of erotic expression, for one's art is part of the public to whom one displays. As nudity becomes commercial entertainment, anything which exposes a person to sexualization exposes them to "risk." What may be erotic in private space often becomes pornographic in public space.

11. May, *Love and Will*, 39, 43, 54, 56.

12. Sherman Silber, *The Male: From Infancy to Old Age* (Charles Scribner's Sons: New York, 1981), 77-78.

13. Ibid.

14. Thomas Weyr, *Reaching for Paradise: The Playboy Vision of America* (Times Books: New York, 1978), 218.

15. Alfred C. Kinsey, et al, *Male* (W.B. Saunders, Co., Philadelphia, 1948), 237.

16. David Reuben, *Everything You Wanted to Know About Sex But Were Afraid to Ask* (David McKay, Inc.: New York, 1970) 13.

17. Christopher Lash, *The Culture of Narcissism* (W.W. Norton and Company: Canada, 1979), 345-347.

Chapter Six

1. "Virginity," *Playboy* (December 1953).

2. "Genital-Wart Virus Found in 46% of Women Tested," *Washington Times* (January 24, 1991).

3. Thomas Weyr, *Reaching for Paradise* (Times Books: New York, 1978), 310.

4. Peter Dally, *The Fantasy Factor* (Weidenfeld and Nicolson: London, 1975), 106.

5. Russell Miller, *Bunny* (Holt, Rinehart and Wilson: New

York, 1984), 117.

6. Frank Brady, *Hefner* (Ballantine Books: New York, 1975), 183.

7. Miller, *Bunny*, 119.

8. Hugh Hefner, *Philosophy IV* (*Playboy*/HMH Publishing Company, Inc: Chicago, 1964), 178.

9. Susan Lurie, "Pornography and the Dread of Women: The Male Sexual Dilemma," *Take Back the Night*, ed. Laura Lederer (Bantam Books, New York, 1980), 153.

Chapter Seven

1. Hugh Hefner, *Playboy* (December, 1983), 42-43.

2. Frank Brady, *Hefner* (Ballantine Books: New York, 1975), 89.

3. Stephen Byer, *Hefner's Gonna Kill Me When He Reads This* (Allen-Bennett: Chicago, 1972), 91.

4. Thomas Weyr, *Reaching for Paradise* (Times Books: New York, 1978), 199.

5. Vance Packard, *The Sexual Wilderness* (Pocket Books: New York, 1970), 121.

6. Paul Robinson, *The Modernization of Sex* (Harper and Row: New York, 1976), 58, 66.

7. Russel Miller, *Bunny* (Holt, Rinehart and Wilson: New York, 1984), 197.

8. Hefner, *Playboy* (January 1989), Preface.

9. Packard, *The Sexual Wilderness*, 25.

10. Ibid., 35.

11. See reprint of *Playboy* editorial statement (December 1953) in *The Realist* (May 1961).

12. Dr. Philip Kotler, *Marketing Management: Analysis, Planning and Control* (Prentice-Hall: Englewood Cliffs, NJ, 1967), 50, 68, 92.

13. Weyr, *Reaching for Paradise*, 310.

14. Barbara Ehrenreich, *The Hearts of Men* (Anchor Press/

Doubleday: Garden City, NJ, 1983), 47.

15. Ibid.

16. Jessie Bernard, *The Future of Marriage* (Bantam Books: New York, 1973), 149-150.

17. Ibid., 153.

18. Leonore Weitzman, *The Divorce Revolution* (Free Press: New York, 1985), overleaf.

19. See "Research on Children and Adolescents with Mental, Behavioral and Developmental Disorders" (National Academy Press: Institute of Medicine, Washington, DC, 1989); "Code Blue: Uniting for Healthier Youth" (The National Commission on the Role of the School and the Community in Improving Adolescent Health: Alexandria, VA, 1989). Especially see Deborah Fink, "Homeless Children..." (National Academy Press: National Academy of Science, the Institute of Medicine, Rockville, MD, 1989) as noted in *Images of Children, Crime and Violence*, iv.

Chapter Eight

1. Gay Talese, *Thy Neighbor's Wife* (Doubleday: New York, 1980), 484, 486.

2. Hugh Hefner, as quoted in the *Cleveland Plain Dealer* (11 January 1976).

3. Dr. Philip Kotler, *Marketing Management: Analysis, Planning and Control* (Prentice-Hall: Englewood Cliffs, NJ, 1967), 347.

4. Dr. Timothy Leary, "Episode and Postscript," *Playboy* (December 1969).

5. Martin Lee and Bruce Shlain, *Acid Dreams* (Grove Press, Inc: New York, 1985), 113-114.

6. Ibid., 114.

7. Dr. Robert Dupont, *Getting Tough on Gateway Drugs* (American

Psychiatric Press: Washington, DC, 1984), xvi-xvii.

8. Patrick Anderson, *High in America: The True Story Behind NORML and The Politics of Marjuaina* (Viking Press: New York, 198), 15-22. Of particular note is Gay Talese's mention in *Thy Neighbor's Wife:* "Christie was clearly the type that would appeal to her father; and by her own admission, they shared a mutural attraction that was far more romantic than familial" (p. 497).

9. Aaron Hass, *Teenage Sexuality* (Macmillan: New York, 1979), 153-161.

10. Hugh Hefner, *Philosophy II* (Playboy/HMH Publishing Company, Inc., 1963), 79.

11. James Petersen, "Playboy Advisor," *Playboy* (December 1978).

12. James Petersen, "Playboy Advisor," *Playboy* (June 1979).

13. Hugh Hefner as quoted in Anderson, *High in America*, 137.

Chapter Nine

1. Any descriptions of photographs, cartoons, or other: images of children in sexually compromising scene found in *Playboy, Penthouse* or *Hustler* are included to document the history of PPH's use of child images and the extent to which they are willing to go to provoke their readers. The actual images were not included in this book due to the author's desire to encourage parents to initiate open discussions with their children regarding their exposure to and knowledge of soft porn. Those serious scholars who wish to obtain a copy of the author's *Images of Children, Crime, and Violence in Playboy, Penthouse, and Hustler*, or the full *Reisman Report*, where copies of the photographs themselves appear, will find an order form in the back of this book.

2. *Spiderman*, a publication of the National Committee for the Prevention of Child Abuse (1984), 6.

3. Joe Goldberg, *The Big Bunny* (Ballantine Books: New York, 1967), 249-250.

4. Frank Brady, *Hefner* (Ballantine Books: New York, 1975), 134-135.

5. Ibid., 115.

6. Russell Miller, *Bunny* (Holt, Rinehart and Wilson: New York, 1984), 161.

7. Ibid., 135.

8. Brady, *Hefner*, 121.

9. Thomas Weyr, *Reaching for Paradise* (Times Books: New York, 1978), 298-299.

10. *Reisman Report*, Institute for Media Education, Arlington, VA (1989), 178-182.

11. Ibid., 6.

12. Dr. Gail Dines-Levy, "Toward a Sociology of Cartoons: A Framework for Sociological Investigation with Special Reference to *Playboy* Sex Cartoons" (Ph.D. diss., University of Salford, Great Britain, 1990).

Chapter Ten

1. See *Images of Children, Crime and Violence in Playboy, Penthouse and Hustler* (Huntington House: Lafayette, LA, 1990), 107-109 for a review of the historical "Santa" research.

2. Thomas Weyr, *Reaching for Paradise* (Times Books: New York, 1978), 303-305, quotes Arthur Kretchmen who states that *Playboy* "orchestrate[s]" their "skin book" so that "its features complement each other."

3. Ibid., 305.

Chapter Eleven

1. While I often use the term *genital* or *genitalia* in this book, we

would do well to reinstate the more accurate and all embracing pre-1948 term *reproductive organs*. This suggestion is not driven by moral imperatives but by the need for authenticity in discussing sex. The post-1948 language maneuver from *reproductive* to *genital* has narrowed our understanding, in my opinion, of human behavior in general and sexual behavior in particular. From a scientific perspective, *sex* organs are primarily designed as reproductive organs since these organs will normally produce babies unless the sex act involves artificial intervention. As these organs do not always even provide pleasure (i.e., the sex act is by no means always pleasurable—as in forced or even boring sex) the notion of *sexual arousal* changes dramatically. In its wider, more accurate dimension, humans experience "reproductive arousal." Animal behavior supports both creationists and evolutionists in that coitus is first an innate drive to reproduce. The sociobiological literature identifies *pleasure* as a means to attain that larger end.

2. The *Attorney General's Report on Pornography* (July 1986).

3. Patrick Buchanan, "Losing The War for America's Culture," *Washington Times* (22 May 1988).

4. Rollo May, *Love and Will* (Dell: New York, 1969), 121-171.

Chapter Twelve

1. M. O'Brien and W. Brea, "Adolescent Sexual Offenders: A descriptive typology, *Preventing Sexual Abuse* 1(3), 2.

2. Ann Burgess and Marianne Clark, *Child Pornography and Sex Rings* (Lexington Press: Lex-

ington, MA, 1984), 78. See *Images of Children, Crime and Violence in Playboy, Penthouse, and Hustler* (Huntington House: Lafayette, LA, 1990) for extensive documentation.

3. Aaron Hass, *Teenage Sexuality* (Macmillan: New York, 1979), 153-177.

4. It has been my empirical observation that while massive data exists, pornography special interests are censoring the research at the federal, state, and even the university levels.

5. Hass, *Teenage Sexuality*, 153-155.

6. Ibid., 153-161.

7. Ibid.

8. Ibid.

9. Ibid.

10. Report to Michigan Legislature, "Sexual Offenses by Youth in Michigan" (Safe Society Resources of Michigan: Detroit, 1988), Executive Summary.

11. John Whitehead, *The Stealing of America* (Good News Publishers/Crossway Books: Wheaton, IL, 1983), 68.

12. Dr. John Briere, Ph.D., assistant professor of Psychology at the University of California said in "Adult Survivors of Sex-Abuse in Crisis," *Behavior Today*, (25 June 1990), 4.

13. John Gagnon and William Simon, *The Sexual Scene* (Transaction Inc.: USA, 1970), 7-8, 145.

14. Of 18,214,000 youths between 15-19 years of age there were 2,059 deaths by suicide in 1988, for a rate of 11.3 per 100,000 or roughly 8 deaths per day according to the National Center for Health Statistics (1988), Table 1-26). Moreverover, the juvenile homicide rates more than double

the number of youngsters dying each day in this child-toxic environment. Kids are killing themselves and each other in record numbers. "In the past five years, juvenile homicide has increased five times faster than homicides committed by adults. . . . Murder is just the awful tip of the ice-berg. . . . In 1989, 2,208 juveniles nationwide were arrested on charges of murder or non-negligent manslaughter, 25 percent more than the year before," stated Dr. Ewing at a news conference sponsored by the University of Buffalo at the American Psychological Association's annual meeting, 12 August 1990.

15. "Clinical Psychiatry News, "As quoted in *National Coalition on Television Violence NCTV News* (April-May 1989), 5.

16. Ibid., 2.

17. James Petersen, "*Playboy* Advisor," *Playboy* (October 1976).

18. Burgess, Hazelwood, Rokous, Hartman, and Burgess, "Serial Rapists and Their Victims: Reenactment and Repetition," Office of Juvenile Justice and Delinquency Prevention Pre-Publication Draft (July 1987), Grant 84-UN-K010.

19. Thomas Weyr, *Reaching for Paradise* (Times Books: New York, 1978), 299, 308.

20. Dr. Marvin Wolfgang, *Report on the Commission on Obscenity and Pornography* (Bantam Books: New York, 1970), 446-447.

21. See Reisman and Eichel, *Kinsey, Sex and Fraud: the Indoctrination of a People* (Huntington House: Lafayette, LA, 1990) for documentation of Alfred Kinsey's fraudulently-based conclusions.

Chapter Thirteen

1. Terri Rosenthal, unpublished manuscript.

2. Phyllis Schlafly, comp., *Pornography's Victims: Official Transcript of Proceedings, Attorney General's Report on Pornography* (Crossway Books: Westchester, IL, 1987), 28-29.

3. Ibid., 86-90.

4. *Playboy* bunnies, lending added credibility to Miki Garcia's testimony before the Attorney General's Commission, reported that rape and even death occurred on the aristocratic grounds of the *Playboy* mansion. Parents, take note. Former centerfold Linda Marchiano states she was forced by battery to star in the infamous film, *Deep Throat.* "I was beaten physically and suffered mental abuse each and every day. . . . Guns were used to threaten the lives of my friends and my family. I've seen the kind of people involved in pornography and how they will use anyone to get what they want." Several witnesses testified that those who were tipped off to the atrocities inflicted on the bunnies ignored the victims' pleas for help or changed the subject. Marchiano continues, "There were guns, there were knives, there were beatings, there were threats on the lives of my family constantly, and after the physical abuse, the mental abuse [was] just as damaging." Regarding charges that she appeared to be enjoying herself while filming, she replies, "That smile is what saved my life," 229-234.

5. Schlafly, *Pornography's Victims: Official Transcript of Proceedings, Attorney General's Report on Pornography*, 91-96.

6. *Take Back the Night*, ed. Laura Lederer (Bantam Books: New York, 1980), 113.

7. Rosemary Agonito, *History of Ideas on Women* (Paragon: New York, 1977). Kinsey/ Hefner, psychologists and sexologists urged Americans to look to "primitive" tribes and Third World nations for a freer, less inhibited sexual life. For example, Kinseyans generally cite the graphic sex imagery of India and Japan, without mentioning that women and children were legally and culturally powerless in both of these countries. See also numerous books touching on this issue: June Hahner, *Women in Latin American History* (UCLA America Center: Los Angeles, 1976); Youssef El Masry, *Daughters of Sin: The Sexual Tragedy of Arab Women* (MacFadden Books: New York, 1963); Kathleen Newland, *The Sisterhood of Man* (Norton: New York, 1979); and *Sisterhood is Global*, ed. Robin Morgan (Anchor Books: New York, 1984).

8. See October 1988 term documentation, 33.

Chapter Fourteen

1. Alfred Kinsey, et al, *Male* (W.B. Saunders Co.,: Philadelphia, 1948) 180.

2. Ibid.

3. Paul Gebhard, et al, *Sex Offenders* (Bantam Books: New York, 1965). "Child molesters seldom commit or attempt rape. . . . Pornography plays little or no part in motivating sex crimes. . . . Drug addicts rarely figure in sex crimes" (Opening page to *Sex Offenders*).

4. Glenn Tinder, "Can We Be Good Without God?" *The Atlantic Monthly* (December 1989), 69-85.

A Con Job On Society About Human Sexuality

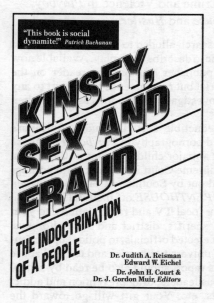

"This book is social dynamite!" *Patrick Buchanan*

KINSEY, SEX AND FRAUD
THE INDOCTRINATION OF A PEOPLE

Dr. Judith A. Reisman
Edward W. Eichel
Dr. John H. Court &
Dr. J. Gordon Muir, *Editors*

Kinsey, Sex and Fraud: The Indoctrination of a People describes the allegedly scientific research of Alfred Kinsey and colleagues, which shaped western society's beliefs and understanding of the nature of human sexuality. Kinsey's unchallenged conclusions are taught at every level of education—elementary, high school and college—and quoted in textbooks as undisputed truth.

"On the cultural Richter scale, the impact of Kinsey, Sex and Fraud *could be close to a 10"—Patrick Buchanan, syndicated columnist*

"The authors raise serious and disturbing questions about the accuracy, reliability and perhaps, truthfulness of the figures given in Kinsey's 1948 book and the methods by which these data were obtained. Because of the obvious importance of Kinsey's work, these questions need to be thoroughly and openly debated by the scientific community."—Walter W. Stewart, Research Scientist, National Institutes of Health

"It is important to understand that the results of this wacky science are taught as truth in classrooms across the nation. . . . Is Kinsey and colleagues' research the "Fraud of the Century?" The documentation in Kinsey, Sex and Fraud *would suggest nothing else even comes close."—New Dimensions*

"In Kinsey, Sex and Fraud *Dr. Judith A. Reisman and her colleagues demolish the foundations of the two reports. . . . Kinsey . . has left his former co-workers some explaining to do."—The Lancet*

divorce . . . suicide . . . abortion . . . child abuse . . . neglect . . . homosexuality . . . promiscuity . . . The systematic destruction of the American family is the direct result of the influential and well-protected "soft porn" industry.

"Soft Porn" Plays Hardball

Its Tragic Effects on Women, Children & the Family

Judith A. Reisman, Ph.D.

Playboy, Penthouse, Hustler and their sex industry spin-offs are enslaving our youth and stripping future generations of their moral fiber and strength.

Order now more copies of *"Soft Porn" Plays Hardball* by Judith Reisman and learn how to fight back!

MORE GOOD BOOKS FROM
HUNTINGTON HOUSE PUBLISHERS

Cover of Darkness (A Novel) by J. Carroll

Jack's time is running out. The network's top investigative reporter has been given the most bizarre and difficult assignment of his life. The powers behind the conspiracy (occult and demonic forces) are finally exposed by Jack. Now comes the real challenge—convincing others. Matching wits with supernatural forces Jack faces the most hideous conspiracy the world has ever known.

ISBN 0-910311-31-5 $7.95

Psychic Phenomena Unveiled: Confessions of a New Age Warlock by John Anderson

He walked on hot coals and stopped his heart. As one of Los Angeles' mos recognized psychics, John Anderson was on top of the world. His ability to perform psychic phenomena converted the most stubborn unbeliever into a true believer in occult power. But John Anderson sensed his involvement in the occul was destroying him. This book was written to expose the trickery behind the New Age magic and address man's attraction to the occult.

ISBN 0-910311-49-8 $8.95

Crystalline Connection (A Novel) by Bob Maddux & Mary Carpenter Reid

Enter the enchanting World of Ebbern, a planet in many ways like our own In the Crystalline Connection our hero, Bracken, returns to his homeland after ten years of wandering. Once there he becomes involved in a monumental struggle gallantly confronting the dark forces of evil. This futuristic fantasy is fraught with intrigue, adventure, romance and much more. The Crystalline Connection artfully discloses the devastating consequences of involvement in the New Age movement while using the medium of fiction.

ISBN 0-910311-71-4 $8.95

Kinsey, Sex and Fraud: The Indoctrination of a People by Dr. Judith A. Reisman and Edward Eiche

Kinsey, Sex and Fraud describes the research of Alfred Kinsey which shaped Western society's beliefs and understanding of the nature of human sexuality. His unchallenged conclusions are taught at every level of education—elementary high school and college—and quoted in textbooks as undisputed truth.

The authors clearly demonstrate that Kinsey's research involved illega experimentations on several hundred children. The survey was carried out on a non-representative group of Americans, including disproportionately large num bers of sex offenders, prostitutes, prison inmates and exhibitionists.

ISBN 0-910311-20-X $19.95 Hardcover

Seduction of the Innocent Revisited by John Fulce

You honestly can't judge a book by its cover—especially a comic book Comic books of yesteryear bring to mind cute cartoon characters, super-heroes battling the forces of evil or a sleuth tracking down the bad guy clue-by-clue. But that was a long, long time ago.

Today's comic books aren't innocent at all! Author John Fulce asserts that "super-heroes" are constantly found in the nude engaging in promiscuity, and atanic symbols are abundant throughout the pages. Fulce says most parents aren't aware of the contents of today's comic books. We need to pay attention to what our children are reading, Fulce claims. Comic books are not as innocent as they used to be.

ISBN 0-910311-66-8 $8.95

God's Rebels by Henry Lee Curry III

From his unique perspective Dr. Henry Lee Curry III offers a fascinating look at the lives of some of our greatest Southern religious leaders during the Civil War. The rampant Evangelical Christianity prominent at the outbreak of the Civil War, asserts Dr. Curry, is directly traceable to the 2nd Great Awakening of the early 1800s. The evangelical tradition, with its emphasis on strict morality, individual salvation, and emotional worship, had influenced most of Southern Protestantism by this time. Southerners unquestionably believed the voice of the ministers to be the "voice of God"; consequently, the church became one of the most powerful forces influencing Confederate life and morale. Inclined toward Calvinistic emphasis on predestination, the South was confident that God would sustain its way of life.

ISBN: 0-910311-67-6 $12.95 Trade paper
ISBN: 0-910311-68-4 $21.95 Hardcover

The Devil's Web by Pat Pulling with Kathy Cawthon

This explosive exposé presents the first comprehensive guide to childhood and adolescent occult involvement. Written by a nationally recognized occult crime expert, the author explains how the violent occult underworld operates and how they stalk and recruit our children, teenagers, and young adults for their evil purposes.

ISBN 0-910311-59-5 $8.95 Trade paper
ISBN 0-910311-63-3 $16.95 Hardcover

New World Order: The Ancient Plan of Secret Societies by William Still

Secret societies such as Freemasons have been active since before the advent of Christ, yet most of us don't realize what they are or the impact they've had on many historical events. Author William Still brings into focus the actual manipulative work of the societies, and the "Great Plan" they follow, much to the surprise of many of those who are blindly led into the organization. Their ultimate goal is simple: world dictatorship and unification of all mankind into a world confederation.

ISBN 0-910311-64-1 $8.95

To Grow By Storybook Readers by Janet Friend

Today the quality of education is a major concern; consequently, more and more parents have turned to home schooling to teach their children how to read. The *To Grow By Storybook Readers* by Janet Friend can greatly enhance your home schooling reading program. The set of readers consists of 18 storybook readers plus 2 activity books. The *To Grow By Storybook Readers* has been designed to be used in conjunction with Marie LeDoux's PLAY 'N TALK phonics program but will work well with other orderly phonics programs.

These are the first phonics readers that subtly but positively instill moral values.

ISBN 0-910311-69-2 $44.95 per set

ORDER THESE HUNTINGTON HOUSE BOOKS !